REGENSBURGER BEITRÄGE
ZUR GENDER-FORSCHUNG
Band 6

Herausgegeben von
Rainer Emig
Anne-Julia Zwierlein

Treasure in Literature and Culture

Edited by
RAINER EMIG

Universitätsverlag
WINTER
Heidelberg

Bibliografische Information der Deutschen Nationalbibliothek

Die Deutsche Nationalbibliothek verzeichnet diese Publikation
in der Deutschen Nationalbibliografie;
detaillierte bibliografische Daten sind im Internet
über *http://dnb.d-nb.de* abrufbar.

COVER ILLUSTRATION

Klaus Brecht GmbH und fotolia

ISBN 978-3-8253-6202-7

Dieses Werk einschließlich aller seiner Teile ist urheberrechtlich geschützt. Jede
Verwertung außerhalb der engen Grenzen des Urheberrechtsgesetzes ist ohne
Zustimmung des Verlages unzulässig und strafbar. Das gilt insbesondere für
Vervielfältigungen, Übersetzungen, Mikroverfilmungen und die Einspeicherung
und Verarbeitung in elektronischen Systemen.

© 2013 Universitätsverlag Winter GmbH Heidelberg
Imprimé en Allemagne · Printed in Germany
Druck: Memminger MedienCentrum, 87700 Memmingen

Gedruckt auf umweltfreundlichem, chlorfrei gebleichtem
und alterungsbeständigem Papier

Den Verlag erreichen Sie im Internet unter:
www.winter-verlag.de

Vorwort zur Reihe
„Regensburger Beiträge zur Gender-Forschung"

Gender ist in überraschend kurzer Zeit von einem Randbereich der Literatur- und Kulturwissenschaft zu dem zentralen Paradigma geworden, als das die Gender-Forschung selbst die Frage nach Geschlecht und Sexualität schon immer gesehen hat. Kaum eine Veranstaltung und nur wenige Publikationen kommen ohne implizite oder explizite Gender-Fragen aus. Dabei ist es noch keine fünfzig Jahre her, dass Geschlecht weitgehend als konstant und universell verstanden wurde: Männer und Frauen hatte es scheinbar schon immer gegeben und würde es immer geben und mit ihnen durch die Natur oder göttliche Gebote festgelegte Geschlechterrollen.

Es waren die Feministinnen, die mindestens seit dem 18. Jahrhundert und schließlich unüberhörbar im 20. Jahrhundert die Frage stellten, ob die Geschlechterbeziehungen „natürlich" und vor allem gerecht geregelt seien, und damit auch, ob Geschlecht gegeben oder gemacht ist. Simone de Beauvoirs berühmte Feststellung „Man kommt nicht als Frau zur Welt, sondern wird dazu gemacht" fasst diese radikal neue Betrachtungsweise zusammen. Sie eröffnet die Möglichkeit, Geschlecht als Konstruktion zu sehen. Das heißt nicht, dass Geschlecht nicht existiert, sondern dass es das Resultat kultureller und gesellschaftlicher Prozesse ist, die sich aus Machtverhältnissen speisen und diese wiederum in aller Regel festigen.

Dieser ersten Phase des modernen Feminismus folgten mehrere Revisionen, in denen unter anderem die Fragen, ob es so etwas wie „die Frau" gibt, ob Weiblichkeit immer gegen Männlichkeit definiert werden muss, und ob es spezifische weibliche Denk- und Ausdrucksformen gibt, kontrovers diskutiert wurden. Diese Debatten riefen dann wieder die Männlichkeitsforschung auf den Plan, die daran erinnerte, dass die gleichen Fragen auch der Männlichkeit gestellt werden müssen. Männlichkeitsforschung war dabei ursprünglich stark von der Homosexuellenbewegung motiviert, die sich mit einer ewigen und „natürlichen" Definition von Sexualität als Heterosexualität nicht einverstanden erklären konnte. Bevor allerdings aus dem Konvolut aus Feminismus, Frauen-, Männer-, Weiblichkeits- und Männlichkeits-forschung die *Gender Studies* in ihrer heutigen Form hervorgehen konnten, brauchte es die Intervention der amerikanischen Philosophin Judith Butler. Ihr *Gender Trouble* (deutsch: *Das Unbehagen der Geschlechter*) aus dem Jahr 1990 nahm die zentralen Engpässe der bisherigen Positionen ins Visier, die in aller Regel an irgendeinem Punkt wieder in essentialistische Haltungen verfielen, in denen bestimmte Festlegungen unhintergehbar wurden. Sie schaffte es auch, sinnvoll Geschlechterfragen mit denen der Sexualität zu verknüpfen, aber auf eine Art und Weise, die bisherige Vorstellungen radikal umdrehte. Butler geht davon aus, dass gesellschaftlich gewollte, verpflichtende Heterosexualität (zur Erhaltung der Nation, von Arbeitskräften wie auch des Militärs) umgekehrt kulturelle Geschlechterrollen bedingt, für die sie den Begriff *Gender* verwendet, für den es im Deutschen kein Äquivalent gibt. Diese kulturellen Gender-Rollen basieren nun nicht einfach auf biologischen Körpern, sondern sie bestimmen deren Bedeutung mit, wenn z. B. Ärzte das Geschlecht von Neugeborenen ohne klare Geschlechtsorgane aufgrund der besten sozialen Lebenschancen bestimmen.

Damit werden Phänomene wie Transvestismus und Transsexualität von Randphänomenen zu zentralen Manifestationen, die gerade die Konstruiertheit von *Gender* aufzeigen. Hier schließen sich an Butler auch die *Queer Studies* an, die im Unterschied zu Studien über männliche und weibliche Homosexualität zu deren Legitimierung generell alle Normen von Geschlecht und Sexualität hinterfragen – und damit geschlechtliche wie sexuelle Normalität selbst.

In diese lebhaften Debatten sind die zeitgenössischen *Gender Studies* involviert, und sie involvieren zahlreiche andere Disziplinen produktiv und manchmal kontrovers in sie. *Gender Studies* sind damit per se interdisziplinär. Die Universität Regensburg trug dem vor wenigen Jahren Rechnung, als sie als erste (und bislang immer noch einzige) Universität Bayerns die *Gender Studies* als „freies Nebenfach" etablierte, das in Veranstaltungen verschiedener Fächer studiert werden konnte. Es ist in kurzer Zeit zu einem Erfolgsmodell geworden. Es profitiert auch von der engen Zusammenarbeit mit und Unterstützung durch die Frauenbeauftragte der Universität Regensburg, die nicht nur in die Planungen von Kolloquien und Ringvorlesungen involviert ist, sondern mehrfach auch einen willkommenen Beitrag zu deren Finanzierung leistete. So erklärt es sich auch, dass diese Reihe in regelmäßigen Abständen, teils in deutscher, teils in englischer Sprache, sowohl neueste Debatten abbilden wie auch eine historische Aufarbeitung des Feldes leisten wird. Wir erhoffen uns von ihr sowohl eine weitere Konsolidierung der *Gender Studies* in den Geisteswissenschaften wie auch vielfältige Anregungen zu neuen und auch kontroversen Ideen.

Rainer Emig
Anne-Julia Zwierlein

Hannover und Regensburg, im September 2010

Table of Contents

RAINER EMIG
Treasure in Literature and Culture: From Motif to Discourse...............................9

JESSICA MALAY
The Trouble with Treasure in Tudor and Stuart England.....................................15

STEFAN HERBRECHTER
Treasuring the Self: Romanticism…in Theory...35

DOMINIQUE CLAISSE
Nathaniel Hawthorne's Mother of Pearl and Other Gems.....................................49

KARIN PREUSS
Family Treasures and Subversive Power Play in Collins' *The Moonstone*................63

RAINER EMIG
Treasure Hunts: Between Decadence and Morality...81

RUSSELL WEST-PAVLOV
Treasure, Value and Signs in Conrad's *Nostromo*...89

MARCIN STAWIARSKI
Treasure and the Desire to Know: Richard Wagner's *Der Ring des Nibelungen*
and Anthony Burgess's *The Worm and the Ring*...99

CARL PLASA
"The Object of His Craving": Loss and Compensation
in Toni Morrison's *Song of Solomon*...117

OLIVER LINDNER
Broken Future, Broken Narrative: Risk and the Threatened Treasure
of the Environment in David Mitchell's *Cloud Atlas* (2004)
and Margaret Atwood's *The Year of the Flood* (2009)......................................133

ELLEN GRÜNKEMEIER
Antiretroviral AIDS Medication in South(ern) Africa – a Treasure?......................147

Notes on Contributors...169

Rainer Emig

Treasure in Literature and Culture: From Motif to Discourse

Treasure is ubiquitous in literature. From the earliest surviving texts onwards, it holds a central place in the construction of narratives, where it frequently acts as the trigger for actions or forms the goal of quests. In other genres it also provides fascinating images and a mysterious element. Its appeal has not lessened in an age in which traditional texts have to compete with many other media for the attention of an audience. Indeed, it is evident that treasure has not only survived well in contemporary writings (see the triumph of the Harry Potter series), but has also effortlessly migrated between the media, as the phenomenal success of *Pirates of the Caribbean* (a series of films based on computer games based on pirate stories) demonstrates.

Considering the lasting popularity as treasure, it is surprising that Literary and Cultural Studies have not taken greater pains to consider treasure more thoroughly. In fact, very little work has been dedicated to it, and if it has appeared as a point of interest, it has very often been dealt with as a mere motif, an image or object around which certain symbolic meanings have accumulated.

This is not in itself wrong, but it underestimates the conceptual and theoretical potential of treasure. The present collection of essays is a first tentative attempt to begin a re-evaluation of treasure along more informed conceptual and theoretical lines. It will show that treasure is generated from and simultaneously triggers certain structural and ideological formations. These in turn form part of important discourses, systems of generating truths and realities that are of central relevance to the establishment, development, but also critical transformation of cultures at any given point. Treasure, it will transpire, is a point of confluence that ties together a variety of important discourses that permit cultural self-definition as well as its distinction from supposed alterities.

Gender is one of the most evident of these discourses, and all contributions to the present volume will in some way or other present treasure and the quests for treasure as gendered. With the notable exception of some children's stories (Edith Blyton is a prominent example), treasure hunters are generally male. Treasure, in contrast, is often given feminine connotations – to the extent that for many centuries in Western cultures treasure was synonymous with a woman's chastity.

Yet gender never appears in isolation from other important discourses. Thus, class is a further issue that treasure foregrounds, and not only in cultures that are particularly determined by fixed class structures, such as the British one. It is no coincidence that the male treasure hunters generally hail from the privileged classes. In British adventure tales of the nineteenth century, a group of treasure hunters will generally be headed by a member of the upper class, at least a gentleman, sometimes even an aristocrat. Those getting the work done will, however, often belong to the middle classes. The antagonists, who wish to defy the treasure hunters and aim at securing the treasure for themselves, are frequently drawn as members of the underclass. They are also sometimes female. The social shifts that British culture underwent at the time are thus clearly mirrored in the fictional set-ups of treasure tales.

The same holds true for colonialism. The cultural alterities underpinning treasure are very evident here: treasures are often relics from the past and frequently the remains of other cultures. In the exotic settings of many treasure stories, the indigenous population generally plays the role of the underclass. If they are supportive of the (generally white, Western, privileged, and male) treasure hunters, they are permitted to play the role of helpers. In some extreme cases, they are even granted the privilege of sacrificing themselves for the treasure hunters. This is especially true for the women among them. Yet if they hinder the treasure hunters or attempt to deprive them of the opportunity of securing what they want, then the natives quickly assume the role of primitive villains. In the same way that the shifts in class structure mirror themselves in treasure stories, the mental set-up of colonial hierarchies and stereotypes (including its chauvinism and heteronormativity) finds its simplistic yet potent depiction there.

All this means that, far from being trivial, treasure stories through the millennia have a lot to tell us. They are linked with those discourses that generate cultural and individual identity in Western cultures. Gender and sexuality are among the most prominent of these. One could even polemically claim that treasure stories act as a mirror, distorting perhaps, but therefore by no means completely untrue, of both the mechanisms of cultural identity creation and their areas of tension, the blind spots that this creation produces. This is why treasure stories are rarely unambiguous, and why triumphant returns of successful treasure hunters are often tampered by the sacrifices they have had to make or by the awareness of who has lost out to secure the treasure hunter's success.

One could take this further, into areas such as psychoanalysis which also has its buried ambivalent treasures in the shape of traumas and repressed memories. One could look at the very mechanisms of interpretation and find treasure structures in the very philosophy that is concerned with unearthing supposedly hidden meaning, i.e. hermeneutics. The essays collected in this volume, although all using theory for their own purposes, represent a number of possible paths into the debate. They have been chosen to explore particular eras and areas of English Literature and British, European, and in one case African culture in which treasure manifests itself in especially telling ways. Some of the essays were first presented at a symposium entitled "Treasure in Literature, Culture and Theory" and Leibniz University Hanover in Germany in May 2009. Others were added afterwards to complement the picture.

Jessica Malay's essay takes us into the formative period of modern Western culture, the Renaissance. It shows that in the sixteenth and seventeenth century treasure acquired the status of what almost amounted to a mass hysteria. In an age when the accumulation of wealth shifted into the realm of individual possibility, residual religious and moral anxieties nevertheless made treasures and treasure hunting problematic territories. Treasure could for instance be associated with angelic as well as demonic forces. Even before late nineteenth-century psychoanalysis located the terrain of trouble in the unconscious, dreams and visions provided outlets for a cultural desire for treasure as well as for moral and religious scruples that came with it. Gender and legal issues provided strong "worldly" complications, and it is the latter to which we owe the survival of Renaissance treasure trouble in court documents.

Stefan Herbrechter's essay takes us into another crucial period for the formation of modern Western identities. The Romantic period, his essay demonstrates, marks the phase when self as treasure becomes the norm of Western thinking. In doing so, treasure also emerges as a constitutive element in theory, both the theory of interpretation where this treasure from then onwards oscillates between author and reader, and in the theory of the masculinist modern self where what it means to be a human being becomes contestable as soon as it has been proposed in its modern individualistic guise. Keats's famous "Ode to a Nightingale" acts as a litmus test for Herbrechter's interpretation of the Romantic self as treasure, which works along poststructuralist and deconstructive lines. The self as treasure as depicted in Keats's poem can, according to Herbrechter, be viewed as a link between a residual Romantic Humanism and the Posthumanism advocated by modern theorists and natural scientists.

Dominique Claisse examines the numerous treasure images in the works of Nathaniel Hawthorne. In his nineteenth-century tales of secrets, betrayals, and quests, treasure occupies a central position and one that aligns it with the shifts in the perception of the self from an enlightened rational being to a psychological one. It the new psychologised perception of the self, that which is hidden and locked away is central, and it is less its objective content that is important than its mystery and the desire for recovery it creates in the percipient. In Hawthorne's tales, Claisse argues, it is ultimately language, the language of fiction itself, that provides both the map for the treasure and the treasure whose recovery is often an ambivalent triumph. It is especially patriarchal norms and values and their reification of women as treasure that Hawthorne's irony undermines. There, finding one's treasure often amounts to a loss of the treasure hunter's self.

Karin Preuss' essay on Wilkie Collins' *The Moonstone* analyses the famous Victorian sensation novel as an intricate web of imperial, gender, and generic issues. According to her reading, the novel displays a shift between the literary genres of the "feminine" Gothic and the emerging "masculine" genre of detective fiction. At the same time, it confuses these gendered models again in the ambivalences of its characters. In the same way it makes a colonial treasure the obvious focus of its narrative, yet by doing so re-evaluates many domestic "treasures", such as the safe division of Victorian existence into private and public sphere, bourgeois respectability, or the respectability of science, medicine, and religion. Treasure thereby acquires more than a double edge: it becomes part of a multifaceted display of values as much as of a complex interrogation of such norms.

Rainer Emig's essay compares three late nineteenth-century adventure stories featuring treasure at their cores: Robert Louis Stevenson's *Treasure Island*, Henry Rider Haggard's *King Solomon's Mines*, and a German classic, Karl May's *Der Schatz im Silbersee* [The Treasure of the Silver Lake]. While discovering key characteristics of treasure stories in all of them, the analysis also detects odd areas of contradiction, especially in the novel's treatment of gender and morality. In keeping with their different position towards imperial endeavours, treasure hunting merits very different evaluations – to the extent of being discouraged altogether in May's tale (only to be replaced by industrial exploitation). In a similar manner, the status of treasure hunting between Divine mission, honest or not so honest labour and decadent thirst for adventure is often combined in a single story. Consequently, treasure becomes a mode of abjection in which that which is valued most (usually determined normative masculinity) can also represent that which one would like to exclude – from one's self-image, ideals of one's class, culture, or indeed nation.

Russell West-Pavlov's essay on Conrad's *Nostromo* concentrates on treasure *ex negativo* by highlighting the many instances in which supposed treasure in Conrad's texts hides an essential absence rather than a presence of identity, meaning, and value. Using Jacques Lacan and Harold Bloom as his theoretical inspirations, his essay shows that language becomes the medium and the means with which masculine identity as absence is created in Conrad's texts. This applies to names as much as to missions. In shifting the notion of meaning away from objective material presence and value, yet not into a direction of psychological interiority, but rather into a fluid semantics of superficiality, Conrad's text are thus as much part of an analysis and critique of the high capitalism and its attendant gender norms that informs the plots of his stories as they contribute to the literary and cultural movement of Modernism.

Marcin Stawiarski reads Richard Wagner's *Ring des Nibelungen* and Anthony Burgess's intertextual response *The Worm and the Ring* with their treasure motifs as allegories of quests for knowledge. Caught between treasure's implicit structure of accumulation, i.e. piling up, and the relational nature of treasure hunts, both Wagner and Burgess make gender and group relations, initiations, alliances, treasons and betrayals their theme. Moreover, they use intertextuality and intermediality to further include their spectators and readers in this creation of networks, in which the quest for value once again becomes a challenge to individual and group identity. The layers of meaning between which the quest for interpretation oscillates thus mirror the layers of identity as well as the layers of the texts and their respective media.

Carl Plasa's essay on Toni Morrison's *Song of Solomon* takes us to the United States and into the post-emancipation debates following the abolition of slavery. That the newly achieved "freedom" is an ambivalent one is shown in Morrison's novel in the father-son relationships. These hint at a continuing crisis in masculine identity, in which the issues of debt and loss, both on a metaphorical and a very material level, play a central part. Using Freudian notions of mourning and repetition, Plasa then opens them up by using the novel's intertextuality, especially towards Greek myths and African oral traditions, to show how the characters in the novel manage to escape from the reified identities to which the treasure structures in their existence tie them. It thus develops a concept of mourning that is liberating – rather than regressive.

Oliver Lindner's essay on two recent dystopian novels dealing with environmental catastrophes, David Mitchell's *Cloud Atlas* (2004) and Margaret Atwood's *The Year of the Flood* (2009), adds Ecocriticism to the range of investigations into treasure and gender in the present volume. Both texts view the environment and nature as treasures that are coveted, but also in need of protection. Both novels moreover display a telling gendering in their approach to nature and threats to the environment. These do not always manage to liberate themselves from traditional patriarchal views that associate nature with femininity and the shaping human spirit that, unfortunately, often threatens to destroy nature with masculinity. Nonetheless, their respective views of environmental protection and destruction and its consequences, read through the concept of 'risk', also permit interesting views of a resulting gender order.

Ellen Grünkemeier's essay on the discourses surrounding HIV and AIDS medication in contemporary South Africa takes the present collection of essays to a postcolonial territory and into Cultural Studies. It is striking to see, though, that treasure structures, especially the ones connected with limiting access and ascribing a tempting value, are as evident in the debates about HIV and AIDS treatment as they were in European Renaissance culture or British Victorianism. Only now treasure once again shifts from the metaphorical level to the pragmatic one when it comes to the question whether South Africa can afford this medication – and for whom. There, gender and sexuality become hotly debated aspects. While pregnant women are more likely to be considered worthy recipients of the "treasure" of HIV and AIDS medication, those who have been infected through sexual intercourse are not, especially if they belong to marginalised groups such as homosexuals or prostitutes.

Taken together, the essays in this collection are designed to open up – rather than fully explore and thereby close – possible debates on treasure. It is to be hoped that more publications and symposia will follow to assess further aspects of treasure and demonstrate that the wealth contained in treasure is worth excavating in literature and culture.

Jessica Malay

The Trouble with Treasure in Tudor and Stuart England

In 1607 a local "cunning woman" or healer was called to the sickbed of Susan Swapper whose symptoms included, "being troubled with treasure." That is, she had dreams and visitations telling of buried riches waiting for her nearby. This would sound to a modern audience more like a boon than an affliction which could be cured with a few hours of labour. Unfortunately, the seeking of treasure in sixteenth and seventeenth century England was a complicated and risky endeavour for a variety of cultural reasons, though many like Susan Swapper were willing to take the risk. In Swapper's visions two green men, or fairies, instructed her to dig in a secluded part of her garden near a summer house and plant sage in order to find the treasure. Susan, along with the healer Anne Taylor, followed this advice. Unfortunately there was no treasure in the garden and no end to Susanna's troubles. Both women were just beginning to be "troubled with treasure."

Indeed, throughout the sixteenth and seventeenth centuries the entire culture was troubled with treasure. This era saw heavy demands on the country's economy due to conflicts abroad and economic fluctuations, which often left large numbers in desperate need of funds for survival or advancement. Thus the hope of finding treasure that haunted many was understandable. Indeed, one could go so far as to say the expectation of finding treasure was not simply an unrealistic dream, but rather a reasonable assumption, and even a prudent activity in which to invest time and energy. The fairly regular discoveries of ancient treasure hoards and more contemporary stashes of goods hidden for security reasons was well publicized throughout the society and whetted the appetites of many. Rumours of vast amounts of wealth stowed away by religious institutions during the time of the dissolution of the monasteries also circulated widely. And while within the English legal system the right to treasure troves was reserved for the monarch, or to those to whom it was assigned by royal prerogative,[1] many certainly hoped to at least retain a part of any find through legal or illegal means. Thus while treasure could enrich, it also entailed a degree of risk. The practical difficulties relating to treasure as a material object were also intensified by long established religious teachings and cultural myths regarding the seeking and finding of treasure. When Susanna Swapper and her confederate Ann Taylor stumbled into these legal and

---

[1] Thomas Blount, *Nomo-lexikon, a law-dictionary* (London: 1670), sig. Sff2v: "Treasure-trove ... the Civil Law give it to the finder, according to the Law of Nature, yet, our Law gives it to the King by His Prerogative, or to some other, who claims by the Kings grant, or by praescription ... The punishment for concealing Treasure found is imprisonment and fine. But, if the owner may any wayes be known, then it does not belong to the Kings Prerogative."

16   Jessica Malay

ideological complications related to treasure, their unadvised sojourn came to threaten their very lives.

Certainly Swapper and Taylor would have been affected by the culturally infused meaning of treasure. This explains the fact that Swapper was "troubled" by thoughts of treasure, rather than delighted. By the sixteenth century treasure as a material object was weighted with centuries of moral, philosophical, religious and practical engagement. This resulted in the object itself functioning as an ambiguous and contested signification of divine satisfaction and as an instrument through which demonic chaos threatened individuals and entire nations.

The connection between treasure and death, both of the soul and the physical body, had been well established through medieval moral exemplum, derived from biblical and philosophical teachings. In visual media the connection between avarice, treasure and death was often explicitly represented. In the fifteenth century manuscript poem, the *Pilgrimage of the Life of Man*, a miniature illumination accompanying the text portrays a merchant, totally engrossed with his treasure. The allegorical figure of Avarice encourages the man in his singular occupation as Death prepares a coffin for the unwary merchant.[2] Avarice and treasure were of course a most congenial couple in medieval iconography. In an earlier medieval manuscript a chest of treasure hangs above the head of Avarice, serving as an emblem for the death of the soul brought about by this figure.[3] Perhaps the most well known exemplum in this tradition is the Pardoner's tale, from Geoffrey Chaucer's *Canterbury Tales*. In this tale three rascals rudely confront an elderly man in their search for Death. The old man obliges by instructing them to go to a particular tree. As the well known story progresses the three find a treasure underneath the tree, which through their avariciousness results in their deaths. Yet, this tale does not simply provide an uncomplicated warning concerning greed. Treasure here, and in many medieval texts, functions not only as a figure of evil but also as an instrument of divine will. The object itself is a neutral entity which serves as a catalyst revealing humanity's fallen nature and its dependence upon divine intervention for spiritual salvation.

While the theological reforms of the Reformation may have challenged and modified many beliefs surrounding humanity's relationship with the divine, treasure and its connection to human depravity survived relatively unchanged, as the sixteenth-century interlude, the *Trial of Treasure* demonstrates. However, this play is not simply an old style medieval allegory trussed up for "in hall" entertainment. Instead, the play reveals developing concerns regarding treasure that go beyond medieval pyschomachy. Here the complex relationship between treasure, the individual and the state becomes explicit, signalling concerns that continued to accumulate around both the conceptualisation of treasure and its function as a material object.

This self described "mery Enterlude" begins by communicating a relatively traditional moral theme:

---

[2] Cotton Tiberius A. VII, f.40, John Lydgate's translation of Guillaume de Guileville's poem *Pèlerinage de la vie humaine*.
[3] BL Royal 19 B. XIII.

The Trouble with Treasure in Tudor and Stuart England 17

> Even so evill men that are not contente,
> Are subjectes and slaves to their lustes and affection
> This lesson unto us may be a direction
> Which way our inclination to bridle and subdewe
> Namely if we labour the same to eschewe…
> The aboundant possessions of this mundaine treasure.[4]

These early lines convey to the audience that this play will provide a moral exemplum that will instruct them in the culture's desired moral position concerning material treasure. In so far as this play functions as a traditional morality play, this is certainly the case. The cast of characters is divided into a recognisable gallery of rogues and saints. The most entertaining, as is typical of this type of drama, are the rogues including: Luste, Natural Inclination, Pleasure and Greedy Gut. The obviously admirable, if slightly dull saints are listed as Sapience, Consolation, Trust, Just, and Contentation. Treasure is introduced in the play as a figure of vice. However, unlike the other allegorized concepts, treasure is problematised in that the vice figure as characterised does not contain the many meanings attached to the concept. The character Treasure does serve as an allegorical figure representing the material object and its traditional role as a catalyst for avarice. However, alternative significations of the term are constantly presented in juxtaposition, complicating the conceptualisation of treasure in a way unique to this particular figure within the play. This can be seen when Sapience contends: "For treasures here gotten are uncertaine and vaine/ But treasures of the mynde do continually remaine." Here "treasure" functions as a both signification of monetary wealth and intellectual understanding. Later Contentation and Trust use the term to refer to spiritual fulfillment, or "treasure celestiall," juxtaposing the treasure of the soul with material treasure (C4v-D1r). Contentation, continuing on this theme, infuses the metaphor of treasure further with the concept of spiritual election:

> Alas should we not have that estimation,
> Which God hath prepared for his dere elect,
> Shoud not our myndes reste in full contetation
> Having truste in this treasure most high in respecte. (D1r)

This metaphorical use of treasure as spiritual wealth is then explicitly compared with an oppositional construct of treasure as representative of material fortune and all the soul destroying vice long associated with the downfall of humanity. After listing several historical figures betrayed by treasure, Contentation concludes, "Howe sone by uncertentie, this treasure doth remove" (D1v). In other words, worldly wealth is fraught with anxiety and quickly lost. Within this juxtaposition of spiritual with earthly treasure is situated the moral message of the play. The wise individual will resist "natural inclination" and eschew material treasure while amassing "treasure of the mynde" (B5v). However, the result of this strategy of comparison is to insert ambiguity into the

---

[4] *A new and merry enterlude, called the triall of treasure* (London, 1567), sig. A2r-A2v. All further references are to this edition; signature marks are included parenthetically.

concept of treasure which affected the cultural relationship with both the concept of treasure and its material reality.

In sixteenth century England this relationship between the material and the spiritual inevitably included the political. This play signals the anxiety surrounding the concept of treasure and its role within the sociopolitical construct of sixteenth century English society. In this play, treasure as a material object could incite a variety of behaviours which threatened the stability of society. At its most innocuous, the play presents treasure as encouraging foolish behaviour. Contentation claims, "What men are more foolish, wretched and miserable/then those [that] in these treasures accompt their whole blys" (D1r). Beyond mere foolishness, the play serves to warn, through Natural Inclination's boast, that Treasure leads to criminal activity:

> The most noble champions by her hath ben murthered…
> Tushe, innumberable at this day spende their breath,
> Sume hange or be hanged, they love her so well. (C4r)

Yet, worse than these individual calamities, Contentation warns that Treasure corrupts "our realme, to our great decaie." Natural Inclination gleefully acknowledges that Treasure has caused the downfall of nations, "She of her power hath whole countries conquered" (C4r). Just explains more pointedly the threat treasure poses for a nation:

> It is often seene that such monsters ambitious,
> As spare not to spill the bloud o the innocente,
> Will not greatly stick to become seditious,
> The determination of God thereby to prevente:
> God graunt everyone of us earnestly to repent,
> And not to set our mindes or this fading treasure… (D1r)

Trust concurs, counseling all to "Fle from love of treasure..." (D1r).

The play ends with Time, an agent of God, confronting Treasure. Treasure is returned to the hell of Vulcan's fire, where she will be beaten to dust, while Just binds Natural Inclination. Trust and Consolation attest to the successful re-inscription of the term treasure, complementing Just for making a "treasure of Truste" (E3v). Within the play, not only does the material object of Treasure turn to dust, even the meaning of the term is appropriated to serve its moral theme. This re-inscription points to the instability inherent in the concept of treasure. It was an instability that existed not only in the linguistic field of a text, but permeated much of sixteenth and early seventeenth century England. The conceptualisations of treasure inherent in the culture were certainly informed by medieval morality. Yet within the changing political and religious climate of the period the ambiguity surrounding the concept of treasure bred a rich, if at times increasingly dangerous and bizarre, cultural relationship with treasure.

Unlike medieval morality plays, which tended to focus on the spiritual struggle within an individual, in the *Trial of Treasure* and other literary texts of the Tudor and Stuart period, the impact of individual moral conflict upon the wider body politic is continually made manifest. The more amusing, if at times disturbing, manifestation of disruption caused to society by the concept of treasure, as publicised in much of the popular writing, concerned the gulling of fools. One of the most entertaining narratives of the genre is a pamphlet entitled, "The Brideling, Sadling and ryding of a rich churle in Hampshire, by the Subtill practice of one Judith Philips."[5] In this tale Philips, hoping to both defraud and humiliate Sir William Kingsman, a knight in Hampshire, promises him buried treasure. The generic elements in this purportedly true tale include a rich but greedy man whose avaricious nature overcomes his common sense. The desire for treasure, as described in *The Trial for Treasure* "plucke from men the sence of their mind/ So that no contentation, therein they can finde" (D1r). In this tale, Judith Philips uses both flattery and folk superstition to lure her victims.

Through judicious use of compliments she is allowed to meet with Kingsman. Upon meeting him, the pamphlet describes Philips as looking at "him strangely in the face." She tells him, "that she knew by certaine signes in his forehead that he was in sute of lawe with some great man of the country, and how he should prevaile in his sute" (6). Considering that very few gentlemen of the day were not engaged in some sort of law suit from time to time, this piece of intelligence should not have had too much of an effect on Kingsman. The text clearly attributes Kingsman and his wife's subsequent bizarre behaviour to their greed, which clouds their judgment. Philips, having earlier planted a few gold coins under a holly tree, convinces the couple that greater wealth is to be had. She encourages them to lay out linen and coins in the house, and then to procure a bridle and saddle. In the yard she meets the couple and proceeds to saddle up Kingsman and rides upon his back between the chamber decorated with linen and the holly tree where the treasure was supposed to emerge (6-8). Philips, after engaging in this ritual humiliation of the knight, slips away with the linen and coins leaving the couple to spend a cold night under the holly tree.

The couple, after realizing they have been defrauded, suffer and repent for their avariciousness which led to such humiliation. Philips is captured, though goes on to commit further offences and is finally committed to Newgate prison (8-10). The writer of this pamphlet goes to great lengths to present this as a true account of the career of Judith Philips, naming places, dates and people involved in her tale. And yet, the narrative functions as a morality tale through which the couple must suffer for their human frailty before they are redeemed. The construct of treasure becomes an instrument of both their humiliation and their redemption.

Material treasure also fulfils this function in a similar narrative of deception recounted by Henry Chettle. In his book, *Kind-harts dreame conteining five apparitions,* he writes of a farmer and his wife near Winchester who are taken in by a cunning woman, again promising treasure. This tale contains the typical elements of the

---

[5] *The brideling, sadling and ryding, of a rich churle in Hampshire, by the subtill practise of one Judith Philips, a professed cunning woman, or fortune teller VVith a true discourse of her vnwomanly vsing of a trype wife, a widow, lately dwelling on the back side of S. Nicholas shambles in London, whom she with her confederates, likewise cosoned: for which fact, shee was at the Sessions house without New-gate arraigned, where she confessed the same, and had judgement for her offence, to be whipped through the citie, the 14. of February, 1594*, Printed at London: By T[homas] C[reede] and are to be solde by William Barley, at his shop in New-gate Market, neare Christ-Church, 1595. All further references are to this edition; page numbers are included parenthetically.

genre: a deceptive agent (generally female), the promise of treasure and the gulling of the foolish. However, Chettle inserts a more disturbing element in his tale. Here the couple, rather than being rich and avaricious are instead honest and simple farmers. The wife, falling into talk with the cunning woman, whom she takes to be a simple peddler, is amazed to hear the woman tell her that "shee shall have such for[tune] as never had any of her kinne: and if her husband were no more unlucky than she, they should be possest of s[uch] infinite a sum of hidden treasure, as no man in England had ever seene the like."[6] In this narrative however, the farmer is cautious, asking relevant and logical questions, including perhaps the most salient question–why if she was so poor in appearance did she not take the treasure herself? The cunning woman responds by alluding to common folklore regarding treasure, that the treasure is "by spirits possest, and they keepe it onely for them, to whome it is destinied."[7] The couple come to believe the woman and follow her suggestions, which end up being nearly identical to those of Judith Philips.

They decorate a room with their best linen and place gold coins around it. The farmer is saddled and bridled, after which the couple in a more menacing manner, are instructed to stay in the chamber and eschew meat and drink until the treasure becomes manifest. Despite being famished the couple keep their vigil until neighbours release them from their watch with news of a cunning woman being taken nearby. When asked why she humiliated the farmer in such a way, the woman replies: "onely to see how like an Asse hee lookt."[8] This tale, despite the obvious plot similarities, does more than simply caution against greedy foolishness. Instead it warns of the dangers and social disruption caused by treasure seeking.

Ben Jonson, never one to let an opportunity for biting satire to pass by, also uses this motif of a promised treasure through which a fool is exposed and humiliated. In *The Devil is an Asse*, performed in 1613, Jonson situates a satire on London's depravity within a narrative of greed. Again, the lure of treasure is the catalyst for much of the fun within the comedy. The miser figure, Fabian Fitzdottrel, obsessed with the desire for hidden treasure, hopes to make a pact with the Devil and secure demonic aid in his quest. With this in mind, he seeks out conjurers and magicians and of course puts himself in the way of exploitation by unscrupulous men. Two of these, Manly and Wittpol, quickly assess the situation in order to lay their plot:

> *Manly*: I would faine see more of him.
> *Wittpol*: What thinke you of this?
> *Manley*: I am past degrees of thinking.
> Old Africk, and the new America,
> With all their fruite of Monsters cannot shew
> So just a prodigie.
> *Wittipol*: Could you have beleev'd,
> Without your sight, a minde so sordide inward,
> Should be so specious, and laid forth abroad,
> To all the shew, that ever shop, or ware was?

---

[6] Henry Chettle, *Kind-harts Dreame Conteining Five Apparitions* (London, 1593), sig. K1r.
[7] Chettle, sig. K1r.
[8] Chettle, sig. K2r.

The Trouble with Treasure in Tudor and Stuart England   21

Manly: I beleeve any thing now, though I confesse
His Vices are the most extremities
I ever knew in nature. But, why loves he
The Divell so?
Wittipol: O Sir! for hidden treasure,
He hopes to finde: and has propos'd himselfe
So infinite a Masse as to recover,
He cares not what he parts with, of the present,
To his men of Art, who are the race, may coine him.
Promise gold-mountaines, and the covetous
Are still most prodigall.[9]

This passage, while certainly fulfilling the requirements of comedy, reveals again the prevailing moral position in relation to the seeking of treasure. Fitzdottrel's inability to recognize and seek spiritual aid in overcoming his depraved human nature marks him out as a fool, a gull, and even, as Manly suggests, a prodigious monster. Jonson, never gentle in his satire, uses the concept of hidden treasure as an instrument of discovery, allowing, as in the case of the knight and the farmer, inner depravity to become outwardly manifest. As Thomas Lodge quips in his tract, "Wits Miserie:"

> Promise him a familiar, and he will take a flie in a box for good paiment: if you long to know this slave, you shall never take him without a book of characters [spells] in his bosome. Promise to bring him to treasure-trove, he will sell his land for it, but he will be cousened [10]

All these narratives function most saliently as moral exempla, allowing for normative behaviour to be reinforced within society. The fools are exposed and humiliated, the deceivers are disposed of to prison or hell, social order is restored. Yet situated within these narratives is a shared cultural anxiety regarding the function of treasure and its ability to disrupt or threaten society, which is not adequately alleviated. The real life disruption of such activities could not be contained within these constructed narratives and thus this anxiety manifested itself in more sinister ways, hinted at in these fictional narratives and displayed more starkly within the institutions of government.

Perhaps the most disturbing element of treasure contributing to this anxiety was the long established connection between treasure and the satanic; a connection taken very seriously by the purveyors of social order. While the comic narratives of cons and gulls include allusions to the satanic, the relationship between treasure and evil was expounded upon in more serious texts. E. Fenton's translation of Pierre Boaistuau's *Sundry Abuses and Wonders of Sathan,* published in 1569, discusses the role of treasure in Satan's dominion over ancient Greece where Boaistuau claims Satan took residence at the site of the Oracle of Apollo and "kept his schole an open shop of villanous

---

[9] Ben Jonson, *The Divell is an Asse* (London, 1641), p. 9.
[10] Thomas Lodge *Wits miserie, and the Worlds madnesse discouering the deuils incarnat of this age* (London, 1596), p. 12.

22   Jessica Malay

crueltie."[11] Upon this site, Boaistuau claims, Satan amassed a "treasure above ten thousand talentes, amounting (according to the order of our accompt) to six Millions of golde," which was "so carefully garded by divels, that no mortal man durst assaile [...] his treasure ammased from so many partes of the world." As the narrative progresses, the role of this treasure in destroying kingdoms is made manifest–a "moving cause of feare to Princes."[12] Boaistuau goes on to catalogue the doom of several ancient princes seduced by the desire for this treasure of Satan's.

Henry Lawrence, in his *A History of Angells* (1649) also discusses the role of treasure in Satan's efforts to sow discord within society:

> Now in this the Divell as in other things juggles with us extreamely, one of the baites and snares, with which hee holds those personally and professedly subjected to him, is some money they shall get, some hidden treasure, these poore captives hee abuseth infinitely, and after severall yeares expectations of some great riches, and many diggings and minings, wherein by breaking some method, or other they faile a thousand times, they meet at last with winde in steed of gold, with that which lookes like it, but prooves leaves or dust when they use it. Remigius[13] reports that of all the moneys, that the witches that fell under his examination, acknowledge to have received from the Divell, there were but three stivers prooved currant, the rest were leaves, or sand, when it came to use; hee doth the same in effect with all earthly men, either hee deludes their hopes, they get not what they expected.[14]

Here we see Satan himself in the role of deceiver, a role that his deputies fulfil in the comic tales of those gulled with treasure. Lawrence also foregrounds the role of witches and witchcraft in the seeking of treasure. Paradoxically, Lawrence infers that while these deluded wretches barter their souls for "winde" the righteous shall be given the very treasure that these dupes of Satan are denied, "the Divell incourageth us to cracke the nut, but God takes away the kirnell, gives it to them that are good, before him; comfort and enjoyment and delight are the portion of his people."[15] Here again the paradoxical relationship to treasure present in the culture emerges. Yet despite this caveat that God could choose to bestow upon the elect the treasures of the world, Lawrence, in keeping with long established moral positions, concludes that the "litle that a righteous man hath, is better then the revenues of many wicked."[16]

John Field, in 1581, also explicitly connects the seeking of treasure with demonic activity. His treatise incorporates anti-papal sentiment with satanic activity both as moral injunction and political diatribe:

---

[11] Pierre Boaistuau, *Certaine Secrete Wonders of Nature*, trans. E. Fenton (London, 1569), p. 2.

[12] Boaistuau, *Certaine Secrete Wonders of Nature*, p. 2.

[13] Nicholas Rémy's Latin *Daemonolatreiae libri tres* (*Demonolatry*) was published in Lyon in 1595. In 1596 it was also published at Cologne and Frankfurt. A German translation, *Daemonolatria: Das ist Von Unholden und Zaubergeistern*, appeared in Frankfurt in 1598 and proved highly influential throughout Europe in the seventeenth century.

[14] Henry Lawrence, *An History of Angells* (London, 1649), p. 101.

[15] Lawrence, *An History of Angells*, p. 101.

[16] Lawrence, *An History of Angells*, p. 101.

The Trouble with Treasure in Tudor and Stuart England 23

> Benedict the second, who was a student of Negromancie, and fetched away by the Divell...appeared after his death on a blacke horse ... to a Byshop an acquaintance of his, to whom he said, he was that unhappy Benedict, being in great torment and shewed then of an hidden treasure, which til it was found he could never be quiet ... either in hell or in purgatory.[17]

Field uses this relationship between necromancy, demonic activity and treasure as part of his attack on papal power. He warns of the political chaos threatening the realm of England from not only seen and acknowledged enemies, but also the enemies of the spirit. This conflation of spiritual battle with the conflicts of nations was a key feature in much political writing of the period. This explains why, while the foolish knight and farmer in the comic narratives of gulling escaped from their treasure seeking fiasco with a lesson in humiliation, Anne Taylor and Susanna Swapper nearly paid for their indiscretion with their lives.

The fear of social disruption, political sedition and treason were all in some ways associated with the seeking of treasure by illicit means, though the definition of illicit means was sometimes vague enough to entrap the unwary. In 1542 the first English statute against witchcraft stated that it was prohibited for:

> any person or persons, after the first day of May next coming, [to] use, devise, practise or exercise, or cause to be used, devised, practised, or exercised, any invocations or conjurations of spirits, witchcrafts, enchantments, or sorceries, to the intent to get or find money or treasure, or to waste, consume or destroy any person in his body, members or goods.[18]

This act was later repealed, but was replaced in 1563 with another act prohibiting witchcraft. The stated reason for the reinstatement of an act against witchcraft was the effect of such behaviour on the stability of the realm:

> Since the repeal whereof [of the Henrician statute of 1542] many fantastical and devilish persons have devised and practised invocations and conjurations of evil and wicked spirits...[for] lewd intents and purposes contrary to the laws of Almighty God, to the peril of their own souls and to the *great infamy and disquietness of this realm.* [italics added].

The act specifically prohibited any person to "take upon him or them, by witchcraft, enchantment, charm, or sorcery, to tell or declare in what place any treasure of gold or silver should be found or had, in the earth or other secret places."[19] The penalties imposed for the seeking of treasure through demonic means in this act were: one year imprisonment for the first offence and imprisonment for life upon being convicted of a

---

[17] John Fielde *A Caveat for Parsons* (London, 1581), p. 13.

[18] 1542. 33 Hen. VIII, c. 8 [Statutes of the Realm, Vol. iii., p. 837]; Barbara Rosen, *Witchcraft in England 1558-1618* (Amherst, Massachusetts: University of Massachusetts Press, 1991 [1969]), p. 53.

[19] 1563. 5 Elizabeth, c. 16. [Statutes of the Realm, Vol. iv. pt. 1, p. 446]; Rosen, *Witchcraft in England 1558-1618*, pp. 54-56.

24 Jessica Malay

subsequent offence. In the 1604 revision of the statute against witchcraft the penalty for a second offence of seeking treasure by witchcraft became death.[20]

And yet the lure of treasure seeking was too much for many to resist, and indeed the cultural ambiguity surrounding the seeking of treasure, despite the statutes of 1563 and 1604, led many to consider treasure a commodity rather than an invitation to mortal death and eternal damnation. E.J. Kent suggests attempts to use supernatural means to find hidden treasure was "fairly common."[21] Certainly, the sixteenth century records concerning illegal behaviour in Essex uncover a number of instances where supernatural aid was sought to find treasure. In 1577 Robert Mantell was questioned for treasure seeking and keeping a familiar. He was also questioned about the activities of a Dr. Spacy [Spacie]. Later a Ralph Spacie was apprehended for conjuring.[22] In 1573 a tailor named Robert Wallys, from the village of Chishall in Essex, defrauded money from a variety of people by pretending he could invoke demons through which the secret whereabouts of hidden treasure would be revealed. He was found innocent of this charge, but was instead found guilty of vagabondage which carried a lesser penalty.[23] When considering the penalties handed down for the crimes related to treasure seeking, the state obviously believed the use of fraudulent claims concerning the ability to find treasure through demonic means to be less threatening to society than the actual use of demons, as in the case of Anne Taylor and Susanna Swapper.

As mentioned at the beginning of this essay, Susanna Swapper, a resident of Rye, in East Sussex, suffered a variety of ailments, including being "troubled with treasure."[24] Strange as it may seem, this was not an unusual ailment in the period. In a letter written to William Cecil, Lord Burghley (and Elizabeth I's Lord Treasurer) John Dee, a scholar well known for his esoteric knowledge, claims to have been "sued unto by divers sorts of people. Of which some by vehement iterated dreams, some by visions (as they have thought,) others by speech formed to their imagination by night, have been informed of certain places where tresure doth ly hid."[25] This letter shows that Susanna Swapper's condition was not unique. And, like the many who contacted John Dee, she also sought a person whom she believed could relieve her of her symptoms, although this was likely a disingenuous way of acting upon the hope that actual treasure could be found.

In her case Swapper enlisted the help of a cunning woman, Anne Taylor, who already had a reputation in the community as a healer. Unfortunately, Swapper's alliance with Taylor was the beginning of very real problems with the Rye officials,

---

[20] Alan Macfarland, *Witchcraft in Tudor and Stuart England*, 2nd ed. (London: Routledge, 1999), p. 115.

[21] E. J. Kent, "Masculinity and Male Witches in Old and New England, 1593–1680", *History Workshop Journal* 60 (2005), 71.

[22] Macfarland, *Witchcraft in Tudor and Stuart England*, p. 303.

[23] Indictment of Robert Wellys, 20 June 1573, T/A 418/22/32, Calendar of the Essex Assize Records, Essex Records Office, Chelmsford.

[24] Papers concerning the trial of Susannah Swapper and Ann Taylor for Witchcraft, Rye /13, East Sussex Records office Rye. See also Annabel Gregory, "Witchcraft, Politics and 'Good Neighbourhood' in Early Seventeenth-Century Rye", *Past and Present* 133 (1991), 31-66.

[25] A letter dated 3 Oct 1574 from John Dee to William Cecil, Lord Burghley, Lansdowne 19, f. 81r-83r, British Lib., London; John Strype, *Annals of the Reformation* (Oxford: Clarendon Press, 1824), p. 559.

The Trouble with Treasure in Tudor and Stuart England 25

both for herself and Taylor. Taylor had up to this time, like her mother before her, managed to serve the community as a healing woman without running afoul of the law. Interestingly, during the examination of these two women it was discovered that a previous tenant at Swapper's home, which Swapper was renting from Anne Taylor's mother, had also suffered from acute feelings of treasure within the vicinity of the property. It is likely this was proffered as a sort of defence to suggest that Swapper was a victim of a malady located in her lodging, and not a result of her own depravity. The addition of this information to her explanation illustrates her belief that the officials would recognize being "troubled with treasure" as a genuine malady. Of course, it was not the ailment that raised official ire; it was Swapper's actions in relation to her troubles that brought her into conflict with the keepers of social order.

Swapper chose to follow Taylor's suggestion that her physical and spiritual ailments would be eased by simply following the instructions of the green men of her visions. Swapper and Taylor "planted" the sage in the appointed place and Swapper's ailments were relieved, though no treasure was uncovered. If the two had stopped at this point it is unlikely they would have attracted the notice of officials. However, like the weak individuals that featured ubiquitously in the literature of the period, the temptation of riches was too much for Swapper. In describing her next adventure she explained that a spirit revealed to her that gold was buried at Weeks Green, outside of Rye. This plot of land had belonged to Taylor and her mother, so it is likely Taylor may have had some part in planting the suggestion that treasure resided there. Swapper describes how she was met by the queen of the fairies and was offered riches if she would do the fairy queen's bidding. Swapper asserted she refused and became ill.[26] Swapper was subsequently found guilty of communing with demonic spirits. The court document stated that Swapper:

> not having God before her eyes and led by diabolical instigation, at Rye aforesaid, wickedly, diabolically, and feloniously "did councell" with certain wicked and impious spirits, and the same wicked and impious spirits "did enterteyne and feed" in order to gain wealth, against the King's peace and the form of the Statute.[27]

Swapper was sentenced to death in 1609, an incredibly harsh sentence given she had no earlier accusations of witchcraft and her "crime" was related to potential material gain only and not the harming of persons. They key to the harshness of the sentence given is probably the phrase, "in order to gain wealth, against the King's peace." Swapper's communing with spirits was seen to threaten society by providing a conduit for these spirits to work in the world. In the end, Swapper was not executed. She was imprisoned until 1611 when she was finally pardoned.[28] Anne Taylor, after further difficulties relating to the use of witchcraft, was acquitted.[29] Unlike the fools and wickedly greedy, which were the steady fodder of moralists and satirists of the day, these two women sought treasure as a means of alleviating the harsh economic

[26] Gregory, "Witchcraft", 35-37.
[27] Mayoralty of Richard Cockram, RYE/47/79/14, East Sussex Record's Office. Lewes.
[28] RYE/47/79/14.
[29] Gregory, "Witchcraft", 36.

26   Jessica Malay

conditions in which they found themselves in a society where the margin between respectability and destitution was at times very thin. Indeed, one of the reasons put forward for Anne Taylor's interest in finding treasure at Weeks Green was the hope of recovering the land which her father had been forced to sell due to economic hardship.[30]

Susan Swapper, in seeking out the aid of Anne Taylor, no doubt believed initially that she was being prudent. The seeking of some sort of legitimacy for one's activities when "troubled with treasure" was commonplace. Certainly this is what Edmund Hunt of Maldon, in Essex attempted to do initially. Hunt claimed in court documents that he was continually disturbed by the thought that treasure was buried in the grounds of Beeleigh Abbey. Again, by claiming he was "troubled with treasure" Hunt was certainly attempting to situate the source of his subsequent actions outside his own moral responsibility. Hunt consulted Thomas Collyne who suggested they send a soil sample to John Dee. Whether Hunt and Collyne were among those that Dee wrote had contacted him is unknown. What is clear is that Hunt was not willing to wait for Dee's more authoritative advice, and was determined to seek treasure with or without the approbation of a more powerful sponsor. Hunt managed to obtain a parchment "full of crosses, characters and strange names" that he believed related to the treasure he sought. He showed this to John Mace while drinking in the White Horse Inn at Maldon. This was not a particularly wise decision on Hunt's part as Mace charged Hunt with use of witchcraft to secure treasure, the parchment serving as a damning piece of evidence against him.[31]

Another treasure seeker, William Hobby, was apparently trying to be more prudent than others with the same interests. In a letter dated 28th April 1589 he contacted Lord Burghley with bizarre request.[32] Burghley, as Lord Treasurer was placed in an unparalleled position of authority within Elizabeth's government, and thus uniquely situated to give permission regarding the seeking of treasure. In Hobby's letter he asks Burghley to allow him to "drive the Devil and his dam" away from treasure he believed to be hidden in the castle of Skenfrith, in Monmouthshire. There is no evidence that Burghley ever responded to Hobby. However, it is clear that Burghley found Hobby's letter disturbing as it was saved with a collection of letters by writers of concern to Burghley, and by extension the state. Many of the letters are from extremist elements within the society, as well as from persons exhibiting signs of insanity. For example, one letter dated 28 June 1587, from Miles Fry claims to be writing to Burghley at the request of God. He purports to be the son of God and Queen Elizabeth, taken away from the Queen at birth by the angel Gabriel and left with a Mrs. Fry.[33] Other letters also contain claims of mysterious high birth and demand the perquisites of their imagined station. Many are rants against various factions in society, including foreign workers, Catholics and Puritans. The fact that Hobby's letter was kept amongst these suggests that Burghley found the request for treasure seeking a matter of possible suspicion. Whether Hobby and the writers of the other letters in the group were placed under some

---

[30] Gregory, "Witchcraft", 39.

[31] D/B 3 1/8, Essex Record Office, Chelmsford, f. 23, 23v, 87v. Kent 72. Marfarlane 296-297.

[32] Letter dated 28th April 1589 from William Hobby to William Cecil, Lansdowne 99, no. 11, British Lib., London.

[33] Lansdowne 99, no. 6, British Lib., London.

The Trouble with Treasure in Tudor and Stuart England 27

sort of surveillance is unclear, but it is obvious the letters created at least a degree of anxiety in Burghley's mind.

Perhaps the most intriguing letter to reach Burghley concerning treasure seeking came from John Dee. Dee opens his letter by rehearsing his scholarly accomplishments and the struggles he has undergone and continues to undergo in an effort to expand his knowledge for the service of God and the state:

> To compare with any in public deserts and learning, I neither dare, nor justly can; but in zele to the best learning and knowledge, and incredible toyls of body and mind very many years, therefore only endured, I know most assuredly, that the learned never bred any man, whose accounts therein can evidently be proved greater than mine.[34]

His purpose in this letter is to secure the funds necessary to provide his "poor family necessary meat, drink and fewel, for a frugal philosophical diet." He proposes that should there be no means available from the government to fund him, he could try funding himself, through treasure seeking and, as can be assumed, treasure finding. Dee reminds Burghley that ancient chronicles recorded treasure being hidden in the land. He also informs Burghley, as noted earlier, that "divers sorts of people" have asked for his assistance after being informed of the whereabouts of treasure in dreams and visions. He notes that these people refrain from actually seeking out this treasure "for fear of *keepers* [i.e. demons] [...] or for mistrust of truth in the places assigned, and for some other causes, have forborn to deal further; unless I should encourage them." Aware of the legal and moral injunctions against seeking treasure by supernatural means, Dee is quick to add, "Wherein I have always been contented to hear the histories, fantasies, or illusions to me reported; but never intermeddled according to the desire of such."[35] Dee's statement here is not quite true, as will be shown. Dee readily acknowledges that the seeking of treasure is controversial amongst theologians and men of learning, but believes that treasure seeking in and of itself is not ungodly. He assures Burghley that he is:

> ready to answer only your lordship most largely, in termes of godly philosophy, when opportunity shall serve; making small account of vulgar opinions in matter of so rare knowledge. But making always my chief reckoning to do nothing but that which may stand with the profession of a true Christian, and of a faithful subject.

By asserting that his intentions are compatible with being a Christian and a faithful subject Dee shows that he is clearly aware of the anxiety treasure seeking elicited in the minds of both secular and religious authorities. He appears to be counting on his reputation for scholarship to counter the obvious objections to his scheme which Burghley might pose. But his comments are more than calculated rhetoric. Dee certainly believed that the reasons he had for seeking treasure and the methods he intended to employ differed from the unlawful methods of a Hunt or a Swapper. In Dee's attitude toward treasure the cultural ambiguities inherent in treasure as a material object emerge.

---

[34] Dee, Letter to William Cecil, 559.
[35] Dee, Letter William Cecil, 560-561.

28   Jessica Malay

Dee believed that material treasure could be the means through which divine intention
became manifest. He clearly felt that his own efforts in seeking treasure were sanctioned
by God, as he reveals in his angelic conversations.

Dee sought out contact with angelic beings in the belief that he could come to a
"pure and sownd wisdom and understanding of some of thy [God's] truths natural and
artificiall [...] to thy honor & glory, & the benefit of thy Servants, my brethern and
Sistern."[36] To this end Dee perfected a system of communication using a skryer (the
most famous of these was Edward Kelley) who claimed to see and hear the angels with
the assistance of a crystal ball (crystology), or at times an obsidian mirror. Deborah
Harkness suggests that the angelic conversations provided "a role for Dee and his
natural philosophy in an apocalyptic redefinition of the relationship between humanity
and the natural world."[37]

In the past many scholars struggled to accommodate Dee's supernatural activity
with his wide-ranging work in natural philosophy, mathematics and other scholarly
pursuits. Recently, several studies on John Dee have concluded that Dee's angelic
conversations form a part of the many contradictory subtexts in Dee's career[38] and were
not out of keeping with intellectual inquiry of the late sixteenth century when, as
Stephen Clucas contends, the boundaries between magical, religious, devotional and
scientific pursuits were often quite fluid.[39] This explains why Dee felt confident that
Burghley would appreciate the difference between his proposal and the mad or
felonious actions of other treasure seekers. The record of Dee's angelic conversations
provides insight to contemporary attitudes and anxieties relating to treasure as a
conceptual construct as well as a material object in a way many other narratives do not.

Dee, despite his assurances to Burghley, did "intermeddle" in the affairs of those
who sought his aid in solving their visions of treasure. In a conversation with the angel
Murifri he seeks counsel in the case of a woman:

> who hath great need, and is driven to maintain her self, her husband, and three children by
> her hand labour, and there is one that by dream is advertised of a place of Treasure hid in
> a Cellar, which this woman hath hired thereupon, and hath no longer time of hiring the
> said Cellar, but till Midsummer next. She, and this dreaming Maiden digged somewhat,
> and found certain tokens notefied unto her: But so left off. I would gladly have your help
> herein, if it pleased God.[40]

---

[36] John Dee, *John Dee's Actions With Spirits*, ed. Christopher Whitby, vol. 2 (New York:
Garland, 1988), p. 8. Deborah E. Harkness, "Shows in the Showstone: A Theater of Alchemy and
Apocalypse in the Angel Conversations of John Dee (1527-1608/97)", *Renaissance Quarterly* 49
(1996), 713.

[37] Harkness, "Shows in the Showstone", 710.

[38] György E. Szönyi, "Paracelsus, Scrying, and the Lingua Adamica", *John Dee: Interdisciplinary
Studies in English Renaissance Thought,* ed. Stephen Clucas (Amsterdam: Springer, 2006), pp.
207-229 (p. 221).

[39] Stephen Clucas, "John Dee's Angel Conversations and the *Ars Notoria*: Renaissance Magic and
Mediaeval Theurgy," *John Dee: Interdisciplinary Studies in English Renaissance Thought*, pp.
231-273 (p. 257).

[40] Dee, John, *A true & faithful relation of what passed for many yeers between Dr. John Dee and
some spirits,* ed. Meric Casaubon (London: 1659), p. 5. All further references are to this edition,

The Trouble with Treasure in Tudor and Stuart England 29

There is no record of Murifri's answer, but other conversations show the angelic guides as reluctant to become involved in the recovery of treasure. In another conversation, Dee hopes to ask the angel Madimi "about Treasure hid in England." In this case Madimi answers obliquely that she has been "charitable" (69). Dee receives no other satisfaction. Another of Dee's inquiries is directed at the angel Raphael, concerning treasure taken from a man called Eccleston and hidden by James Bolton. The angel Raphael appears uncomfortable with the subject of treasure as befits an angel and admonishes Dee, "I Raphael do now tell thee, that this matter, and all such like unto it, are not for me to enter into, neither for any such as be of that high Society and Calling as I am of." However, he does condescend to allow lesser angelic beings to ensure the return of the treasure to the rightful owner, Eccleston, because this is "God's pleasure" (39).

At times, the angels become impatient with Dee's regular questions regarding treasure, Raphael chides, "John Dee, be not too much inquisitive, but what shall be best to your liking in any good cause whatsoever you or he shall think good to be done for your good, God will put his assistance and help that you shall perceive Gods favour therein" (43). Later in this conversation the topic of treasure emerges again, and this time the narrative reveals the cultural myths and social prejudices surrounding the hiding and seeking of treasure. The conversation also validates for Dee the widely held belief that an enormous amount of treasure continued to lay hidden in the country.

In this conversation the angel Raphael discusses with Dee the case of a man called George Sherman who was "troubled with treasure." This man continually dreamt that treasure "in times past" was buried under the wall of the ruined Delapre Abbey near Northampton and close to the house of Sir William Tate. Raphael proceeds to explain the exact location of the treasure and how the treasure came to be hidden:

> That man [George Sherman] may lawfully have it, if he take heed [...] for it is for the greatest part under the bottom of the wall, and many roots of thorns and trees that will let and hinder the working for it [...] go under the roots, the which he may well and lawfully do. So doing, he may well obtain his purpose; and now you have plainly understood the truth. The one part of that Treasure was laid by an old Nun, that was of that house, at that time, and one that was her brother, and the other was [...] hid at the same time by one of the Lords that was there killed, and so it hath remained ever since, the one place more easier to come at then the other, but with the favour of God, and in his mercy, that good fortune to be desired at parties hand, it may be had and compassed by the said party. (43)

In its generic elements this narrative is not significantly different from the story Susanna Swapper confessed to her inquest. A divine being directs a deserving subject towards a treasure that will ensure good fortune. However, through the transformation of particular agents the tale is changed from one of transgression to one of divine election – the will and favour of God rather than the demonic whim of a fairy queen. One can easily identify the element of wish fulfilment on the part of Dee in this narrative. When

page numbers are included in the text parenthetically. Casaubon transcribed the notes for angelic conversations after 1583. For a modern edition of the transcription of John Dee's angelic conversations, including the angelic conversations that took place between 1581 and 1583 see Whitby, vols 1 and 2.

the angel Raphael asserts that Sherman may "lawfully" have the treasure, celestial law replaces common law. The treasure trove at Delapre Abbey, should one be found, would have been the property of the Queen, or those granted the right to treasure trove in that manor. It is likely in this case that Sir William Tate would have held this right. And while Dee may have been perfectly satisfied with Raphael's disposing of the Queen's rights believing that celestial permission had greater authority than secular law and custom, it is likely that Burghley would have been decidedly more cautious.

In fact Dee's letter in effect asks Burghley to assign Dee the rights of treasure trove which had for centuries been a royal prerogative. Dee cleverly infers that his methods for finding treasure will also be useful in finding veins of precious metals of which he has no interest, but is content for the profit of these to go to the state, "The value of a mine is matter for a king's use, but a pot of two or three hundred pounds hid in the ground, jarr, or tree, is but the price of a good book, or instrument for perspective, astronomy, or some feat of importance."[41] Dee finishes by asking for the Queen to give him "letters patent" to all treasure he recovers through use of his scholarship. He also offers to give Burghley half of all treasure he finds.

Again, as in the case of Hobby, there is no record of Burghley's reply. And while there is no obvious clue to signal that Burghley was uncomfortable with Dee's request, his silence on the matter of treasure is telling. The right to treasure trove was a complicated issue in the period. Deeds and grants to manors and families throughout the centuries created a legal tangle, as the conflict between Sir John Oglander and the Gard family on the Isle of Wight reveal. On the 18th of May 1631 Richard Jarvis discovered a treasure trove worth 110 pounds under the floor of a barn on land Nicholas Gard inherited from his uncle, Richard Gard. Thus began a contentious exchange over the ownership of the treasure. Nicholas Gard claimed the treasure was simply his own money which he had secreted away as a precaution. Sir John Oglander, as deputy Governor of the Isle of Wight believed the treasure had been buried by Richard Gard. As Richard Gard was dead, his hidden treasure legally became the property of the crown or his assignees. This is why Nicholas Gard asserted so vehemently that the treasure was his. The crux of the case hinged upon whose treasure was actually hidden under the floor boards. Oglander clearly believed the treasure was not the property of Nicholas Gard and sought to gain control of the treasure as this letter to Henry Knowles makes clear:

> I delivered to My Lord Treasurer your [Oglander's] letter with the examinations about the treasure trove. The Council were clearly of the opinion that it was the Kings, when I received a petition on behalf of Richard [actually Nicholas] Gard claiming that the money belonged entirely to him.

Oglander apparently believed that he would personally benefit from at least a portion of the treasure recovered should he be able to get his hands on it. However, by July 1631 the treasure continued to remain in the possession of the Gards, much to Oglander's irritation: "I have laboured what I could to get the moneys into my custody, but Nicholas Gard is ruled by his father, one Peter Garde, a rich curr, one that affects and

---

[41] Dee, Letter to William Cecil, 561.

The Trouble with Treasure in Tudor and Stuart England 31

desires altogether opposition." The matter was still not resolved by the following June (1632) when a letter from William Lake to Oglander affirms that Lake will carry the business forward. There appears to be no record of the final resolution of the matter.[42] The Gard family was a large and prosperous family on the island. Indeed, Oglander himself has served as one of the executors of Richard Gard's will. This episode obviously created a degree of discord within the community. The tenacity with which both the Gards and Oglander pursued the matter would have justified many contemporary attitudes concerning the negative effect of treasure upon individuals and communities.

The Oglander/Gard conflict also reveals the widely held belief that treasure was a commodity which could benefit the person who managed to gain or maintain possession of it. The surveyor, John Norden clearly believed that treasure was part of the value of many manors, as he explains in his *Surveyors Dialogue*:

> Treasures, which, as long as they lie unknowne, benefit not the Lord: but when they are found, they are called Treasure trove, as Silver, Gold, Plate, Jewels, and such like, before time hidden, which appertaine unto the Lord. So doe minerals of Lead [...] Copper, and such like.[43]

It is the caveat "unknowne" that may have given Burghley pause before disregarding Dee's request. For as Bernard Georges noted in his preface to a 1596 translation of Paracelus: "there commeth no commoditie or profit of hidden treasure."[44] In a country that viewed itself as the last bastion of Christianity locked in an apocalyptic struggle with the forces of the Anti-Christ represented by Spanish dominion, hidden treasure within the country was a commodity whose potential value was very attractive. John Dee's interest in treasure stemmed at least in part from his ambitious hopes for a British imperial project. The funds treasure could provide were seen by Dee as a means to this end and he hoped to convince Burghley of this as well. Despite this important consideration, Burghley, and indeed John Dee himself, decided it was more prudent to leave the discovery of hidden treasure in the hands of a providential God.

The most likely reason for this decision is revealed in anxiety surrounding the actual seeking of treasure that permeates Dee's conversations with angels in the same way it permeated society. The angel Nalvage, like a character in a morality play, advises Dee in one conversation that it is the "entrance into the secret mysteries of God" that bring eternal glory, "which is the greatest Treasure" (64). Dee acknowledges to the angel Juban that "the treasures of the Lord are not scant, to them whom he favoureth" (23). The angel Ave speaks to Dee of the "Treasures of the Heavens" and chides Dee for his interest in the "Treasures of the Earth," explaining that the treasures of the earth when used for earthly means corrupt men (187). And yet despite the obvious distaste the angels constantly assert for earthly treasure, Ave does acknowledge that from this

---

[42] The Oglander Collection , OG/BB/227, 228, 231, 268, Isle of Wight Records Office, Newport.
[43] John Norden, *The Surveyors Dialogue* (London, 1607), p. 66.
[44] Bernard Georges, preface, *Paracelsus, A hundred and fouretene experiments and cures of the famous physitian Philippus Aureolus Theophrastus Paracelsus*, trans. John Hester (London, 1596), sig. B2r.

32 Jessica Malay

corrosive wealth could come the substance and means for Dee to continue what he believed was his divinely sanctioned scholarship:

> *Ave*: The good Angels are ministers for that purpose [to provide Dee with financial support.]. The Angels of the 4 angles shall make the Earth open unto you, and shall serve your necessities from the 4 parts of the Earth.
> *Dee*: God make me a man of wisdom in all parts, I beseech him. (188)

In this particular conversation with Ave Dee notes that he was concerned with "my part in Devonshire Mines: and of the Danish Treasures which were taken of the Earth," and sought divine approval for his activities.[45]

Dee, in his angelic conversations, desired to obtain knowledge and understanding beyond that available to him within the scholarship and common lore of his culture. Instead, at least in regards to treasure, what the angelic conversations do is to rehearse long held cultural myths regarding treasure. Dee's experiences confirm that in the sixteenth century treasure, in both its physical and linguistic manifestations, functioned as a sort of palimpsest allowing simultaneous meanings to exist. In this way treasure could signify both satanic depravity and chaos while at the same time symbolise the means through which divine intention could become manifest on earth. This palimpsestic quality clearly allowed for the deployment of the sign in an apparently contradictory fashion. Treasure, as a material object, could be appropriated as a commodity which served to bolster a robust and, at times, apocalyptic imperialism, while at the same time fomenting discord in society by encouraging disharmony within communities, criminal behaviour, and even a providing a portal through which demonic forces could threaten the realm.

The government, itself acting upon pragmatic concerns and inherited cultural mores, sought to control the effects of treasure, positioning itself as both the guardian of social stability and spiritual health. It attempted to accomplish these dual roles, in a manner typical of governments of the time, by limiting authority over treasure to the crown and his/her designees. The right to hidden treasure, or treasure-trove, resided with the crown, though these rights were often devolved by monarchs to individuals or organizations.[46] Yet even within the actions of government the multiple and contradictory meanings inherent in the concept of treasure were present. The right to treasure trove was often given along with the rights to waifs and strays as well as the goods of felons and fugitives. Thus, even in legal documents where rights to treasure were given as a sign of monarchic favour, the term was contiguous with the disasters and depravity of human existence.

---

[45] p. 188. There is no evidence that Dee ever received funds from a treasure trove or mining operations, so perhaps when he speaks of his part, he alludes to his part in a project to find mines and treasure.

[46] For instance, Henry VI granted John Carpenter, Bishop of Worcester, and his successors "all manner of deodands and treasure trove, the goods and chattels of felons, fugitives and others" in letters patent dated 13 February 1446. Ms 34444/435327, Birmingham City Archives, Birmingham.

Despite strategies to contain the concerns that surrounded treasure both as a material object and a concept, Tudor and Stuart Britain continued to be "troubled with treasure." The narratives of treasure which they fashioned for theatres, literature and legal documents reveal not only the age old connection between greed and treasure, but more contemporary issues. Religious attitudes and prejudices developing out of the Reformation are displayed in these tales of treasure. Concerns about the effect of economic changes upon the structures of society are also alluded to within many narratives. Individuals are shown negotiating their temporal and spiritual identities when confronted with treasure in its material and conceptual forms. These negotiations reveal their attempts to incorporate the particular demands of their society with the often contradictory edicts of contemporary religious belief. As such, these narratives remain fascinating, if discordant, tales through which the competing desires of a culture and its resultant anxieties are displayed.

Stefan Herbrechter

Treasuring the Self: Romanticism...in Theory

> ...at once it struck me, what quality went to form a Man of Achievement especially in Literature & which Shakespeare possessed so enormously – I mean *Negative Capability*, that is when man is capable of being in uncertainties, Mysteries, doubts, without any irritable reaching after fact & reason...[1]

Secret Treasures

> It has been rightly said: "Where your treasure is, there will your heart be also"; our treasure is where the beehives of our knowledge are.[2]

The word 'treasure' seems to provoke the most romantic associations of deserts, islands and ancient monuments, hiding at once terrible and dangerous secrets and promising the most gratifying booty. They are perfect screens of our desires and anxieties, and thus represent the very essence of who we are, i.e. the treasure and me, or the treasure of my 'self', myself as treasure. The notion of treasure is evidently shot through with metaphysics and is therefore closely connected to the question of identity, literature, meaning, truth and presence – all those questions that have been dealt with by this very specific twentieth-century academic discourse called theory and, before that, by the Romantics. It therefore seems promising to look at treasure not so much as a motif but as a symptom or maybe a crypt of a very specific metaphysical necessity. In fact, it is more the verb, the dynamic process of treasuring that might be of help here, and which this essay wants to investigate through what might be taken as an exemplary Romantic poem – Keats's "Ode to a Nightingale". It will do so in relation to theory, which in the context of the present paper is really shorthand for poststructuralism and deconstruction, and the question of what their futures might hold in store.

The *Oxford English Dictionary*, this treasury and thesaurus of words, promising the instantaneous and complete fullness of meaning, defines treasure as "wealth or riches stored or accumulated; esp., in the form of precious metals... A store or stock of anything valuable... Anything valued and preserved as precious". While the verb, 'treasure', refers to "put away or lay aside (anything of value) for preservation, security,

---

[1] John Keats, *The Letters of John Keats, 1814-1821*, 2 vols, ed. Hyder Edward Rollins (Cambridge, Massachusetts: Harvard University Press, 1958 [1817]), vol. 1, p. 193.
[2] Friedrich Nietzsche, *On the Genealogy of Morals*, § 1, cited in Daniel W. Conway, *Nietzsche and the Political* (London: Routledge, 1997), p. 60.

or future use; to hoard or store up... to furnish or endow with treasures... to enrich... to cherish, prize". It seems as if the very ambiguity of Derridean *différance* (with its ever-deferring 'fullness' or 'presence' and its ever-differing meaning from it(s)self as the impossible foundation of 'Western metaphysics') is at work in the very concept of treasure and treasuring.[3] In the storing aspect of treasure, which we might call the archival dimension, the identity of treasure seems secured or at least determinable as value, its preciousness based on rarity, difference and economy. The very storing of the treasure, however, is future-oriented, based on deferred enjoyment, as a source of desire that is based on hiding. This we might call the secretive aspect of the treasure whose essence or truth must remain hidden and postponed. In an almost classical Derridean sense, the treasure, therefore, haunts. Its metaphysical drift, like that of any metaphysics, is towards a 'hauntology', namely a presence promised to itself that nevertheless must remain a ghostly and insistent, deferred, Other. Treasure's essence, one might say, lies in this yearning, which is the fundamental drive of its underlying metaphysical humanism – as manifest in literature, and especially Romantic poetry – a desire to become transparent to one's self, or to Nietzsche's fusion of becoming and being, pure acting, life and art.

Keats – Autobiography of a National Treasure

> Literature keeps a secret that doesn't exist, in a sense.[4]

Why Keats? Why the "Ode to a Nightingale"? In a sense, both are national treasures, of course, perhaps even treasures of world literature. Keats's life has fired up people's imagination, while the "Ode to a Nightingale" keeps on puzzling its readers as to what extent it might possibly be an autobiographical crypt. In fact, this combination constitutes an almost perfect example of the idea of the 'secret of literature' and the 'secret in literature'. According to Derrida, literature harbours an absolute secret of alterity, namely the structural unknowability of the other as other, which is the necessary space for any fictionality to become possible. In other words, radical undecidability between fiction and fact and the idea that literature, at least 'in theory', must be allowed to say anything, is what constitutes the impossible identity of fiction and possibly the very principle of identity in general. In addition, the essence of any secret (literature, identity…) is something that cannot be shared *as* a secret, even though it is the essence or truth of every bond. Nowhere is this more insistent than in autobiography, which, for Derrida, is the very "locus of the secret",[5] and thus the unresolvable, unrecoverable continuity and identity of poet and poem, or their mutual

---

[3] Jacques Derrida, "Différance", in *Margins of Philosophy*, trans. Alan Bass (Chicago: University of Chicago Press, 1982).

[4] Jacques Derrida, *Paper Machine*, trans. Rachel Bowlby (Stanford: Stanford University Press, 2005), p. 162.

[5] Jacques Derrida and Maurizio Ferraris, *A Taste for the Secret* (Cambridge: Polity Press, 2001), pp. 57-59.

inscriptions as a 'writing self'.[6] Both, the poet's and the poem's identity, are suffering so to speak from a troubled identity, which is precisely not some identity trouble but rather a problematisation of identity as such, perhaps even the deconstruction of identity.

Herein lies the attempt to link treasure, secret and self with a 'symptomatic' reading of Keats's "Ode to a Nightingale" as a textual crypt that challenges the identity of meaning and the meaning of identity. Keats is thus not just any example, he is exemplary of a question that is as old as humanity, if there is such a thing, a question which touches on the very foundation of humanism and anthropocentrism: who (or what) am (or is) 'I'? "I is an other|", another poet, Rimbaud, will write, on his "drunken boat", in 1871. 'What is man?' is the question that haunts the entire tradition of philosophical anthropology. Günter Anders, representative of a whole generation of post-WWII intellectuals, speaks of man's 'antiquatedness' (1961). "What *was* man?" Michel Foucault asks in *Les Mots et les choses* (1966), and today, when the human is threatened with yielding his or her last remaining secrets, when the door to the safe is almost unlocked, so-called 'posthumanists' or even 'transhumanists' – often a strange mixture of cognitive, bio- and neuro-scientists and media and cultural theorists – speak either of the evolutionary supersession of the human species by cyborgs and machines, computers, neuronal networks and artificial intelligence, or, in stark contrast to this posthuman euphoria, of a new holistic, neohumanist, or new-age inspired return *of* nature (as opposed to the Romantic return *to* nature).

In many ways, Keats is the embodiment of the Romantic poet. A statement like the one made by Furniss and Bath is quite symptomatic in this respect: "Keats seems to embody our collective idea of the quintessential poet, and his 'Ode to a Nightingale' (1819) is often thought of as an exemplary poem".[7] As the youngest of the 'second Romantic generation' (together with Byron and Shelley) Keats and his work are characterised by a short but intensive creative period. His short life full of suffering, illness and loss fulfils all the expectations raised by the image of a tormented, emotional and heroic 'genius' of a poet. When Keats died of consumption, in 1821, at the age of 25, like his mother and younger brother Tom (just a year) before, he had been a practising poet for only about seven years (of which merely five years were dedicated to poetry full time). Not having had the privilege of receiving a classical humanistic education like most of his Romantic peers, he had first learned the trade of a surgeon and apothecary and pursued medical studies until, encouraged by one of his mentors and editors, Leigh Hunt, he decided to abandon medicine and become a professional poet. The works that make him one of the most important and essential English poets are collected in one single volume, published in 1820 (*Lamia, Isabella, The Eve of St Agnes and Other Poems*). Among the "Other Poems" that the title refers to are Keats's great odes: "To Psyche", "Ode to a Nightingale", "Ode on a Grecian Urn", "Ode on Melancholy", "Ode on Indolence" and "To Autumn". His short intensive creative phase,

---

[6] Cf. also "Others are Secret Because They Are Other", in: Derrida, *Paper Machine*, pp 136-163; and Jacques Derrida, "This Strange Institution Called Literature", in: *Acts of Literature*, ed. Derek Attridge, London: Routledge 1992), pp. 33-75.

[7] Tom Furniss and Michael Bath, *Reading Poetry: An Introduction*, London: Prentice Hall, 1996), p. 4.

full of promise and potentiality, contributes to a certain stylisation, mythologisation and heroisation of Keats's person and of the figure of the Romantic poet as such. It also usually leads to an emphasis on something like Romantic unity or essence, which literary critics have always been looking for (and have usually found, of course) in Keats. He thus tells us as much about historical Romanticism as about changing aesthetic criteria and cultural political and moral values in criticism. Cultural poetics and cultural politics are inextricably linked in Keats's work, his biography and his reception. As a case study in literary treasury, hardly any other poet than Keats (with the possible exception of his great model, Shakespeare) might serve better to ask the question of the identity of the poet, of poetry and the poetic experience.

Keats's entire oeuvre in fact could be seen as a self-stylised, spiritual autobiography. His letters are impregnated with his poetic creativity and represent the search of a young agnostic for undogmatic knowledge, freedom and sensual experience. Just like Goethe's Werther (and his modern followers, from Baudelaire and the *poètes maudits* to Jack Kerouac, the beatniks and all kinds of modern and postmodern subcultures) Keats belongs to the category of the rebelling teenager, who is constantly looking for a true and authentic self – an ontological treasure-hunt after the innermost secret truth. In contrast with his somewhat more egotistic Romantic peers, however, Keats seems more reserved, secretive and mysterious, but also more sensitive and empathic, more positive, even ethical – the kind of emotional softie, perhaps even the equivalent of contemporary goths and emos, and, for that reason, perhaps also less obsolete than many of his fellow Romantics. It could even be argued that it is the Keatsian searching 'I' that we associate with youth and with whom, as adults, we tend to fall out and by which we might even feel challenged, embarrassed or disturbed.

Literary criticism of Keats usually comes in two forms: one that takes Keats's thoughts expressed in his letters and poems as cues for an explanation of an aestheticised philosophy of life, which usually evolves from juvenile aesthetic ('objective') idealism to more or less disillusioned scepticism, nostalgia, maybe even nihilism. The other form of criticism normally emphasises the sensuality in Keats's poetry and stresses not so much development but the inevitable, maybe even intended, contradiction within Keats's 'genius'. This genius is therefore often represented as ambiguous in order to illustrate the tension between sensations and thoughts that underlies Keats's work.

Central in these evaluations are of course Keats's notions of 'negative capability' and that of the 'chameleon poet'. Both might be clarified in a close reading of the "Ode to a Nightingale". One could argue that this ode continues the initial logic of 'exemplarity' in the form of a condensation. Romanticism (at least a certain understanding of it) is personified in Keats and the further substitution, the example of the example so to speak, occurs in taking the "Ode to a Nightingale" as some kind of essential Keats (other forms of essentialism are of course always imaginable, however, and that is one of the main points, any of these processes are an essential part of 'treasuring', in the sense of a double move of revealing the essence as value and hiding its secret, its crypt or 'truth').

First of all, the ode as a genre has of course a long and venerable history, from its Pindaric origins, to Horatian classicism, and to European and English Romanticism, during which it was practised by virtually all major poets (for example, Wordsworth's

"To Immortality", Coleridge's "Dejection", Shelley's "West Wind", or Byron's "Ode to Napoleon" and "Ode to Venice", or, in France, by Lamartine and Hugo, in Germany, by Klopstock and Hölderlin). The ode is at once a solemn address and an aesthetic self-performance. Usually dedicated to the celebration of an object or a mythical figure, the ode contains a paradox between its personification (*prosopopoeia*) or animated apostrophe (*invocatio*) and its extreme self-reflexivity and visionary character. Keats, who is arguably the master of the ode in English, manages to tailor what might otherwise be a very constraining genre to his very own needs. And in this context the "Ode to a Nightingale" takes up another exemplary function, namely it is here that Keats uses for the first time a form that combines the strength of his sonnets (for example "On First Looking Into Chapman's Homer", "On Seeing the Elgin Marbles", or "When I have Fears That I May Cease to Be", right up to his last work, "Bright Star") with the intrinsically dialectic form of the ode. He returns to the regular Horatian ode stanza (instead of the irregular form preferred by Wordsworth and Coleridge) and invents a ten-line stanza with a Shakespearean quatrain and a rhyme scheme of *abab*, followed by a Petrarchan sestett of *cdecde*, containing a metric variation of a trimeter in line eight to complement the iambic pentameter throughout. This will be the form that Keats uses in all his 'great odes'.

The ode with its rhetorical, metrical and rhythmic complexities in fact develops into the ideal form to express essentially Romantic, psychological ideas surrounding the identity of the poetic or 'writing self' and the function of aesthetic or poetic communication. Keats manages to combine the perfection of the genre with sincerity in the expression of emotion and dialectical oppositions of metaphysical themes (for example, the opposition between art and reality, happiness and sadness, truth and appearance, etc.) which can then be taken as the basis for a general statement about the *conditio humana*.[8] This is precisely what constitutes Keats's already mentioned but not entirely unproblematic topicality and relevance today.

The Secret of Identity – "Ode to a Nightingale"

> Now... we all do nominalism *sans le savoir*, as if it were a general premise of our thought, an acquired axiom.[9]

The topic of the "Ode to a Nightingale" is of course an established theme, a *topos*, derived from the ancient myth of Philomela. There are a number of Romantic nightingale poems, for example Coleridge's "To the Nightingale" (1796) and "The Nightingale: A Conversation Poem" (1798).

The poem starts somewhat unexpectedly not with an apostrophe or *invocatio* but with the introspection of the poetic self. It characterises the process of poetic creation

---

[8] Cf. M.H. Abrams, *Natural Supernaturalism: Tradition and Revolution in Romantic Literature*, New York: Norton, 1971), p. 67, on Keats's "humanistic naturalism".
[9] Jorge Luis Borges, *The Total Library: Non-Fiction 1922-1986*, ed. Eliot Weinberger, (London: Penguin, 2001), p. 135.

40 Stefan Herbrechter

with all its metaphysical and emotional contradiction. "My heart", "my sense" – the contradiction suffered by the poet is at once heightened and dampened as if under the influence of drugs. Introspection, in fact, starts with the extraordinary sensitisation of the I, or the writing self. Only at the beginning of the first sestet does the direct address to the nightingale occur in reply to its song. However, it is from the start a selfless listening and feeling, not guided by envy of the bird's serenity and happiness. Almost immediately therefore there is a relation to Keats's ideal of the poet's 'negative capability', which says that poetic genius cannot be located in identity but, on the contrary, depends on the poet's temporarily being able to suspend or transcend his self, which allows him to overcome superficial oppositions. Lacking epistemological insight he instead focuses on the essence of sensual experience, namely the privileging of freed imagination as the way to the hidden treasure, i.e. truth that lies in beauty.[10]

The idea of ecstatic epiphany is continued in the second stanza in which the poet craves for wine and dance as another form of self-disappearance: "leave the world unseen, / And with thee fade away into the forest dim" – a self-dissolution taken up again at the beginning of stanza three: "Fade far away, dissolve, and quite forget". The imaginary dialogue with the non-human animal Other remains however anthropocentrically motivated, for the poet longs for an escape from the *conditio humana*, the "vale of soul-making", which is a woeful but nevertheless necessary precondition for self-transcendence. What the nightingale has never known, namely the human knowledge of mortality and finality, the suffering, aging and mourning that constitutes the human species – personified in Keats's younger brother, whom Keats had nursed until his death at the age of nineteen, the year before: "Where youth grow pale, and spectre-thin, and dies". Thinking, in typically Romantic, anti-Enlightenment fashion, is equated with the experience of "despair" and "sorrow" – a state of the mind which is not capable of knowing either "beauty" or "love".

The mood of the poet is elevated in his exclamation: "Away! Away! For I will flee to thee", whose assonance resembles that of the nightingale's call. He realises that neither the drugs nor medicine of the first, nor the wine of the second stanza can lead to a union with the free creature, but only the 'blindness' of poetry itself ("the viewless wings of Poesy"). The "dull brain" is evoked almost clinically, neurologically, but its role is deception because it "perplexes and retards". As if in trance the poet experiences the synaesthetic apotheosis of the plentiful vegetation, the starlit summer night replete with scent and humming. However, in the midst of this sensual intensity, in stanza six, the I becomes aware of the reality of death: "Darkling I listen; and, for many a time I have been half in love with easeful Death". Half in love with easeful death, whom Keats's poetry so often invokes, the I comes to. The song of the nightingale recalls the poet to consciousness and a barrier falls between the poet's self-identity and his non-human animal other: "While thou art pouring forth thy soul abroad / In such ecstasy".

This is where the intensifiying and reversing role of the eighth line becomes fully apparent. "In such ecstacy" refers both to the poet's innermost emotional state and to his surroundings, so that the I becomes aware of the impossibility of a fusion or an appropriation, i.e. a self-realisation through identification with the other: "Still wouldst thou sing, and I have ears in vain – To thy high requiem become a sod". The nightingale

---

[10] Cf. Keats's letter to his brother George, 22 December 1817; in: Keats, *Letters*, vol. 1, p. 184.

has already started its requiem for the human, while it itself belongs to immortality: "Thou wast not born for death, immortal bird!"[11]

However, the poet's self-realisation appears ambiguous – there is both sadness and joy at having found the mortal self, at possibly having elevated it. It is only in stanza seven that the poet becomes aware of the humanist, mythological importance of the scene: "The voice I hear this passing night was heard / In ancient days by emperor and clown", signifying the process of human self-alienation and self-exilation, of the existential (Heideggerian) 'thrownness' of the human as yearning (cf. the image of the "alien corn" and "lands forlorn").

The repetition of "forlorn" finally turns the poet's attention to language itself. The first "forlorn", meaning "vast" or "desolate", leads to the questioning of the identity of linguistic meaning as such, because the second "forlorn" ("desperate" or "miserable") clearly refers to the poet's inner state: "Forlorn! The very word sounds like a bell / To toll me back from thee to my sole self!" It is not difficult to imagine how a deconstructive reading of the poem would begin precisely here, in claiming that it is the very alterity of language, the lack of identity and selfsameness in language as such, which prevents self-presence, a being-at-one-with-one's-self in the sense of 'fullness' or 'richness'. Instead, the treasure of selfsameness remains a promise, a secret and a crypt, deferred and always differing from itself, as proposed above, an example of Derridean *différance* – as an impossible but necessary precondition that only ever manifests itself as a trace. The treasured self is and will remain a fortress, a safe, locked. In fact, the value of the treasure lies in its secrecy, which is the inevitable effect of treasuring. "Forlorn" designates experience of self as such; its symbol is the tolling bell, the word, and meaning in general. Even though language and thus poetry cannot do justice to the

---

[11] Jorge Luis Borges famously used this line to explain the distinction between "Aristotelian nominalists" and "Platonic realists". For the former, Keats's notion of the nightingale's archetypal immortality remains a "secret", whereas the latter see reality located in the "idea" or "class" rather than any individual bird. Borges elaborates on this in "A History of Eternity" (in: *The Total Library*, p. 135) in the form of a "general history of eternity": "Or rather, of eternities, for human desire dreamed two successive and mutually hostile dreams by that name: one, realist, yearns with a strange love for the still and silent archetypes of all creatures; the other, nominalist, denies the truth of the archetypes and seeks to gather up all the details of the universe in a single second. The first is based on realism, a doctrine so distant from our essential nature that I disbelieve all interpretations of it, including my own; the second, on realism's opponent, nominalism, which affirms the truth of individuals and the conventional nature of genres". Borges, of course feels uncomfortable with the absence of eternity in nominalism, as he explains: "Without an eternity, without a sensitive mirror of what passes through every soul, universal history is lost time, and along with it our personal history – which rather uncomfortably makes ghosts of us" (p. 136). This passage clearly anticipates Derrida's notion of "hauntology" and goes to the heart of the ambiguity of the self that Keats seems to be struggling with in the Ode and which is highlighted by (its self-)deconstruction. Borges's subsequent proposal of his own "personal theory of eternity" (p. 137), entitled "Feeling in Death", almost sounds like Derrida's idea of a "messianism without messiah" (Jacques Derrida, *Specters of Marx*, trans. Peggy Kamuf, London: Routledge, 1994), *passim*): "Mine is an impoverished eternity, without God or even a co-proprietor, and entirely devoid of archetypes". However, Borges seems unaware that this proposition itself constitutes a (proto-)deconstruction of the opposition between realism and nominalism.

42 Stefan Herbrechter

yearning of the poet, it nevertheless remains his only hope of expressing and overcoming his "sole self", his utterly decentred subject.

Negative capability could thus be interpreted as the Romantic version of the linguistic process of self-deconstruction (an economy of an ongoing deconstruction of the self, a deconstructing by itself) of the 'metaphysics of presence', which of course is the ultimate target of theory, and Derridean deconstruction in particular.

The elf's (or the nightingale's) deceptive spell, however, is broken by now: "The fancy cannot cheat so well… deceiving elf". The desire for self-identity is once more deferred. It seems as if the poet in the last ten lines of the ode, while the nightingale's song disappears into the next valley, is completely re-evaluated. The poet's nostalgia turns into disappointment, almost resentment. "Adieu! Adieu! Thy plaintive anthem fades", for the second and last time the nightingale's song is fused with the poet's perception through onomatopoeia. This time, however, it means farewell, complaint and mourning ("plaintive anthem"), while the bird is nestling in the next vale of soulmaking. Thus it is the non-human animal other whose memory trace allows the human I of the poet to experience himself as another, at least for a moment, through deferral and detour. But this is no ontological foundation on which to build, no treasure to hold in one's hand, nothing that could be made present, but a phantasm, a vision: "Was it a vision, or a waking dream? Fled is that music… Do I wake or sleep?" What remains is the ambiguity as most foundational experience of human identity.

Romanticism... in Theory

Keats has no theory…[12]

Job done, one could argue. Keats in particular and Romantic poetry in general may be identified as more or less (self-)conscious precursors to deconstruction. From a slightly more cynical point of view, however, it could be said that literary criticism and (literary) theory – this very peculiar kind of treasure hunt – in the end always finds what it has been looking for. The text or poem was always going to yield (its meaning, its innermost, its treasure, the returned investment). T.S. Eliot's and Keats's Modernist critics understood 'negative capability' as a kind of spiritual disinterestedness (an almost Heideggerian *Gelassenheit*, a self-abandoning, i.e. the precursor to the postmodern 'death of the subject'). Even though Eliot did not directly comment on Keats's odes or his poetry as such but focused on his letters,[13] in Eliot's opposition to Shelley and other Romantic poets, it is Keats who arguably comes closest to his ideal of the poet's 'impersonality', for as opposed to Shelley and Wordsworth, Keats did not have a theory, according to Eliot, and was not even interested in developing one. "Keats

---

[12] T.S. Eliot, *The Use of Poetry and the Use of Criticism* (London: Faber & Faber, 1950 [1933]), p. 102.

[13] Cf. Eliot, "Shelley and Keats", in: *The Use of Poetry*.

has no theory", yet, as befits a true poet, he has, like Shakespeare, "a philosophical mind".[14]

In this sense Keats's poetry must come close to Eliot's ideal of a 'unified sensibility' and the achievement of an 'objective correlative' in a poet and his poetry – ideals which, according to Murray Krieger, also form the basis of New Criticism. Keats's "Ode to a Nightingale" must exemplify, then, Eliot's notion of the poet's self-abandonment which is "a continual surrender of himself as he is at the moment to something which is more valuable. The progress of an artist is a continual self-sacrifice, a continual extinction of personality".[15] However, this process of depersonalisation which is the core of Eliot's impersonal theory of poetry, and which thinks of the poet's self as a mere catalyst between tradition and the individual talent, between emotion and sensibility, is launched precisely through the contradiction that Eliot tries to overcome, namely the experience of ambiguity, the kind of ambiguity Keats's poetic I experiences in relation to the singing nightingale. According to Eliot, poetry should not be a detachment from emotion but the flight from emotion, not an expression of personality but an escape from personality. However, Eliot is quick to add that only those poets who have emotions and personality in the first place may know what it means to escape from them.[16]

From Eliot's idea of 'catalytic' or almost scientifically 'clinical' poetry to the idea of immanentism in literary criticism, i.e. the New Criticism, there is only one relatively small step. Neither the subjectivity of aesthetic experience nor the so-called 'intentional fallacy' can reveal the treasure, the key to the safe lies in establishing the 'objectivity', that is to say, the identity of the text, or poem, or, in this case, the nightingale's song (to) itself. This objectification of the text, in turn, allows for correspondences between New Criticism and Structuralism, even though New Criticism never took Eliot's impersonality too personally and instead carried on emitting aesthetic value judgments, usually barely disguised in notions like 'harmony', 'unity' etc., and went on to draw moral or pedagogical conclusions from these 'objective' outcomes.

What poststructuralist and deconstructive literary criticism gives back to the object of aesthetic communication and experience is the process character of meaning that is *produced* (cf. the emphasis on so-called 'signifying practices'), its radical contextuality, its literality as opposed to literarity, and the shift in accent from intention to reception and interpretation. Roland Barthes's 'death of the author' or rather the incredulity towards the 'authorial function', is the political price (i.e. the persistence of ambiguity) that will have to be paid for the liberation and plurality of meaning and interpretation. The inherent Romanticism of this gesture has not gone unnoticed. Its initial radicality is still all about self-assurance, only this time it is the confidence of a split self – the one that loses and finds itself in the process of poetic production and the other, who, through identification in reading, can be communicated and embodied. In this way, the poet's individualism passes over to the reader and Eliot's principle of impersonality becomes an issue at the other, the receiving and decoding end. Does an 'ideal' reader have to

---

[14] Eliot, *The Use of Poetry*, p. 102.

[15] T.S. Eliot, *Selected Prose*, ed. Frank Kermode (London: Faber & Faber, 1975 [1919]), p. 40.

[16] Eliot, *Selected Prose*, p. 43.

abandon, or suspend at least, his or her personality in order to, like the poet, hear the nightingale sing or even become (one with) it?

At this point one should look at Paul de Man's ideas concerning Romanticism, which state that Romantic literature invests general validity in an experience without ever breaking off the contact with the individual self in whom this experience first arose.[17] Again, one could take Keats as an example of Paul de Man's idea of rhetorical 'disfiguration'. In "Shelley Disfigured" de Man develops the notion that in Romantic poetry in particular there is a play of figuration in the use of rhetorical tropes (a process which constitutes the very ability of visual representation in a text) and disfiguration (to be understood as the very structure inherent in a text that erases these tropological meanings).[18] As Keats's ode has demonstrated, it is as much an act of remembrance as it is an act of forgetting, namely the forgetting of the I as a means of remembering. The nightingale functions as a metonymy, as a trope for the poetic process, which is why the nightingale and its meaning – i.e. the personification of the I – can neither be fully present nor absent. Instead it has a haunting ability, an entirely uncanny presence. Its only point is to create the illusion of self-presence and the guarantee of meaning, which nevertheless cannot be articulated. The conclusion that a deconstructive reading *à la* de Man would draw from this is that the I itself is nothing but an autobiographical trope (namely a *prosopopoeia*) that must constantly articulate and dearticulate itself.[19] De Man shows how *prosopopoeia* can indeed be taken as the general condition of all language, namely as the permanent construction of masks of human self-identity – a fact that manifests itself in particular through the repressive function at work in the ode's constant questioning. The poetic I with its autobiographical desire to be at-one-with-its-self, or with its structure of *différance*, in fact becomes a constant process of self-annihilation, disfiguration as the forgetting of the trope as trope, as de Man explains in *The Rhetoric of Romanticism*. Since Keats's "Ode to a Nightingale" is an act of self-interpretation or an 'auto-communicative' act, or in de Man's words an 'allegory of reading', one is allowed to apply this insight to the reading of the poem itself, and arguably to any act of reading: reading is at once the appearance and disappearance of understanding. The price of understanding is thus the annihilation of the I, or permanent self-deconstruction.

The mentioned topicality of Keats, and his modern and postmodern interpreters from Eliot to de Man, lies in the fact that Keats's model of impossible self-realisation seems to have become the standard understanding of any autobiographical I. It is somewhat like the original trope of the modern and postmodern self or subject which constantly finds itself and in finding itself disappears or loses its self – an endless dialectic deferral of being-with-one's-self as promise, or, indeed, a 'self-treasuring'. It is in this context that de Man's comment on Keats as a purely future-oriented poet begins to make

---

[17] Cf. Paul de Man's "Introduction to the Poetry of John Keats", in: *Critical Writings 1953-1978* (Minneapolis: University of Minnesota Press, 1989), p. 197.

[18] Paul de Man, *The Rhetoric of Romanticism* (New York: Columbia University Press, 1984), pp. 93-123.

[19] Cf. "Autobiography as De-Facement", in: de Man, *The Rhetoric of Romanticism*, pp. 67-81.

sense.[20] The prospective questioning in Keats's poetry in general is the expression of a haunting dream whose truth always remains in the future.

Keats is the least narcissistic poet of English Romanticism because the deferral necessarily demands a forgetting of self, and *not* Wordsworthian introspection or self-reflexivity. Negative capability for Keats means empathy with the other or others as a replacement for an I, or a kind of self-undoing, but in a positive sense. Nothing is more despicable for Keats than the 'sole self' or the 'habitual self'. For him the role of imagination is not finding an authentic self but the abandoning of the self, which is why he constantly faces the criticism of being irresponsible or lacking in self control. Evidently, de Man would interpret the "forlorn" in the "Ode to a Nightingale" as that moment when the repressed 'real' self, parallel to Freud's notion of the unconscious, returns, and in doing so, destroys the poetic illusion of an auto-heterogenesis.

Treasuring the Self

We have lost the *mystique* of the self.[21]

It is Romanticism's chief merit, according to de Man, to have shown that general philosophical insight has to be rooted in authentic self-understanding, or that self-assurance is the necessary first step towards any moral judgment. It is certainly no exaggeration that the big treasure hunt for the self has greatly intensified in the age of so-called 'postmodern identity politics'. Postmodern society is obsessed with identity and views identity – like its Romantic precursors – as task in the double meaning of *Aufgabe* in Walter Benjamin's "The Task of the Translator": namely as task (or promise) and abandonment (or disappearance).[22] The abandoning of the metaphysical Cartesian subject leads to an accumulation of minoritarian identities or, as Stuart Hall would say, "minimal selves".[23] Identity is not an essential given but the temporary end product of a continuous, incompletable, process, literally a 'pro-ject'.

Here is therefore Keats's continued but problematic relevance, because already in Keats are we shown the limits of this somewhat naive self-proliferation and self-stylisation.[24] The impossibility of identity – the self as disappearance and as promise, or

---

[20] Paul de Man, "An Introduction to the Poetry of John Keats", in: *Critical Writings, 1953-1978* (Minneapolis: University of Minnesota Press, 1989), pp. 179-197.

[21] Lionel Trilling, *The Opposing Self: Nine Essays in Criticism* (Oxford: Oxford University Press, 1980), p. 40.

[22] Walter Benjamin, *Illuminations*, trans. Harry Zohn (New York: Schocken. 1968), pp. 70-82.

[23] Stuart Hall, "Minimal Selves", *Identity: The Real Me, ICA Documents* 6 (1988), 134-138.

[24] It might be useful, in this context, to draw parallels between Mark Sandy's argument in *Poetics of Self and Form in Keats and Shelley: Nietzschean Subjectivity and Genre* (Aldershot: Ashgate, 2005) about Nietzsche's fundamental ambiguity towards Romanticism, and Romanticism in theory. Despite Nietzsche's apparent negative attitude towards Romanticism and art as "redemptive shelter from the suffering of existence", according to Sandy, "Nietzsche's own account of the self and world as involving fictions and fictionalising illuminates comparable concerns in the poetry of Keats and Shelley" (vii). According to Sandy, the "Keatsian and

as repression – is by no means made more tolerable through loss and celebrated pluralisation. On the contrary, the dispersal of the initial 'problem' only increases the desire for self-discovery – i.e. it intensifies the metaphysics of treasuring. The answer to the impossible quest for a unified self, one could argue, is already given by Keats himself, and this answer is, strictly speaking, an ethical one, almost in the radical sense given to ethics by Emmanuel Levinas, namely the insight that the self is itself a kind of answer to a prior question: the necessary precedence of the other for any self. Identity, precisely, is an answer not a question, an effect not the cause of alterity – an asymmetrical relation which turns every I into a hostage of the Other in all its forms. Or, in other words, the infinity of the I does not correspond to any totality. In opening itself up towards the other in the shape of a nightingale, or nature etc. and in becoming self-aware through facing an or the Other, the Keatsian I also pre-empts another trend in contemporary literary and cultural criticism, a development one might call 'critically posthumanist',[25] or 'post-anthropocentric' or even 'post-psychological'. These latest 'postisms' seem to find their expression, for example, in cognitive, neuro- and eco-criticism.

Keats's anti-Cartesian reference to the "dull brain" in the "Ode to a Nightingale" might be recalled here. It seems as if current literary criticism is attempting to overcome the fundamental gap between author, reading and text through new holistic, maybe even new monist, approaches. The holistic nature of the communicative or aesthetic-poetic process is being stressed once again, however this time without recourse to any humanist moral ideal of self-realisation or pedagogy. Instead the new understanding of the poetic process might resemble something like posthumanist neuropsychology. The new image of the human in the age of the demystified "dull" brain no longer clearly distinguishes between the individual subject and its natural and cultural environment. Just as any I is the extension of an embodied mind, the body is a network of technical, cultural and natural extensions and interventions. Conscience, communication and aesthetics literally are complex effects of neural affects and Keats, the surgeon and student at United Hospitals, with its most advanced teachers in the new brain science might have sensed this. Keats's "dull brain", which belatedly and in a state of perplexity capitulates in front of the immediacy of sensual experience because it ultimately cannot extricate itself from dualism's imprisonment – consciousness somehow always comes too late, brain and self never meet, even less do they become one. As Alan Richardson explains in *British Romanticism and the Science of the Mind*,[26] the Romantic period witnesses the foundations of modern neurology. He coins the phrase "neural romanticism" with particular reference to Keats and especially his odes. One could even go so far, mindful of the Romantic beginnings of contemporary holistic-psychological

---

Shelleyan treatment of poetic identity anticipate a Nietzschean understanding of the self as a site of conflict" (viii). Sandy insinuates the parallels between Nietzsche's (anti-)romanticism and Nietzsche's "re-absorption into theoretical literary commentaries on romanticism" in figures like Deleuze, Derrida, Foucault, de Man, Bloom, Hartman and Hillis Miller (1-2).

[25] Stefan Herbrechter and Ivan Callus, *Critical Posthumanism* (Amsterdam: Rodopi, 2013).

[26] Alan Richardson, *British Romanticism and the Science of the Mind* (Cambridge: Cambridge University Press, 2001).

approaches and posthumanist neuro-aesthetics, as to speak of Keats as the first 'neuro-mantic', or indeed 'Roman-tech'.

What does all this mean for the treasure, and the self? Is the age of brain science the ultimate loss of the "mystique of the self", taking up Lionel Trilling's somewhat nostalgic epigraph? Does it spell the end of literature and poetry, or the generalisation of its secret, its fictionality? Is the Romantic irresistibility of theory a 'triumph' or a 'downfall', to recall de Man on theory?[27] Is Nietzsche's proto-posthumanist image of human knowledge as "beehive" really the end of any metaphysics of treasure and the triumph of nihilistic disenchantment? We shall have to ask the nightingale...

---

[27] Paul de Man, *The Resistance to Theory* (Minneapolis: University of Minnesota Press, 1986).

Dominique Claisse

Nathaniel Hawthorne's Mother of Pearl and Other Gems

In Nathaniel Hawthorne's works, treasure hunting may have various objects: a scarlet gem in "The Great Carbuncle", a heap of gold artefacts in "Peter Goldthwaite's Treasure", immeasurable tracts of land in *The House of the Seven Gables,* or Venus' statue in *The Marble Faun,* among others. The theme also provides a host of misleading clues, and long-lost parchments abound: Surveyor Pue's manuscript in *The Scarlet Letter*, Colonel Pyncheon's forgotten message in *Seven Gables*, or a blood-stained document in *Septimius Felton*, for example. The reader is invited to go in search of secrets, or try to unveil mysteries that will most often remain unsolved. A heuristic approach, built upon successive interrogations, might help to find one's way through the Hawthornean maze: is treasure hunting a matter of discovery or recovery? Hilda's dream about the seven-branched golden candlestick, in *The Marble Faun,* suggests the question: "When it is found again, and seven lights are kindled and burning in it, the whole world will gain the illumination which it needs."[1] Is there any person – an alchemist perhaps – entitled to discourse on the very nature of treasures, or confirm their existence? Are the expected valuables all-important, or does the container also matter? In *The French and Italian Notebooks*, Nathaniel Hawthorne had an intuition, when he was in the Louvre in Paris: "[but] I must confess that the vast and beautiful edifice struck me far more than the pictures, sculpture, and curiosities which it contains; the shell more than the meat inside."[2]

This analysis will have the appearance of a quest, considering, first, the traditional aspects of treasure hunting, through Nathaniel Hawthorne's tales and romances: the impact of letters, for instance, or the sources of confusion and ambiguity. Interpretation will then try to focus on a potentially subversive approach, the positive identification between the feminine and the treasure, the constellations of instructive images, the sense of possession, or the powers of transformation.

---

[1] Nathaniel Hawthorne, *The Marble Faun: or, The Romance of Monte Beni*, ed. Richard Brodhead (London: Penguin, 1990), p. 371. All further references are given parenthetically in the text.
[2] Nathaniel Hawthorne, *The French and Italian Notebooks*, ed. Thomas Woodson, The Centenary Edition of the Works of Nathaniel Hawthorne, vol. XIV (Columbus, Ohio: Ohio State University Press, 1980), p. 15.

50 Dominique Claisse

Treasure Hunting

"The Great Carbuncle" and "Peter Goldthwaite's Treasure" were published in *Twice-Told Tales*. In the latter, Peter's house is said to hold an "immense hoard of the precious metals", buried by a long-forgotten ancestor, somewhere in a place that looked like a "sepulchre", or "vault".[3] In order to lay hands on the treasure, Peter starts pulling down the interior, gradually turning the house into an empty shell. The hunt goes on for some time, "But, as yet, no treasure!" (532); he eventually finds out, in "a cavity, or concealed closet", an old chest, whose contents turn out to be worthless paper money: "Oh, what a ghost of dead and buried wealth had Peter Goldthwaite raised, to scare himself out of his scanty wits withal! Here was the semblance of an incalculable sum [...]. What then, in sober earnest, were the delusive treasures of the chest?" (540). In "The Great Carbuncle", a treasure-trove is the occasion to display a series of different human facets: it can be buried deeper, sold, or reduced to "its first elements" by an alchemist; the Cynic can even deny its very existence. The pilgrims who go in search of the scarlet gem will get the reward they deserve: it can be deception, bondage, blindness or death. Only young Matthew and his beloved bride, Hannah, escape unharmed: "For it is affirmed, that, from the hour when two mortals had shown themselves so simply wise, as to reject a jewel which would have dimmed all earthly things, its splendor waned."[4]

In either tale, the treasure is reified, turned into a visible object, within reach of the hunters' hands. In Nathaniel Hawthorne's longer works, the traditional magic coffer is also present, as in *Septimius Felton*, for instance: "Septimius looked at this ugly, rusty, ponderous old box, so worn and battered with time, and recollected with a scornful smile the legends of which it was the object; [...] He felt strongly convinced that, inside this old box, was something that appertained to his destiny" (154-155).[5] A similar revelation is expected to come out of Surveyor Pue's "heaped-up rubbish", on the second storey of the Custom House, in *The Scarlet Letter*: "There was something about it that quickened an instinctive curiosity, and made me undo the faded red tape, that tied up the package, with the sense that a treasure would here be brought to light."[6] In the same romance, the narrator's attitude finds an echo in Roger Chillingworth's mood, "probing every thing with a cautious touch, like a treasure-seeker in a dark cavern" (146). The disquieting nature of mysterious treasures also appears in *The House of the Seven Gables*, where Hepzibah Pyncheon mentions the possible existence of long-lost

---

[3] Nathaniel Hawthorne, "Peter Goldthwaite's Treasure", in: *Tales and Sketches*, ed. Roy Harvey Pearce (New York: The Library of America, 1982), pp. 522-541 (pp. 525 & 527). Further references are given parenthetically in the text.

[4] Nathaniel Hawthorne, "The Great Carbuncle", in: *Tales and Sketches*, pp. 435-449 (p. 448). Further references are given parenthetically in the text.

[5] Nathaniel Hawthorne, *Septimius Felton, The Elixir of Life Manuscripts*, ed. Edward H. Davidson, Claude M. Simpson and L. Neal Smith, The Centenary Edition of the Works of Nathaniel Hawthorne, vol. XIII (Columbus, Ohio: Ohio State University Press, 1977), pp. 154-155. Further references are given parenthetically in the text.

[6] Nathaniel Hawthorne, *The Scarlet Letter and Selected Tales*, ed. Thomas E. Connolly (London: Penguin, 1986), p. 60. Further references are given parenthetically in the text.

riches, hidden somewhere within the walls of the old mansion, and she keeps a vigilant watch over her brother's miniature portrait, hidden in a secret drawer, like an innocent treasure.[7]

The different examples mentioned above already point to some characteristics. The treasure house is the centre of attraction, the place that either contains, or perhaps is, the treasured object. The shift from exteriors to interiors is made more perplexing because of the vertical axis along which the search also seems to be moving. Peter Goldthwaite starts his exploration in the garret, and gradually goes down to the kitchen. The narrator in the Custom House goes upstairs in order to begin his narrative, and the treasure hunters have to go up a mountain, in "The Great Carbuncle". Ascent and descent are parts of the initiatory journey which is expected to provide a key to open the box, or clear up the riddle. In a different context, Miles Coverdale, in *The Blithedale Romance*, goes up a pine tree in order to observe his companions, but the final answer, if any, might be found deep down in the river, after Zenobia's suicide.[8]

Looking for what can still be called an object implies going up and down, in order to make one's own way, between skies and graveyards, heavens and the underground, perhaps ethereality and reification.

In addition, in the examples analysed so far, possession of the treasure is never the reward: no matter how great the expectations, the promise is never fulfilled. The discovery of the treasure conventionally signals the end of a narrative and its free play of imagination, but, in Hawthorne's vision, it is often distorted, somehow, by irony. Reversal and delusion are often the real conclusion, as illustrated in "The Celestial Railroad": "A very pretty girl bartered a heart as clear as crystal, and which seemed her most valuable possession, for another jewel of the same kind, but so worn and defaced as to be utterly worthless."[9] This tale is written in imitation of Bunyan's pilgrimage, where Christian goes in search of the ultimate treasure, the Celestial City. Still, in "The Celestial Railroad", the narrator's viewpoint cannot be compared to Christian's belief in a happy end. The final object is a source of disappointment, and irony and ambiguity permeate the final exclamation: "Thank Heaven, it was a Dream!" (824).

The quest has now been turned inwards, focussing all attention on the repository itself: the receptacle seems to be protected by a maze, suggesting the labyrinthine intricacies of human nature. A magic, radiating out of the word "treasure" itself, stirs up the imagination and begins a quest, which is invigorated by incentives as varied as will-power, greed, Eros or spiritual pursuit. Hawthorne's fiction, though, keeps confusing the issue: desire generates a discourse which is often rich in worthless clues, forgotten maps, disturbing memories, irrelevant advice or lost letters.

"Peter Goldthwaite's Treasure" had its own "dusty piece of parchment" (533), but the literary recourse to letters has become considerably more complex in the romances. Hester's scarlet letter, the capital A, is a source of confusion and polysemy. *Seven*

---

[7] Nathaniel Hawthorne, *The House of the Seven Gables*, ed. D. Gross (New York: Norton, 1967). Further references are given parenthetically in the text.

[8] Nathaniel Hawthorne, *The Blithedale Romance*, ed. Annette Kolodny (London: Penguin, 1986). Further references are given parenthetically in the text.

[9] Nathaniel Hawthorne, "The Celestial Railroad", in: *Tales and Sketches*, pp. 808-824 (p. 819). Further references are given parenthetically in the text.

Gables mentions a missing document, left in a dark and feminine recess, under the protection of a gigantic and male portrait of the Ancestor. Once disclosed, the parchment becomes a dead letter. Septimius Felton's mystery lies in an abstruse manuscript, written in old English, Latin, Greek, hieroglyphics and cyphers, which has been partly damaged by a bullet, and is stained with crimson blood: "Septimius unfolded the parchment cover, and found inside some fold of manuscript, closely written in a crabbed hand; so crabbed, indeed, that Septimius could not at first read a word of it, nor satisfy himself, indeed, in what language it was written" (49). Words have to be decoded, or, like objects, dragged out of the crypts where they have fallen. Letters are capital, and discourse has now become a participant in the quest for treasures: Nathaniel Hawthorne's cryptic writing strives to revive language, and words, like new-found treasures, are gradually revisited.

"Treasure" is just a word, but words are also treasures: this apparent connection is a refreshed source of fruitful ambiguity, which opens onto further interrogation, and has to be treated as a preliminary to interpretation.

In modern psychology, the house is an image of the self, and the crypt is the place where ghosts find their refuge. Exploring ancestral vaults and intimate recesses also means going in search of one's own psyche and its spectral antagonists, Eros and Thanatos.

Treasures, at the individual or collective level, emerge from the past. *There* is the receptacle, under the earth, as Nathaniel Hawthorne suggests in *The French and Italian Notebooks*: "How the whole world might be peopled with antique beauty, if the Romans would but dig!" (518). However, treasures are only one facet of the legacy from the past: secrets can be a promise or a curse, as is shown by Matthew Maule's imprecation against the Pyncheon family, in *Seven Gables*, or Arthur's scorching mystery in *The Scarlet Letter*. The equivocal nature of secrets and the potentiality of treasures are illustrated by Clifford Pyncheon: he is an impressive illustration of the return of the repressed, before the phrase itself was coined by psychoanalysis. He comes into the story as a ghost, the unconscious guardian of the secret spring that gives access to the missing parchment, and he is gradually materialized into the narrative: eventually, he participates, as a character, in a partial restoration of order and justice. His return combines a return to the origins of traumas, a return to the missing letter, and a return to childhood, which is the very time and place of the original and womb-like treasure, the Arcadian dream. Clifford, however, fails to recover this original treasure. His development has been stopped by injustice, and he is trapped in regression: he will never grow out of childhood. A valid return to Omphalos, or the central room, only makes sense if a mutation occurs in the process.

The fiery struggle for treasures can have widely different effects. It can be destructive: the search for gold and land sets ablaze the Judge's heart, in *Seven Gables*, and he dies from a form of blood congestion. It can also be beneficial, as in Hester's case, in *The Scarlet Letter*: she is transformed, little by little, and clarifies the positive values of her Letter, which is eventually turned into Affection.

Appearances are deceptive, as Nathaniel Hawthorne humorously suggests in a letter to his future wife, Sophia, when he is in Brook Farm. Manure, despite ill-smelling appearances, is a promise of plenty, which Mother Nature will turn into another form of gold:

Nathaniel Hawthorne's Mother of Pearl and Other Gems 53

Sometimes it almost seemed as if I were at work in the sky itself; though the material in which I wrought was the ore from our gold mine. Nevertheless, there is nothing so unseemly and disagreeable in this sort of toil, as thou wouldst think. It defiles the hands, indeed, but not the soul. This gold ore is a pure and wholesome substance.[10]

Exploring crypts or catacombs has revealed the ambiguous nature of secrets, and returning to origins has shown the deceptions of apparent realities: the very nature of treasures now needs further investigation and interrogation.

Ethereal Longings

Some examples testify to the perils incurred by the potential treasure-seekers, and point to Nathaniel Hawthorne's possible subversive approach. Alice's tale, inserted into *Seven Gables*, starts as a traditional fairy tale, which then turns into a nightmare. Her covetous father, Gervayse Pyncheon, sacrifices her innocence and integrity in order to capture the alleged 'Pyncheon treasure'. Her psychological rape by Matthew Maule will not permit to unveil the mystery and penetrate the secret chamber. Man's desire to break through the sacred barriers of intimacy and femininity has killed her. Her father offers her up and fails to realize that she is his real living treasure. She is victimized by one more patriarchal and unrelenting father figure. The narrative delivers a similar sentence, when Gervayse's descendant, Judge Jaffrey Pyncheon, is portrayed:

> Men of strong minds, great force of character, and a hard texture of the sensibilities, are very capable of falling into mistakes of this kind. They are ordinarily men to whom forms are of paramount importance. Their field of action lies among the external phenomena of life. They possess vast ability in grasping, and arranging, and appropriating to themselves, the big, heavy, solid unrealities, such as gold, landed estate, offices of trust and emolument, and public honors. (229)

In that sense, "Ethan Brand" may appear as another example of the dangers of appropriation: in defiance of God's principles, Ethan Brand, like a new Prometheus, goes in search of the Idea; this "Unforgivable Sin", might be a negative version of the treasure. His quest turns into a curse, and eventually drives him to suicide.[11]

In Nathaniel Hawthorne's works, discourse is often destabilizing: language is subject to reversals, and so-called realities or conventions are treated upside down. Here are some examples of the inversions of language, all related to treasure hunting: in *Seven Gables*, Ned Higgins is an inverted version of Jonah, who devours his ephemeral treasure, a gingerbread whale, offered by Hepzibah; The egg is traditionally considered as a promise of wealth, but Chanticleer's little chicken "looked small enough to be still

---

[10] Nathaniel Hawthorne, *The Letters, 1813-1843*, ed. Thomas Woodson and L. Neil Smith, The Centenary Edition of the Works of Nathaniel Hawthorne, vol. XV (Columbus, Ohio: Ohio State University Press, 1984), p. 542.

[11] Nathaniel. Hawthorne, "Ethan Brand": in: *Tales and Sketches*, pp. 1051-1067.

54   Dominique Claisse

in the egg, and, at the same time, sufficiently old, withered, wizened, and experienced, to have been the founder of the antiquated race" (151). The ironical structure of language also appears in a profusion of apparently contradictory terms: Hepzibah, for example, is "enriched by poverty", or "developed by sorrow" (133). Values are threatened by confusion, as in ambiguous metaphors: Roderick Elliston's "hoarded sin" in "Egotism; or, The Bosom-Serpent", for example.[12] Irony also structures, or unstructures "Feathertop". Created by a witch out of a scarecrow, Feathertop goes in search of his betrothed and her dowry: "Now, depart, my treasure, and good luck go with thee!", exclaims Mother Rigby.[13] Defeat and decay will eventually be his lot.

As the analysis is coming closer to the nature of treasures, it appears that distortion, confusion in values, or equivocation prevail. Three elements participate in Nathaniel Hawthorne's specific alchemy, namely Woman, Art and Language. Tradition has it that the treasure-seeker is a man, a hero who solves the mystery, secures the hoarded riches and wins the young Lady's heart, *en passant*. In Nathaniel Hawthorne's tales and romances, there are no heroes but a good many alchemists: Doctor Cacaphodel in "The Great Carbuncle", Doctor Rappacini in "Rappacini's Daughter",[14] Aylmer in "The Birth-mark",[15] Roger Chillingworth in *The Scarlet Letter*, or Doctor Portsoaken in *Septimius Felton*. They are male, solitary and often patriarchs. They are all looking for the diamond body, the lapis, or the philosopher's stone, using fire in order to transmute base metal into gold. Their search is often nocturnal, and always detrimental to human integrity, at least in Hawthorne's vision. Septimius Felton, who is another aspiring alchemist, has prepared the drink of immortality in a "jewelled goblet" (187), inherited from ancestors, but the scarlet, or bloody, beverage will drive him to insanity and death. The only exception to this series of ill-fated researchers might be Holgrave, in *Seven Gables*. He eventually recovers a threefold treasure: Judge Pyncheon's properties through his marriage with a Pyncheon, his forefather's name, Maule, and the heart of the pure and white Phoebe. Holgrave has escaped the doom that awaits most treasure-seekers, and the feminine presence of Phoebe has been decisive in his success.

There seems to be a sort of identification between the feminine and secrets, and women may sometimes appear as living treasures. Some female characters are associated with pure and transparent pearls. Phoebe's "golden texture" (139), incited E. Whipple, an early 1851 critic, to qualify her as "a pearl of womanhood".[16] In *The Scarlet Letter*, Pearl herself is a budding treasure, "a lovely and immortal flower", a promise:

> Her Pearl! – For so had Hester called her; not as a name expressive of her aspect, which had nothing of the calm, white, unimpassioned lustre that would be indicated by the

---

[12] Nathaniel Hawthorne, "Egotism; or the Bosom-Serpent", in: *Tales and Sketches*, pp. 781-794 (p. 789).

[13] Nathaniel Hawthorne, "Feathertop", in: *Tales and Sketches*, pp. 1103-1122 (p. 1113).

[14] Nathaniel Hawthorne, "Rappacini's Daughter", in: *Tales and Sketches*, pp. 975-1005.

[15] Nathaniel Hawthorne, "The Birth-mark", in: *Tales and Sketches*, pp. 764-780. Further references are given parenthetically in the text.

[16] Edwin Percy Whipple, *"The House of the Seven Gables": Humor and Pathos Combined*, ed. D. Gross (New York: Norton, 1967, pp. 356-360 (p. 359).

comparison. But she named the infant "Pearl", as being of great price, – purchased with all she had, – her mother's only treasure! (113)

However, the metaphors that link the feminine and precious stones bring a distinction to mind. Other women may be treated more ambiguously: for example, in *The Blithedale Romance*, Zenobia is used to having an exotic flower in her hair. This "floral gem" (45) is "an outlandish flower", "a flower of the tropics". As the narrative moves on, the flower goes through "a cold and bright transformation": "it was a flower, exquisitely imitated in jeweller's work, and imparting the last touch that transformed Zenobia into a work of art" (164).

In the same way, the carbuncle is Miriam's favourite jewel, in *The Marble Faun*. As a character, she clearly associates femininity, secrecy, treasures and sin: "Unless I had his heart for my own, [...] it should never be the treasure-place of my secret. It is no precious pearl, as I just now told him; but my dark-red carbuncle – red as blood – is too rich a gem to put into a stranger's casket!" (130). She shows off a garnet, which is perhaps, like Hester's embroidered letter, a reminder of her sin:

> The effect [...] was partly owing to a gem which she had on her bosom; not a diamond, but something that glimmered with a clear, red lustre, like the stars in a southern sky. Somehow or other, this coloured light seemed an emanation of herself, as if all that was passionate and glowing, in her native disposition, had crystallized upon her breast [...] (396)[17]

Thus, Woman is an ambiguous treasure, and can be either a maidenly pearl, or a coloured gem. But, through Phoebe, Hilda or Pearl, treasures seem to have been embodied in maidens or young girls, and to have slipped out of the grasping hands of old alchemists or patriarchs.

Art is another facet of Nathaniel Hawthorne's interpretation of treasures. Feminine statues even turned him into another treasure-seeker. The Venus de' Medici, in the Uffizi Palace in Florence, which Hawthorne visited in June 1858, is a "perfect and indestructible" idea, the essence of womanhood: "I felt a kind of tenderness for her; an affection, not as if she were one woman, but all womankind in one."[18] He wrote a few days later: "[...] mortal man may look on her with new delight from infancy to old age, and keep the memory of her, I should imagine, as one of the treasures of spiritual existence hereafter." "She is a miracle",[19] he exclaims, but she is also made of cold marble, and so fragile. The episode has a correspondence in fiction. In *The Faun*, Kenyon also finds a treasured statue, in "a cellar-like cavity" (422), but the figure is headless and broken, a "poor, fragmentary woman": "'What a discovery is here!' thought Kenyon to himself. 'I seek for Hilda, and find a marble woman! Is the omen

---

[17] Margaret Fuller, the brilliant feminist, who was close to the Hawthornes when the young couple lived in Concord, may have inspired some aspects of fictional Miriam. Margaret, or "Pearl" in Greek, also admitted her preference to the "blood-red, heart's blood-red carbuncle", in "The Magnolia of Lake Pontchartrain", for instance.

[18] Hawthorne, *French and Italian Notebooks*, p. 298.

[19] Hawthorne, *French and Italian Notebooks*, pp. 307-308.

good or ill?' " (423). Interpretation makes the treasure, but a lifeless marble artefact, for all its aesthetic beauty, is not to be compared to a promising maiden.

In addition to the Feminine and Art, the Word is also engaged in Hawthorne's creative process. Jewels and statues are metaphors and suggest that language, being metaphorical itself, is also a treasure. Recurrent combinations of words are spun all along the various narratives, and give birth to successive constellations of images: colours like scarlet and crimson are often associated with letters, gems, femininity, blood or flowers, as illustrated by Septimius' crimson flower, the *Sanguinaria Sanguinissima*; Venus is related to sexuality, culture and cold white marble; bubbles, made up of water and air, are bright and impalpable illusions that are evocative of another, more spiritual world; hands can be treated negatively, when Aylmer, in "The Birth-mark", for example, tries to remove Georgiana's stain, shaped like a crimson little hand, or positively, when Kenyon secretly carves out of marble a replica of Hilda's white and delicate hand. "The hand is a reminiscence" (121), he exclaims, and his treasure, which he keeps in a "little, old-fashioned, ivory coffer" (120), speaks of Love and Truth. Metaphors materialize images, and they are now within the apparent reach of eyes and hands. Judge Pyncheon, Peter Goldthwaite and the protagonists of "The Great Carbuncle" may have been deceived by a beguiling metaphor, the word "treasure" itself. But it still remains that metaphors *are* treasures. Lest they should become mere accumulations of dead letters, buried deep in old and arcane texts, they have to be excavated, transformed, and then revived by a writer's imagination, who offers them as presents to his reading public. Like the quest, they are means of transport, or means for transports.

Thus, through the writer's innovative alchemy, the treasure appears as equivocal, and the ambiguity of its nature has been revealed successively through Woman, Art and Language.

At this stage, a narrative entitled "Foot-prints on The Sea-shore" might be a relevant illustration of his approach. A narrator scrutinizes the shore, which reveals ambiguous sea treasures: a dead seal, a bone, "bejewelled with barnacles and small shell-fish", or a bird, perhaps "the identical albatross of the Ancient Mariner".[20] His dreams of travels and escape take shape along the beach, and he addresses the reader:

> If your imagination be at all accustomed to such freaks, you may look down into the depths of this pool, and fancy it the mysterious depth of ocean. But where are the hulks and scattered timbers of sunken ships? – where the treasures that old Ocean hoards? – where the corroded canon – where the corpses and skeletons of seamen, who went down in storm and battle? (566)[21]

The shore is the starting point for voyages towards imaginary treasure islands, but it is also an intimation of the fateful destiny of male explorers. The obsessional

---

[20] Nathaniel Hawthorne, "Foot-prints on the Sea-shore", in: *Tales and Sketches*, pp. 561-570 (p. 565). Further references are given parenthetically in the text.

[21] The apparent confusion between treasure and death may be explained by a meaningful episode in the writer's childhood: Nathaniel Hawthorne's father was a sea captain. He died during a voyage to the East, in 1808. His son was only four years old.

omnipresence of death and loss encourages the narrator to secure a little place, in a womb-like cavity: "It is a recess in the line of cliffs, walled round by a rough, high precipice, which almost encircles and shuts in a little space of sand" (567). It has the appearance of a refuge, so close to the motherly sea, a place where the child can return, escape the existence of the common run of men, perhaps also to relieve the burden of his own neurotic self. *There* is his treasure-place, a vantage point which permits the observation of natural scenery:

> trailing wreaths of scarlet flaunt from the summit downward; tufts of yellow-flowering shrubs and rose bushes, with their reddened leaves and glossy seed-berries, sprout from every crevice; at every glance, I detect some new light or shade of beauty, all contrasting with the stern, grey rock. […] There is a magic in this spot. (567)

The treasure is now being redefined: it is forever receding, volatile and fluid, like water or quicksilver.

In conventional narratives, the apparently logical outcome of any search for treasures is possession, but the very words treasure and possession seem to be antagonistic here: there can *be* treasures, but *having* one is a source of evil. Matthew Maule, for example, manages to take possession of Alice's mind, in *Seven Gables*: "She is mine! […] Mine, by the right of the strongest spirit" (206). Alice has become "Maule's slave" (203), but a relation based on possession is detrimental both to the possessed and the possessor. Matthew Maule is an illustration of male desire: most treasure-seekers are longing for an unattainable goal, which, like Pothos in Greek myth, is associated with death. The treasure becomes a metaphor for absence, and points to their incapacity to compensate for incompleteness. The Other may be the treasure, but not to be possessed like a treasure. Both Alice and Phoebe Pyncheon are human treasures, but one has been instrumentalised, while the other is allowed to preserve her virtue. Holgrave is attracted to Phoebe but he resists the temptation: "Let us allow (Holgrave) integrity, also, forever after to be confided in; since he forbade himself to twine that one link more, which might have rendered his spell over Phoebe indissoluble" (212).

The narrator's treatment of the theme of exploration, in "Foot-prints on the Sea-shore" or *Seven Gables* point to Hawthorne's singularity, but this originality can also be detected in his appreciation of the mother-country. America is symbolically a synonym for treasure land, captured by Pilgrim Fathers who applied the age-old rule of 'finders keepers'. "The Custom House", the opening of *The Scarlet Letter*, however, raises the issues of legitimate ownership of the land, or the violence left by legacy and appropriation. *Seven Gables* can also be interpreted as a story of doubtful ownership, and Maule's curse breeds disorder and prevents the recovery of the legitimate Indian deed. In consequence, desire of the other's property, or propriety, becomes the source of repeated illustrations of injustice, over seven generations.

The right answer to human desire and the aspiration to find out treasures may be found in Nathaniel Hawthorne's perception of the individual or intimate sphere. Mutual love may conciliate male desire and attraction to feminine treasures. Phoebe and Hilda are dreamlike literary creations, but they find a counterpart in real life, in Hawthorne's wife, Sophia Peabody. His love letters are explicit, and little by little, turn Sophia into a living treasure: "[...] you are a woman – *the* woman; [...] an immortal and pure spirit".[22] Love is a form of alchemy, a refuge, almost a religion, that reconciles physical desire and ethereal longings:

> Remember always that thou art not thine own, but that Providence has entrusted to thy keeping a most delicate physical frame, which belongs wholly to me, and which therefore thou must keep with infinitely more care than thou wouldst the most precious jewel. (464)

A few weeks later, he writes again: "Oh, unutterably ownest wife, no pen can write how I have longed for thee, or for any the slightest word from thee; [...] God bless thee, thou belovedest woman-angel" (548). The love transports of this original treasure-seeker were neither forgotten nor denied until his death. His quest combined outward aspirations to reach the other, with his own inner search: discovering his 'treasure' in Sophia may also have permitted a partial recovery of inner riches, or, in Jungian terms, the ultimate form of the anima, known as the Sophia.

The treasure might be the outcome of concomitant exterior and interior visions, which, at once, transform the beholder's inner self, and turns the object of desire into another person. In the process, his eyes and hands now recognize the Other as the only real treasure. *Transformation* is the other title of the romance known as *The Marble Faun*, and the word itself is adapted to Kenyon's and Hilda's love: the feeling transforms this new American couple, which may be a rejuvenated version of Nathaniel and Sophia. More generally, Love also changes the original quest for gems, jewels or gold:

> As beheld from the tower of Monte Beni, the scene was tenderly magnificent, with mild gradations of hue, and a lavish outpouring of gold, but rather such gold as we see on the leaf of a bright flower than the burnished glow of metal from the mine. Or, if metallic, it looked airy and unsubstantial, like the glorified dreams of an alchemist. And speedily [...] came the twilight, and, brightening through its gray transparency, the stars. (266)

Nathaniel Hawthorne had this capacity to dress up desire in words, and the world has recognized *The Scarlet Letter* as a literary treasure. It is his most accomplished signature, and its letter A its most prominent sign. A is a return to the origins of language, the Alpha in western culture. As first letter of the alphabet, it is also a collective convention, which combines with other letters and becomes a source of polysemous confusion: the letter A that was originally, and blatantly, a sign of infamy, becomes the A of Arthur, America, Angel, Affection, a substitute for the offensive I of Incest, or the origin of so many other words, according to the analysts' wishes. Still, the sign now makes sense. The letter A is capital: it generates discourse and there is no end to interpretation, as every reader can capture the letter and make it their possession. It is a Woman's ambiguous ornament, which becomes a work of Art: it is coloured in red and ornamental, rich in gold embroidery. The most banal of all letters – a mere indefinite article, all-too visible, almost laid bare before the puritan community and despised by all – is gradually dressed up and lavishly adorned. The primal metaphor has

---

[22] Hawthorne, *Letters*, p. 345. Further references are given parenthetically in the text.

been renewed and it changes its nature at the occasion of successive trials and errors. This letter A is a genuine treasure, indeed, but the quest to determine its nature goes through a narrative reversal: offered to full view and obvious from the very beginning, it gradually gets blurred, and eventually ends up in a cryptic sentence, a renewed mystery encoded in a volley of capital letters: "On a field, sable, the letter A, gules" (276). Revelation has become a synonym for veil and secrecy again. The metaphor, however, has been revived, and it becomes a treasure in three different senses: as an object, first, in the feminine hands of Hester, the Artist; from a collective viewpoint, this scarlet letter A also encloses the word America and supplies the new-found treasure land with letters patent of nobility. At a better distance, the letters turn into characters: Pearl is given flesh and blood and becomes the incarnation of a letter which now stands right in her heart. Hester is Pearl's mother, and the words that make up her story shape it into a womb-like receptacle: the Mother of Pearl, in turn, generates an imaginative and resplendent literary gem. Some late works have been left unfinished, like *Septimius Felton*, and their letters are irretrievably lost or incomprehensible. Still, *The Scarlet Letter* is probably the most brilliant treasure of all. Its heuristic power associates a scarlet gem and a living symbol, a translucid pearl. American Indians used sea-shells as a means of exchange, or a trading currency: mother-of-pearl was then a real value in their eyes, the very receptacle that was evocative of a true treasure. Likewise, Hester and her daughter are symbols of the eternal dual unit made up by the mother and her child: in them, Nathaniel Hawthorne found both the pearl and the jewel case, the shell and the kernel, all in one *Scarlet Letter*.

Conclusion

> [Grandfather] felt that the past was not taken from him. The happiness of former days was a possession forever. And there was something in the mingled sorrow of his lifetime that became akin to happiness, after being long treasured in the depths of his heart. There it underwent a change, and grew more precious than pure gold.[23]

The existence of the Hawthornean treasure requires a correspondence between an adequate state of mind of the finder and an object that deserves to be called a treasure. Riches do not exist outside the beholder's conscience, the certainty that they have a value, that they are valuables. Nathaniel Hawthorne has a specific insight when he exposes appearances and determines what is *not* a treasure: he is often in contradiction with the conventions of his contemporaries. Landed property, hoarded gold, puritan rules or even women, when they are considered as a property, are just collective illusions. All along his life, he had financial difficulties: providing for his family was a real concern, until, at least, the relative success of *The Scarlet Letter* and the other romances helped him to cope with material problems. Still, he never gave in to the

---

[23] Nathaniel Hawthorne, *A Wonder-book; Tanglewood Tales; Grandfather's Chair* (Newcastle upon Tyne: Cambridge Scholars, 2008), p. 144.

temptation of cheap writing: the bonanza of domestic novels had no real attraction for him.

In his vision, a real treasure is the result of a triangular process, which involves the finder, the object and the other's approval: it should not be stored up but offered to the world. The living treasure is transient and fragile, often embodied in the feminine Other.

An ultimate return on Hawthorne's work might become a source of effervescence, to use one of the writer's favourite words. *The Whole History of Grandfather's Chair* is a popular historical tale that Nathaniel Hawthorne wrote for the young, in 1841. A dialogue between the Chair, turned into a speaking object, and Grandfather, is helpful to determine the origins and nature of true treasures:

> "As long as I have stood in the midst of human affairs," said the chair, with a very oracular enunciation, "I have constantly observed that Justice, Truth, and Love are the chief ingredients of every happy life".
> "Justice, Truth, and Love!" exclaimed Grandfather. "We need not exist two centuries to find out that these qualities are essential to our happiness. This is no secret. Every human being is born with the instinctive knowledge of it." (257)

This apparently ingenuous coalescence, which associates childhood and ideals, may become the obverse of his negative denunciation of collective false values. Still, Nathaniel Hawthorne never pretends to be a guide: he never lets out his secret, and that attitude has given birth to the so-called Hawthornean Riddle.[24]

Just after writing *The Scarlet Letter*, which was soon considered as a masterpiece, he turned to *Seven Gables*, which has sometimes been regarded as a romance about a treasure that never comes out. In 1853, he travelled to Europe with his family. Separation from the motherland, or, more probably, the poor health of his wife, Sophia, the almost fatal disease of his elder daughter, Una, and his own frequent disorders, may account for his change in perspective: the treasure, which was once massive and substantial, had been transmuted into another fluid and elusive element, the Elixir. Again, its deceptive powers were denounced, in *The Marble Faun*, first. The narrator refers to the myth of the Sibyl and her misfortune, "when she obtained the grievous boon of immortality" (302).

The dream of immortality is the ultimate and ominous form of treasure that the author explored: his last two unfinished romances, *Septimius Felton*[25] and *The Dolliver Romance*, are also known as *The Elixir of Life Manuscripts*. They may have represented his last irretrievable object, the literary objective that remained beyond reach, the sign of his literary incapacity to determine the true value of human life, and to complete the quest. However, the author's alleged failings or shortcomings hardly matter, if the treasure is along the way, if the treasure is the way. All through the writer's works, the reader's own quest for treasures has been improved in quality and colours, and his Ariadne's thread has been ornamented with better gold. But this ultimate disposition might be just as naively hopeful as Hilda's, in the last lines of *The Marble Faun*. The

---

[24] Since the development of psychoanalysis, his obstinate efforts to conceal the origins of his traumas have been interpreted as possible signs of a neurosis.

[25] *Septimius Felton* has another version, also unfinished, *Septimius Norton*.

Nathaniel Hawthorne's Mother of Pearl and Other Gems 61

following quotation can be opened up like a jewel case, with prying, though restrained, impatience: the object here is an authentic treasure-trove, snatched out of the ghostly hands of seven long-buried forefathers.

Memory and imagination soon come into play and transform it into dark legends, the Seven Etruscan Tales.[26] That object is a circle, which, by connecting together its seven elements, becomes a symbol of completeness. In the romance, it is first the possession of a Woman, Miriam, whose rectitude is questioned, and its secret is misinterpreted. The pure Maiden who then comes into the legacy, Hilda, is the adequate reader, or translator. *She* knows, and her vision shows elevation and brilliancy. She holds the treasure in her hand, and, in the process, her hand becomes the treasure, at least for Kenyon. She can now be offered as a present, in a ceremony that will have the appearance of a recognition, or a coronation:

> Before they quitted Rome, a bridal gift was laid on Hilda's table. It was a bracelet, evidently of great cost, being composed of seven ancient Etruscan gems, dug out of seven ancient sepulchres, and each one of them the signet of some princely personage, who had lived an immemorial time ago. Hilda remembered this precious ornament. It had been Miriam's; and once, with the exuberance of fancy that distinguished her, she had amused herself with telling a mythical and magic legend for each gem, comprising the imaginary adventures and catastrophe of its former wearer. Thus, the Etruscan bracelet became the connecting bond of a series of seven wondrous tales, all of which, as they were dug out of seven sepulchres, were characterized by a sevenfold sepulchral gloom; such as Miriam's imagination, shadowed by her own misfortunes, was wont to fling over its most sportive flights.
>
> And, now, happy as Hilda was, the bracelet brought the tears into her eyes, as being, in its entire circle, the symbol of as sad a mystery as any that Miriam had attached to the separate gems. For, what was Miriam's life to be? And where was Donatello? But Hilda had a hopeful soul, and saw sunlight on the mountain-tops. (462)

---

[26] The first unpublished collection of Tales that Nathaniel Hawthorne wrote in 1824 was entitled *Seven Tales of my Native Land.*

Karin Preuss

Family Treasures and Subversive Power Play
in Wilkie Collins' *The Moonstone*

The Moonstone as Subversive Fiction

Collins' *The Moonstone* (1868), which T.S. Eliot called "the first and greatest of detective novels",[1] is a great cover-up. This novel simultaneously expresses and suppresses the generic and ideological with greater subtleness and intricacy than the works that preceded it. Critics have praised *The Moonstone* for its flawless transformation of the Gothic into the detective novel, a genre that brings to light and banishes the hidden secrets so prominent in the Gothic. The tension between Gothic and detective fiction in the novel is indicative of Collins' continued and heightened ambivalence about his literary project. If the novels of *No Name* and *Armadale* represent a bold critique of Victorian conventions and gender roles, considered at the time as particularly shocking and sensational.

The popularity of *The Moonstone* relied on the fact that Collins was a kind of literary outlaw. Setting most of *The Moonstone* in the same insurgent atmosphere of 1848-49 that he had chosen as the setting for *The Woman in White*, he creates a narrative that carefully focuses on the fate of subversion in the fiction. Drugs, Imperialism, and theft of a precious stone (the treasure) are subsumed into the larger question of family relations (cousinly or closer) which is at the heart of *The Moonstone*. "What is the Victorian family and whose purposes does it serve?", Collins asks, and the answer that he gives is not in favour of the family.

The aim of the present essay is to analyse the central image of the novel, the theft of the Moonstone, as it not only represents an exposé of Victorian culture and family secrets, but also recognises the links between types of domination – of the colonisers over the colonised, of the upper over the lower classes, and men over women. Furthermore, the theme of the early detective novel will be closely examined alongside *The Adventures of Sherlock Holmes* (1892), as the general ideal of melancholic male alliances, as embodied in the pair of Franklin Blake and Ezra Jennings (*The Moonstone*) served as role model for such figures as Dr. Watson and Sherlock Holmes. Finally, the topic of drug addiction so present in these fictions will further help to illustrate the point that opium and its trade are comparable to the treasure hunt of nineteenth century imperialists in India.

---

[1] T.S. Eliot, "Wilkie Collins and Charles Dickens", in: *Selected Essays New Edition* (New York: Routledge, 1950), p. 413.

Between Psychosexual Symbolism and Anti-Imperialist Critique

The mystery plot of *The Moonstone* has often been interpreted in the light of psychosexual symbolism, i.e. by focussing on Franklin Blake's theft of Rachel's jewel from her bedroom at night. This Freudian reading of the theft as "symbolic defloration", associates detection with the analyst's work of interpreting a psychological and familial narrative, since Blake's unconscious motivations are bound up in his role as his cousin's suitor. John Reed, for instance, in his examination of *The Moonstone's* anti-imperialist implications, argues forcefully concerning the diamond's status of a sacred gem and stolen object:

> In itself ambiguous, its significance lies in its *misappropriation*. Because it is so desired by *men*, it signifies *man's greed*. [...] More particularly, however, the Moonstone becomes the sign of England's imperial depredations – the symbol of a national rather than a personal crime.[2]

Reed here oversimplifies this polyvalent novel in his historical account to a mere symbolic reading, like most psychoanalytic interpretations have done before.[3] Nonetheless, John Reed's insights can easily be linked to the theme of treasure and are therefore helpful. Rachel Verinder has no more right to the diamond than Godfrey Ablewhite – it belongs in fact to the Indians from whom Franklin and Betteredge try so hard to protect it and to whom it is finally returned. It functions like a woman's virginity, which, in Victorian times, was considered her greatest value of exchange. For, as Luce Irigaray notes, "only virgins are exchange value for men. Once violated (divided, cut up, married) they become use value, recognised only for their ability to reproduce themselves."[4] Rachel and her uncut treasure are both valued more highly for their potential in a capitalist economy than for themselves. Only Hindu priests, who are outside of English life and its capitalist aspirations, are able to value the diamond for itself. Similarly no one (except for Frank Blake) seems to be able to esteem Rachel for herself.

This is why Lady Verinder tries to protect Rachel's inheritance from a too voracious consumer such as Godfrey Ablewhite. Nonetheless its greatest treasure is a symbolic one: it is less valuable to the possessor (Rachel) than the desirer (whether Ablewhite or the Indians). It is most precious as an exchange value and the desirer is only and always male. The diamond thus targets two possible objectives: outwardly, the English colonies

---

[2] John R. Reed, "English Imperialism and the Unacknowledged Crime of *The Moonstone*", *Clio* 2 (1973), 281.

[3] See Lewis A. Lawson, "Wilkie Collins and *The Moonstone*", American *Imago* (1963), 61-79; see also Albert D Hutter, "Dreams, Transformations and Literature: The Implications of Detective Fiction", *Victorian Studies* 19 (1975), 181-209. Both critics draw attention to symbolic representations of sexuality, such as paint-stained shirts and the fact that Blake gives up cigar smoking during his courtship, all of which are immediately associated with symbolic seduction, which can only be resolved in an honourable marriage of the hero and the heroine.

[4] Luce Irigaray, *This Sex Which is Not One*, trans. Catherine Porter, with Carolyn Burke (Ithaca, NY, Cornell University Press, 1985 [1977]), p. 186.

Family Treasures and Subversive Power Play in Collins' *The Moonstone*   65

and their treatment by the British, and inwardly the situation of British families at home. Rachel's insistence on maintaining control defies both of these corresponding power structures: she refuses to treat the treasure as a prize, and she refuses to give up her own independence and her own judgements, preferring to keep the diamond in its native setting (the Indian cabinet).

These psychosexual and historical analyses have yet to be fully integrated. The novel itself is centred on the private world of English families and the public feature of Imperialism. Imperialism is therefore a key aspect in *The Moonstone* and a thematic bridge between the foreign and the English worlds and its narrative. The novel is framed by its references to Imperialism, tracing the history of British rule in India which begins with a crucial moment, the storming of Seringatpatam in 1799, the sway of East Indian Company, and ends with the return of the treasure to its temple by the Indians. Collins, however, unlike most of his contemporaries, was very modern in his interpretation of the Indian Mutiny of 1857, as he claims that the source of violence is rooted in Imperialism itself. Gabriel Betteredge's comment in the novel thus voices the common Orientalism of the Victorians that opposes inside and outside, English to foreign, and good to evil: "here was our quiet English house suddenly invaded by a devilish Indian Diamond."[5] Yet *The Moonstone* also blurs these binary oppositions, to the effect that the novel's narrative illustrates, according to Charles Dickens, "a wild and yet domestic scenery".[6] Whereas the Indians are motivated by an apparently "English" sense of justice, Englishmen like Blake appear to the horrified eyes of Betteredge to have turned foreign. Indeed, the distinction between English and Indian order in the interior and chaos in its exterior is radically disrupted when the thief of the Moonstone is uncovered and Blake is convicted. Nonetheless, the novel's Orientalism is reinforced as the decadently foreign Blake steals the treasure under the influence of the Eastern drug opium. Collins' decision to have a second Englishmen steal the Moonstone is yet a kingpin for his radical interpretation of British culture. Just as the history of Imperialism becomes a family story – the revelation of Herncastle's guilt is "extracted from a family paper" (1) – so the "strange family story" (7) of Blake's theft reflects on a larger scale the narrative of Imperialism. The analogies Collins draws between the two thefts of the diamond – the first in India, the second in England – demonstrate a mutual interpretation of the realms of empire and domesticity. It shows how the hierarchies of gender and class that stabilise as well as destabilise British culture replicate the politics of colonialism. Collins suggests an analogy between sexual and imperial domination.

That Rachel is dark emphasises her likeness to the Indians: "Her hair was the blackest, I ever saw. Her eyes matched her hair" (58). This repetition echoes the desire to explore and control the colonial possessions, as well as the Dark Continent that Rachel's femininity represents. Moreover, just as a colonised territory loses its authenticity when it is subordinated to an imperial power, Rachel's loss of independence within Victorian marriage is anticipated by Blake's theft of the jewel. Indeed this secret theft symbolically corrects Rachel's longing for self-sufficiency. As the male characters in the novel are only too happy to point out, her main "defect" (58)

---

[5] Wilkie Collins, *The Moonstone*, ed. Sandra Kemp (London: Penguin, 1998), p. 46. Further references are given parenthetically in the text.
[6] Kirk H. Beetz, "Wilkie Collins Studies 1972-83", *Dickens Studies Annual* 13 (1983), 333-5.

is her tendency to shut herself "up in her own mind" to think (303), an image that suggests that the jewel, which also has a single flaw, signifies not merely her virginity, but what Bruff calls her "self-dependence" (303) as well.

Victorian ideologies of Imperialism and gender go hand in hand in the novel as Blake's motives for the theft are clearly presented in a more positive light by Ezra Jennings: he stole the jewel in an unconscious state and moreover because he unconsciously wished to protect Rachel from the Indians lurking outside the house. The connection between Blake's fears, the paranoia of female chastity and the hysterical fury aroused by the Mutiny also reveals to the reader that his innocence is a rhetorical construction. Blake's reason for stealing the jewel reveals the rationale of Imperialism as "the white man's burden", protecting people who presumably cannot take control of themselves. As Ray Ashish rightly states:

> In so eagerly embracing with equal enthusiasm the improper gift and then in being beguiled by its Indianness with equal enthusiasm, the virginal Rachel's "little flow of nonsense" forms a collusive opening for the amoral forces already at work. However, in as much as the nonsensical improprieties of this "weak and guilty" sexuality are put to work for more lucid purposes, they keep the otherness signified in the diamond with it awful money light "beyond the pale".[7]

The Trouble with Gender and Genre

The trouble with gender roles also manifests itself as a generic confusion: the novel's most scientific detective, Jennings, is also its most Gothic figure, not merely in his flamboyantly weird appearance, but in his embodiment of the Gothic plot of silence and potential subversion. In a conversation with Blake he describes himself in female terms and thus becomes an image of a potentially dangerous radicalism. In this context, Jennings's wish for amnesia, "Perhaps we should all be happier [...] if we could but completely forget" (410), expresses the novel's own impulse to erase its origins in the Gothic and in radical Romanticism. The script that Jennings writes for his "experiment" that acquits Blake is the novel's climatic example of how it obliterates both its generic predecessors and its seditiousness.

Jennings re-enactment of the theft begins as a Gothic narrative, casting him in the role not only of Frankenstein's monster but also of Frankenstein himself, the Promethean overreacher and daring scientist whose theories incite, as Jennings puts it, "the protest of the world [...] against anything that is new" (463). Jennings convinces hostile witnesses like Betteredge or Bruff that he is right, and he persuades Rachel's proper chaperone Mrs Merridew that he is not as disruptive a force as she had feared, causing Blake to comment that "there is a great deal of undeveloped liberal feeling in the world after all" (480). Yet Mrs Merridew's fears about Jennings are enlightening, as she is certain that his experiment will set off an explosion that most likely would make

---

[7] Ray Ashish, "The Fabulous Imperialist Semiotic of Wilkie Collins' *The Moonstone* ", *New Literary History* 24:3 (Summer 1993), 153-170 (163).

Family Treasures and Subversive Power Play in Collins' *The Moonstone*   67

literal his association with a revolutionary "flash of light". She is appeased in the end, however, because, as she explains after the experiment, "Explosions are infinitely milder than they were" (480).

What makes this comment so funny, of course, is the reader's knowledge that there was no explosion. The absence of disruption implies that the 'Victorian Romantic' is not 'explosive' like that of his predecessors, but instead serves domestic ideology. Jennings is not Frankenstein, who builds a creature out of dead bodies and animates it. Nor is he the monster that attacks families, but a physician who cures their ills. In this role he resembles Dickens, Collins's great model for this kind of literary activity, whose domestic fiction diagnoses social malaise and at the same time stabilises the family and normalises gender roles.

Yet Jennings, who engineers the happy ending, never makes it to the wedding of Franklin Blake and Rachel, when for the duration of the festivities he was to have been a "guest in the house" (479). Even though he has been a figure for the writer of domestic fiction who has reassured the reader that all will end in married bliss, Jennings dies before he himself can enter the house, or the terms of the domestic ideology he has served so well.

The novel, however, does not forget its ideological duplicity, but rather underscores it: like Jennings and Collins – the author within the text and the author outside it – *The Moonstone* never manages to be respectable enough. The narrative ends twice, once in England, the second time in India. The relation between these two endings is not only the novel's double voice, but the English ending in particular reflects the suppression of all that is outcast and other.

Detectives on Drugs

In *The Moonstone* power and human professionalism are portrayed in a psychosocial way, as two men collaborate in order to recover the treasure, although in terms of their character they are totally opposite personality types. Collins bridges differences by allowing such a team work to happen. At the same time, however, both men share some common aspects: they are separated from the woman they love as a consequence of having been falsely accused. They have both abused opium and share a psychic connection as both represent a polarisation of melancholia and narcissism. On the one hand this empathy derives from Jennings' "melancholy view of life" (367), while Blake is more self-absorbed in his "lively, easy way" (15), which makes Rosanna Spearman fall for him, with fatal consequences for herself. This social bond between the scientist and the humanist is complimentary to their emotional alliance. Jennings is a medical assistant, while Blake is a so called "universal genius: he wrote a little, he painted a little, he sang a little" (15). As Audrey Jaffe has rightly observed, parallels to yet another more famous detective couple can be drawn here, namely Sherlock Holmes and Dr. Watson:[8]

---

[8] Similarities between the male characters in *The Adventures of Sherlock Holmes* (1892) and *The Moonstone* (1868) were suggested by Rainer Emig at the Treasure symposium, for which I am

Holmes, it has often been stressed, is a model of the "gentlemanly amateur, relaxed and disinterested". When Watson first meets Holmes in *A Study in Scarlet*, he has difficulty figuring out his profession. Given what Holmes seems to know, it is not clear what he is suited for: "Knowledge of Literature. – Nil ... Knowledge of Chemistry – Profound..."[9]

By bringing these two different characters together, a blending of skills can take place. Holmes does not simply gather random information; indeed, by his own account his methods are completely practical. Despite his practicality, however, Holmes maintains an attitude of gentlemanly disinterest; therefore he maintains the professional characteristic tension between productivity and lack of productivity. The idea of Holmes as "amateur" is a mystification of professional labour: his capital, Holmes's laugh suggests, is purely intellectual, his work a function of desire and a source of pleasure rather than a matter of necessity. It makes sense, then, that "The Man with the Twisted Lip", concerning whom Holmes confesses a fascination, is another professional who manifestly enjoys his work: "I have watched this fellow more then once", he says of Boone, "before ever I thought of making his professional acquaintance, and I have been surprised at the harvest which he has reaped in a short time" (120). Holmes boasts, at the end of the tale, fascinated here by Boone's seemingly effortless production of income, that he can solve the case simply "by sitting upon five pillows and consuming an ounce of shag" (132).

Victorian anxieties about lack of productivity are also clearly visible in connection with the opium den. Holmes famously has no private life, only a bohemianism that dramatises the absence of one. The uncovering of his true identity in the opium den requires no scrubbing, but only, apparently, an act of will, a change of mood – or on Watson's part a slight change of perception. Anxiety about opium use in the late nineteenth century was associated with theories of degeneration of the middle class. The anti-opium movement helped spread the belief that "opium smoking was somehow threatening in its implications for the indigenous population."[10] Holmes emphasises the bohemianism that seems to draw him away from his profession, but in fact registers the absence in his life of anything else.

Dedicated to a profession he himself has invented and of which he is the only member ("I suppose, I am the only one in the world, I am a consulting detective", he states in "A Study in Scarlet"; 29), Holmes's work is completely in line with his nature. In this sense his opium addiction is the expression of fulfilment for him; losing oneself in one's work is the same as finding oneself in it. Yet this fantasy of a purely professional self exists alongside this first idea and depends upon producing everyone else's divided self. It is acquired at the expense of those who image that they can wear

---

very grateful. Further to this point Sir Arthur Conan Doyle may well have used the figure of Ezra Jennings and Franklin Blake as role-models for Holmes and Watson, by slightly inverting their types. The theme of drug addiction is present in both fictions as well.

[9] Audrey Jaffe, "Detecting the Beggar: Arthur Conan Doyle, Henry Mayhew and 'The Man with the Twisted Lip'", in: *Arthur Conan Doyle, Sherlock Holmes: The Major Stories with Contemporary Critical Essays*, ed. John A. Hodgson (Basingstoke: Macmillan, 1994), p. 422. Further references are given parenthetically in the text.

[10] See Virginia Berridge and Griffith Edwards, *Opium and the People: Opiate Use in Nineteenth Century England* (London: Yale University Press, 1987) p. 175.

one identity in public and preserve another, private one, secretly for themselves. Yet these 'divided' personalities are exactly the ones who provide their culture with the reassurance about identities it desires. The world stands still while Holmes moves about, and it consists of identities into which he, temporarily, disappears. Holmes produces the ordinary world on which he depends for his labour, clearing the way for his own practice.

In *The Moonstone*, Collins moves from writing in the sensationalist style to writing a modern detective story, in which the medical assistant Jennings puts science to a more benign purpose than the charlatan Dr. Le Doux has done in *The Woman in White* or Holmes in his investigations. He succeeds because Jennings possesses an in-depth knowledge of science and its practical applications. In doing so, he adjusts the visionary scientism of Edgar Allan Poe's Dupin stories and foresees the mixture of legal with the medical science that Arthur Conan Doyle's Sherlock Holmes undertakes in his Baker Street laboratory at the height of the detective genre's popularity at the end of the nineteenth century.

Jennings claims that "science sanctions my proposal fanciful as it may seem" (385), but his decoding of Dr. Candy's delirium relies on remarkably literary techniques. For instance, he gives a plausible background story to the incoherence of the doctor's notes. On the other hand, Blake's reservations on the subjects of medicine, police work and, above all, law that are mentioned earlier in the novel are contradicted by his enthusiasm for Jennings expertise, while Jennings remains an unconventional experimentalist whose fanciful result produces "a serious difference of opinion" between himself "and physicians of established local repute" (367).

The rise of the detective novels can on the one hand be related to the sensation novels that Collins advances quite significantly in the 1860s. On the other hand these fictions are directly connected with the so called *Newgate Novels* that romanticised the lives of criminals.[11] *The Moonstone's* significance is due to the methodical way in which it reconstructs the past by using technical advances of the nineteenth-century science of criminology and the practices of criminal investigation it also partly inspired.

Science and Imperialism

That science becomes so central to *The Moonstone* is very impressive, given that the novel begins as the most evidently political of Collins' novels with its detailed account of the bloody plundering of a colonial village in India by occupying British troops and the conspiracy of vengeance that violence produces. In the context of the legendary curse of revenge that the treasure is said to carry, the readers (like the victims) are immediately taken in by the fact that the three devious Indians, who appear at the Verinder estate before the theft, are responsible for the crime. But the sacred Moonstone, first stolen from its murdered owner as a result of a political crime in the colonies, becomes the focus of intense scientific enquiry and perseverance, as well as a

---

[11] Winifred Hughes, *The Maniac in the Cellar: Sensation Novels of the 1860s* (New York: Princeton University Press, 1980), pp. 78 & 35.

political proclamation. The rise and widespread approval of one of the most enduring forensic techniques demonstrate this juxtaposition of science and politics vividly, and its history is closely linked to the political-scientific issues in *The Moonstone*.[12] The theories of evolution were employed by criminologists and empire-builders in a similar way to connect political agendas, native rituals and scientific theory. They were also appropriated by law enforcement agencies to mark individuals biologically and in order to bestow an identity on them.

Unlike Poe's Dupin before him or Sherlock Holmes after him, Jennings is a scientist by profession. Analogous to Dupin and Holmes, however, his act of analysis embodies the concurrence of the political and the scientific in his assessment of material evidence and scientific research material to solve the case. Jennings is the assistant to the senior physician in the novel, Dr. Candy, whose argument with Blake about the precision and power of chemistry and the medical profession is the cause of much mystery. In setting out to solve this problem, Jennings designs and conducts the experiments that confirm that Franklin Blake himself, as unbelievable as it may seem, the man most enthusiastically pursuing the investigation, has committed the theft of the Moonstone unconsciously under the influence of laudanum and driven by a nervous impulse.

Science is the sanctioning authority in *The Moonstone*, putting the law on hold and then, eventually, collaborating with this latter institution to reveal the truth. Throughout the experiment, what does indeed begin as the most political of Collins' novels investigating the criminal implication of an illegal act of plundering in British India and the vengeance of the Empire, ends by being the most scientific. The focus of the enquiry is shifted from international politics to experiments in the laboratory. Here the meaning of science is evidently loaded with powerful political implications and consequences.

First, much of the chemistry behind the crime and the experimentation that solves it is rooted in the effects of opium, the substance from India that has taken hold of Colonel Herncastle's body and Jennings' as well. Like the diamond, this powerful drug brings its own curse back upon the colonisers in England. An illicit substance and at the same time a legitimate medical treatment, opium is an apt representation of the Empire's complex and controversial place in nineteenth-century Britain and in the novel. The use of opium was an essential component in nineteenth-century arts circles. It was supposed to broaden the mind and give new insights into the imaginative power of the writer. Coleridge, de Quincey and Wilkie Collins were known for their addiction to the substance.[13]

As a commodity, however, opium was as important in the nineteenth century as oil is nowadays. From 1832 onwards, the annual shipment of opium to China amounted to 30,000 chests. In 1836 the total opium imports valued 18 million US $, which was considered the world's most valuable single commodity trade in the nineteenth century,

---

[12] See for instance, Ronald R. Thomas, "Detection in the Victorian Novel", in *The Cambridge Companion to the Victorian Novel*, ed. Deirdre David (Cambridge: Cambridge University Press, 2000), pp. 169-191.

[13] For opium addiction and Victorian authors see Richard D. Jackson, "James Hogg and the Unfathomable Hell", in: *Romanticism on the Net* 28 (November 2002), 1467-1255 (digital). See also Donald Wigal, *Die Faszination des Opiums in Geschichte und Kunst* (New York: Parkstone Press, 2004), p. 62.

another treasure of the British Empire, so to speak. In fact the commodity opium ended up financing much of Britain's colonisation of India.[14]

It is worth noting that Collins himself was under the influence of the drug during the time he wrote *The Moonstone*, as was his protagonist Franklin Blake (unknowingly) when he took the diamond from Rachel's room thanks to Dr. Candy's experiment performed upon him. Jennings' opium addiction finds itself mirrored in Sherlock Holmes's substance abuse. Jennings represents two sides of the same coin, like the drug that is agent of both healing and debauchery: being part English, part Indian, he is quite literally a child of the British Empire, a mysterious point of intersection between two worlds. At the same time he is located at the very heart of the detective story and the imperial intrigue. While Herncastle is described as a villain and his actions are plainly condemned, Blake's are not. The unconscious nature of Blake's theft and his good intentions to keep the diamond safe seem to excuse his criminal act, and Rachel ultimately forgives and marries him.

The Treasure of Romantic Love versus the Desire of the Other

Rachel is central to the action of the plot, and her virtue remains incontestable. Her love for Franklin Blake is the antithesis of Herncastle's lust and selfishness, which prompts him to steal the diamond in the first place. The Moonstone gem is timeless, while Rachel's and Franklin's love is bounded by time. For Collins, romantic love is the most positive human trait, the Western equivalent of Eastern religious reverence. Like the Hindu priests who are responsible for keeping the diamond safe, Rachel and Franklin are tested by experience and self-sacrifice. Blake recovers Rachel, just as the Brahmins restore the diamond to its rightful place. Their mutual love and affection, Collins seems to indicate here in a romantic fashion, is a treasure worth keeping.

During Collins' lifetime and his literary career spanning nearly fifty years, the British abolished slavery in their possessions (1834), defeated the Chinese in the Opium Wars (1840-1842 and 1860), brutally squashed the Indian Mutiny (1857-1858), and designated Victoria "Empress of India" (1876). While for many these events functioned as a legitimating narrative for the British Imperialists, others like Collins questioned their moral mission, especially concerning the Opium Wars. As in earlier works, Collins again ties class resentment to a desire for revenge among the colonised: "The Moonstone will have its vengeance yet on you and yours!", a dying Brahmin warns Herncastle (4). So, too does the working-class resentment and the call for revolution expressed by Lucy Yolland who "flam[es] out" against Blake (183), blaming him for the suicide of her lovelorn friend, the housemaid Rosanna Spearman. The rhetorical power that shows an obvious struggle to rescue a fellow female from male domination does not appear in the figure of the virtuous Rachel, but in the disabled fisherman's daughter "Limping Lucy", who has a distorted foot. She attacks masculine denigration

---

[14] Wigal, *Die Faszination des Opiums*, pp. 22-25. See also Alethea Hayter, *Opium and the Romantic Imagination* (London: Faber and Faber, 1968), pp. 55-63.

of female intelligence and character. Lucy's affection for Rosanna proves instrumental in resolving the Moonstone's mystery.

Paradoxically, even as Collins' art is combined with the male science of detection, in *The Moonstone* it becomes increasingly more feminine, subverting the official version of what has happened with devious hints and ironies. In this way, the feminine Gothic space of Shivering Sand, where conflict is hidden beneath the veil of secrecy, becomes a striking symbol in the novel. This hush-up becomes understandable in the scene where Blake reads Rosanna's letter after discovering on Shivering Sand that he is guilty of the crime of theft. This is a far more painful moment in his detective investigation "from darkness to light" (369). Rosanna's text is stranded in darkness because she (like Rachel and Miss Clack) does not correctly interpret what she sees; all these women either suspect or know that Blake has taken the diamond, but they cannot know why he has stolen it.

One of the more subversive analyses of gender and class is the moment in which Rosanna reveals in her letter to Franklin Blake that in the matter of suppression she is more knowledgeable than he. The letter can also be interpreted as the secret treasure map that reveals some of the mysteries surrounding the theft of the Moonstone. When Blake, appalled about his actions, refuses to finish Rosanna's letter, handing it over to Betteredge half read, the novel draws attention to how Blake continues to ignore Rosanna or her narrative, which implies a criticism of concessions given to the upper class.

As the detective plot of the novel unfolds, the social critique implied by Collins is buried so deep that the reader can only uncover its traces by digging them up again. In *The Moonstone* the reader is confronted obsessively with images of alienated writers who censor themselves.

Rosanna's suicide is certainly the most drastic example of self-erasure, as she jumps into the quicksand that buries the letter and silences her lips forever. Once again, Blake is spared because of a woman's love for him. This implied criticism of what women are willing to do for love is a recurrent theme in Wilkie Collins's novels. This is clearly stated in *The Woman in White*: "No man under heaven deserves these sacrifices from us women", exclaims Marion Halcombe to Laura Fairlie when she is angered by the thought of Laura's coming entrapment and subjection in a loveless marriage undertaken because Laura has given her father a death-bed promise.[15] Likewise, it could be argued that Rosanna's love for Blake and her ultimate sacrifice are unnecessary, as Franklin is unaware of her affections and would not have given her a chance because he is in love with Rachel, who is also from his social class.

The greatest clash between female Gothic and male detection, however, occurs in the scene where Blake confronts the quicksand to rescue from it Rosanna's letter and the stained nightgown:

> In this position my face was within a few feet of the surface of the quicksand. The sight of it so near me, still disturbed at intervals by its hideous shivering fit, shook my nerves for a

---

[15] Wilkie Collins, *The Woman in White*, ed. Julian Symons (Harmondsworth: Penguin, 1974), p. 33. See also Mark M. Hennelly, Jr., "Reading Detection in *The Woman in White*", *Texas Studies in Literature and Language* 22 (1980), 449-467.

Family Treasures and Subversive Power Play in Collins' *The Moonstone* 73

moment. A horrible fancy that the dead woman might appear on the scene of her suicide, to assist my search – an unutterable dread of seeing her rise through the heaving surface of the sand, and point to the place – forced itself into my mind, and turned me cold in the warm sunlight. I own I closed my eyes at the moment when the point of the stick first entered the quicksand. (343)

The mysterious feminine desire recalls related types of puzzling Otherness in the novel. The Sand's "fathomless deeps" and its "false brown face" (342) remind the reader of "the unfathomable" and "yellow deep" of the Indian diamond (68) and, synecdochically, of the East. Like Mr. Murthwaite's travels "penetrating into regions left still unexplored", detective work maps and colonises these Dark Continents.

Blake's confrontation with the id, or "a threatening second self",[16] is pinpointed by various psychoanalytic readings of this text. In fact, he does not learn so much about the Other within himself as the Other external to it. As in earlier approaches to the Sand, female sexuality marks a disobedient revolt that is potentially beyond the control of the Englishman. At the site of Rosanna's buried desire Blake witnesses the return of the repressed, the reawakening of feminine sexuality signified by the "hideous shivering fit" of the quicksand. A sense of the threat (already vividly suggested by the name Spearman) that this female sexuality poses to his masculine identity pervades the language that he uses to describe his reaction to the Sand. Not only are his nerves shaken, as if he were suffering from neurasthenia, but he confesses to an overpowering fear at the moment he penetrates the quicksand: "I own I closed my eyes". Rather than expressing a horror of female sexuality, as many critics have eagerly suggested, I would interpret this scene as being scared of death and the haunting of the dead, represented by the fantasy that he is haunted by Rosanna's ghost.

The stillness of the Shivering Sand, that site of all that is hidden and buried, is an image of the novel's focus on Gothic silence, for instance Rachel's silence, around which its mystery plot is constructed. The scene of the Sand is a prelude to the climatic scene where a male detective crosses the threshold of female mysteries. Hoping she can prove his innocence, Blake arranges a meeting with Rachel in order to persuade her to tell him what she knows.

Knowledge and Power

Collins's depiction of this scene shows it as a battle over the control of knowledge. Once again it is connected with the breaking of a woman's silence. In Foucauldian terms, this knowledge is an expression of power:[17] Blake's role as a detective, his attempt to repossess Rachel's knowledge, reinforces the control over women that

---

[16] Sue Lonoff uses this expression in *Wilkie Collins and His Victorian Readers: A Study in the Rhetoric of Authorship* (New York: Dover Publishing, 1982), p. 198.

[17] See Stuart Elden and Jeremy W. Crampton, "Introduction – Space, Knowledge and Power: Foucault and Geography", in: *Space, Knowledge and Power: Foucault and Geography*, ed. Stuart Elden and Jeremy W. Crampton (Aldershot: Ashgate, 2007), pp. 1-16.

Victorian gender ideology gave to men within courtship and marriage. In an exchange that reads both like a love scene and an interrogation, Blake gets answers to his pounding questions by assuming once more the role of Rachel's suitor: "while her hand lay in mine I was her master still" (383). When he asserts that, after more of this urging, "she willingly opened her whole mind to me" (384), he implies that Rachel's eagerness to open her mind readily reverses her previous reluctance to have the drawer opened and her jewel stolen. When he provokes the disclosure most detrimental to his case – that she has witnessed him stealing the diamond – his rebuke to her silence ("if you had spoken, when you ought to have spoken") initiates him resolutely to lose "his influence" over her: "the few words I had said seemed to have lashed her on the instant into a frenzy of rage" (388). So powerful is Rachel's outrage that it provokes a reaction in Blake that is comparable to what he has experienced at Shivering Sand: "The hysterical passion swelled in her bosom – her quickened convulsive breathing almost beat on my face" (393). At the end of this scene Franklin simply bursts into tears.

Rachel's hysteria subverts the language of Victorian courtship and marriage. Castigating Blake with a "cry of fury" (388), she accuses him of deceit: "he wonders, I did not charge him with his disgrace the first time we met: 'My heart's darling, you are a Thief! My hero whom I love and honour, you have crept into my room under the cover of the night, and stolen my Diamond!'" (389). In this passage, Rachel's words express repulsion at the thought that her hero has so badly deceived her. If we think in materialistic terms, this can be equally disturbing to a young lady. It has often been equated with sexual violation, but this interpretation suggests that a young woman of the upper class knows nothing of material values.

The construction of woman in the public space as an object of desire in need of protection helped tame the threat independent women posed to the family (by implicitly calling into question the equation between domesticity and respectability). At the same time, the sexualisation of woman in the private sphere as reproductive body served to legitimate her invisible labour in the home not merely as civilizing moral agent – the mid-Victorian angel in the house – but as mother of the race and domestic consumer. The concomitant rearticulation of her labour as a civic responsibility was aided by the increased permeability between the private and the public sphere.

Rachel's silence, however, cuts both ways: while protecting Franklin, it puts herself under suspicion. While Rachel remains silent, the truth will remain hidden. Thus the mystery plot – the discovery of the diamond – is inextricable from woman's passion and her identity. Not only must Rachel conceal her passion for Franklin until he becomes a proper suitor, but the Moonstone itself becomes a prawn in the marriage negotiations. Money and marriage are often related, both in the novels and in life. Rachel's suitors take on roles that mask their suitability, however: Godfrey appears as the "Christian Hero" and Franklin as philandering debtor and suspected thief (239). According to Kennard, when these roles are sorted out – this implies the key to the mystery – the marriage plot can be traditionally and adequately concluded.[18] The sorting out in Collins' novel thus in fact muddles "the poles of value": we establish that Godfrey is both a philandering debtor and a thief, but we never really establish that Franklin is

---

[18] Jean E. Kennard, *Victims of Convention* (Boston, Massachusetts: St Martin's Press, 1978), pp. 13 & 18.

Family Treasures and Subversive Power Play in Collins' *The Moonstone*   75

neither. Godfrey is constrained from returning to England "by some unmentionable woman", and on his return he borrows money from Lady Verinder to repay an earlier debt (48). The conclusion of the courtship plot, however, literalises "the poles of value": Franklin, who has inherited his father's wealth, is simply worth more than Godfrey.

The introduction to the theme of hysteria, however, causes the blurring of gender roles. By making the manly detective cry, the references to hysteria work more strongly to reinstate the notion of sexual difference. Hélène Cixous has pointed out "that silence is the mark of hysteria",[19] so that Rachel's silence is not just a way of protecting her lover, but also a sign of helplessness, of her difficulty in voicing her need. During the period of her estrangement from Blake both her silence and her hysterical outbursts suggests her frustration at the separation, as she herself admits her disillusioned feelings of love to Godfrey Ablewhite and then asks: "Is there a form of hysterics that bursts into words instead of tears?" (262).

But despite these disputes and doubts, Franklin is Rachel's choice even before his father's death makes him wealthy. So while convention demands a fortune for the novel's heroine, Collins also provides her with passion. Rachel's love for Franklin survives her conviction that he is a philanderer, a debtor, and even a thief – it is only his seeming pretence in calling the police which threatens to destroy her love. For the reader, her passion is an ill-kept secret.

Female secrecy is, of course, not unique to *The Moonstone*. Elaine Showalter believes that "secrecy was basic to the lives of all respectable women" of the mid nineteenth century.[20] Collins, however, seems to suggests that these rules are not designed to protect female modesty or propriety, but rather conceal the criminal underpinnings of the Victorian family.

Acting for his uncle "the Honourable John" in bringing the Moonstone to Yorkshire, Blake is linked to the East Indian Company and its suspect practices from the outset. His involuntarily consumption of opium turns the tables on the colonisers, just as their home country is invaded by the Hindus, which can be seen as a moment of reverse colonisation. When Blake expresses scepticism about the benefits of medicine, the local doctor underhandedly adds an opiate to his drink to prove him wrong. Like those subject to British rule and forced into economic and physical dependence on opium, Blake experiences under its influence a loss of selfhood and autonomy that mirrors the condition of the colonised.

---

[19] Hélène Cixous, "Castration or Decapitation", trans. Annette Kuhn, *Signs* 7 (1981), 49. In the Freudian discourse, hysteria is a sign of women's fruitless rebellion against the things that they secretly desire but will not acknowledge: heterosexuality and the subordination to men that its institutionalisation represents. See *The Standard Edition of the Complete Psychological Works of Sigmund Freud*, 2nd ed., trans. and ed. James Strachey and others (London: Imago, 1953-64), here vol. IV.

[20] Elaine Showalter, *A Literature of their Own: British Women Novelists from Brontë to Lessing* (Princeton, New Jersey: Princeton University Press, 1999), p. xii.

Restoring Heteronormativity

Despite its mysterious underpinnings, Rachel's dilemma is not unlike that of any other courtship heroine: any such heroine must not speak of love until she is spoken to. According to Kennard she must also learn to read her suitor correctly and "must adjust…to society values".[21] Rachel still emerges from her nightmare of doubt in both herself and Franklin as a strong character. By reuniting Rachel with Blake, Jennings' experiment replaces the hysteria that "bursts into words instead of tears" with conventionally feminine language. Jennings describes her response to his letter explaining the circumstances of the theft as: "A charming letter… She tells me in the prettiest manner, that my letter has satisfied her of Blake's innocence" (442).

This charming and pretty female text is a paean to romantic love: "the rapture of discovering that he has deserved to be loved, breaks its way innocently through the stoutest formalities of pink and ink" (442). Jennings himself becomes (appropriately enough in this novel that alludes to *Robinson Crusoe*) a kind of Man Friday who serves the upper-class Blake. He also becomes an image of a writer who reconciles himself to the social order instead of challenging it.

This channelling of female writing into the expression of heterosexual desire precedes the re-enactment of the theft in which Rachel reprises her role as silent witness of Blake's theft: "She kept back, in the dark, not a word, not a movement escaped her" (473). Whereas Blake's theft has represented men's domination of women, this repeat performance stages the ritual with the woman's consent to her own invisibility. Unlike her horrified silence during the original theft, Rachel's silence during the experiment expresses her happy anticipation of her impending marriage. Watching Blake sleep off the effects of opium, she reverses the effects of her hysteria by bursting into tears instead of words: "She looked at him in a silent ecstasy of happiness, till her tears rose in her eyes" (477). At last her patience and endurance pay off, Collins seems to suggest.

Rachel is ultimately rewarded with love, marriage and a child, her new treasure worth safeguarding from now on. All this dedication to the non-conformist bachelor Blake has finally made him a family man. These facts stand in sharp contrast to the figure of Godfrey Ablewhite. It is Betteredge who makes Ablewhite's character clear: "Female benevolence and female destitution could do nothing without him" – for he uses female benevolence to create female destitution (89). Ablewhite's broken engagement to Rachel and his secondary theft of the Moonstone are both evidence of his deviance from acceptable behaviour. As Barickman and others rightly observe:

> Godfrey Ablewhite's secret […] involves Victorian sexual roles at their worst; he hypocritically becomes a champion of charitable ladies while he is keeping a mistress, embezzling another man's money, and preying upon Rachel in order to gain control over her money.[22]

---

[21] Kennard, *Victims of Convention*, p. 18.

[22] Richard Barickman, Susan MacDonald and Myra Stark, *Corrupt Relations: Dickens, Thackeray, Trollope, Collins and the Victorian Sexual System* (New York: Colombia University Press, 1982), p. 143.

Family Treasures and Subversive Power Play in Collins' *The Moonstone*   77

It is not so much Ablewhite's preoccupation with wealth as his love of the self and sensual pleasure which condemns him. Ironically he is guilty of exactly the kind of hypocrisy of which Rachel suspects Blake. Even more ironical is the circumstance that it is ultimately this negative character that facilitates the recovery of the diamond. Godfrey's crime is both a family scandal and a police matter. The two spheres are permanently linked, and no amount of artistic license can separate them. Collins seems to make a case for the claim that no family is secure from the dangers of necessary concealments.

Conclusion: A Multifaceted Gem

To Wilkie Collins the Moonstone is the signifier of all the things that humanity can and should strive for, material as well as spiritual. He begins the novel by demonstrating that the history of the Moonstone is a history of crime and theft. In having his initial narrator state "that crime brings its own fatality with it" (38), Collins underscores the fact that nemesis attends every worldly expropriator of the Moonstone, which to its temporary European holders is a bauble and a commodity, but which to its guardians, the Brahmins, is a sacred relic beyond price. Collins claims in his preface to the first edition of *The Moonstone* of 1868 that the great diamond was based both on the "Orloff" (one "Orloff" diamond forms part of the Russian crown jewels, while another "Black Orloff", also called called "the Eye of Brahma", was, according to legend, stolen from an Indian temple) and the British crown's "Koh-i- Noor" (meaning "mountain of light"). The latter was previously owned by the Persian conqueror Nadir Shah, who had in turn obtained it by duplicity from a Mogul Emperor in 1739). In the text, the gem is also never really English or England's, for the novel also begins with an account of various thefts.[23] The novel opens in India with Herncastle's purloining the gem in battle (the opening lines are specifically "written in India") and closes with Murthwaite's account (dated 1850) of the restoration of the gleaming "yellow diamond" to the forehead of the Hindu deity of the Moon "after the lapse of eight centuries" (472).

The Moonstone subverts not only the conventions of the Sensation Novel, but also the traditional tenants of nineteenth-century British Imperialism. The Brahmins are hardly mindless primitives, and the British army is not shown as intervening to prevent bloodshed between rival factions. The conquering English are not superior enlightened beings attempting to confer the benefits of European culture and Christian morality upon benighted savages.

The British are in fact incapable of rendering justice to the Indians. The Indians are "committed" for a week, for, as Betteredge suggests, "Every human institution (Justice included) will stretch a little, if you can only pull it the right way" (91).

[23] See Patrick Brantlinger, *Rule of Darkness: British Literature and Imperialism 1830- 1914* (Ithaca: Cornell University Press, 1988), pp. 200-235. See also Jaya Metha, "English Romance, Indian Violence", *Centennial Review* 39 (Autumn 1995), 611-57.

The Englishmen at the Verinder estate are even incapable of solving the mysteries inside the home. As was pointed out above, the chief analytical instrument that helps Ezra Jennings (who himself has foreign elements in his "English blood"; 367) to solve the mystery, i.e. opium, is a colonial product.

It seems that Imperialism in the novel produces troubling self-images: a wicked colonel and a white thief. One can detect an obsessive need to present and represent peripheries, as there is a realization that the periphery determines the centre.

Returned to its proper guardians, then once again placed in the forehead of the Moon god, the Moonstone once again reverts to a metaphysical rather than a capitalist signifier. *The Moonstone* becomes a sign whose meanings lie beyond cultural misperceptions and hegemonies. In the idol, the treasure inspires faith in the community of believers, while as a useless bauble it excites lust, greed and even murder:

The Indian connection gave Collins an additional dimension for his crime and detection novel, for it suggested light-dark imagery, aspects of the surface versus subsurface, external events versus background, history and its shadows. If nothing else, the Indian strategy reinforced the pressure of the past upon the present.[24]

When Betteredge urges Franklin to believe in the prophetic powers of the novel *Robinson Crusoe* during the novel's open ending, the butler encourages Blake to remember his English roots. This novel stands as symbol of imperial domination that England unthinkingly enjoys over its own colonies. Betteredge uses Daniel Defoe's first novel about early British Imperialism (Crusoe leaves England and conquers a foreign, exotic island) as a prophetic text for his own life. Although Franklin is English, his education is largely foreign:

> [Blake] had come back with so many different sides to his character, all more or less jarring with each other, that he seemed to pass his life in a state of perpetual contradiction with himself [...] He had his French side, and his German side, and his Italian side – the original English foundation showing through, every now and then [...] (35-36)

Betteredge here appeals to Franklin's Englishness, and Blake in the final statement of the butler's tale claims to be "convinced at last" that *Robison Crusoe* has a prophetic quality (463). Yet one could equally well claims that Collins merely gives the reader a conventional ending, revealing a desire on the author's part to assimilate and conform. Betteredge, after all, retires hereafter. This may be an indication that his approval of Imperialism as described in *Robinson Crusoe* has also come to an end.

Franklin Blake, although a sceptic by nature, stays in England with his new family obligations and never returns to India. The imperial justification that racial identity is an inescapable essence that defines people and fixes them in their place, however, is challenged in the portrait of Murthwaite, the English expert on India, who has an affinity for Indian culture, which he prefers to the "humdrum" of English life (65). Yet his ability to transcend racial identity and pass as an Indian is not shared by other Englishmen. Ablewhite's masquerade as a dark sailor is simply washed off, and he is killed as a consequence. Indirectly, he is punished for his greed for the treasure.

---

[24] Karl Frederick, "Introduction", in: Wilkie Collins, *The Moonstone* (Scarborough, Ontario: Signet, 1984), p. 18.

Both Blake and Murthwaite acknowledge that the precious stone belongs to India. They both are tolerant towards other nations. Murthwaite plays an active part in the restoration of the Moonstone, as he brings it back to the Hindus in the final chapter of Collins' novel.

When it comes to a mutual understanding between the coloniser and the colonised, Collins clearly wishes for a diplomatic solution. Bloody oppression is no solution for international conflicts. Along these lines, the open ending of the Indian tale can be regarded as subversive, as the grounds of racial difference are shown as arbitrary and shifting.

Rainer Emig

Treasure Hunts: Between Decadence and Morality[1]

> *quid non mortalia pectora cogis,*
> *auri sacra fames!*
> (Virgil, *Aeneid III,* 11. 56-57)

"To what do you not drive mortal hearts, cursed craving for gold!" – this classical quotation already incorporates the simultaneous fascination and anxiety that treasure hunts create. For "auri sacra fames" of course also translates as "this *sacred* hunger for gold". Even the earliest literary texts, *Beowulf* for instance, contain treasure motifs, and many Structuralist analyses of narratives list elements associated with treasure hunts, such as trial and reward, as prototypical plot elements that motivate action and characters.[2] There are indeed common features that define treasure: wealth whose original owner has disappeared (otherwise a treasure hunt would be theft), and valuable objects that are hidden or difficult to access, whose retriever must invest intelligence in his enterprise and often take risks.[3]

Nonetheless, the meaning of treasure and treasure hunts always depends on ideological contexts that decide, for instance, whether the hunt for treasure is to be applauded or condemned. In the present essay I want to explore the ambivalence of the phenomenon in an era that can itself be regarded as an extended metaphor for treasure hunts, the heyday of imperialism and colonialism in the late nineteenth century. I will compare three texts that were first published within a decade of each other – Robert Louis Stevenson's *Treasure Island (1883),* Henry Rider Haggard's *King Solomon's Mines* (1885) and Karl May's *Der Schatz im Silbersee* [The Treasure of the Silver Lake] (1894)[4] – but which stein from rather different backgrounds.[5] Stevenson's *Treasure*

---

[1] This chapter first appeared in *New Comparison: A Journal of Comparative and General Literary Studies,* 35-36, "Money" (Spring/Autumn 2003), 187-195.

[2] This is already evident in Vladimir Propp's formalist study *Morphology of the Folktale,* 2nd edn, ed. and trans. Laurence Scott (Austin and London: University of Texas Press, 1968).

[3] Zoja Karanovic illustrates the unbroken fascination with the idea of buried treasure, and its indebtedness to very old literary and folkloristic paradigms, in "Fact and Fiction in Today's Stories of Buried Treasure", *Artes Populares,* 16-17 (1995), 409-415.

[4] The novel first appeared in serialized form in a boys' magazine, *Der gute Kamerad (The Good Comrade),* in 1890-1891.

[5] The editions used for this essay are: Henry Rider Haggard, *King Solomon's Mines,* ed. Dennis Butts (Oxford et al.: Oxford University Press, 1998); Robert Louis Stevenson, *Treasure Island,* ed. Wendy R. Katz (Edinburgh: Edinburgh University Press, 1998); Karl May, *Der Schatz im Silbersee,* ed. Hermann Wiedenroth and Hans Wollschläger (Nördlingen: Greno, 1987). All page references are given parenthetically in the text; translations from May are by Rainer Emig.

Island is the first successful tale by a Scotsman who had fled from multiple constraints – a career in law which had been imposed on him, a respectable family, and Scottish Presbyterianism – to California, where he married a divorcee ten years his senior.[6] Rider Haggard's *King Solomon's Mines,* on the other hand, is a tale by a writer who (also after an unsuccessful start as a lawyer) managed to forge first a career as a civil servant and then as a writer out of his work as a member of the staff of Sir Henry Bulwer, Lieutenant-Governor of Natal, in South Africa. May, finally, is the most successful German purveyor of boys' adventure stories, variously set in the Wild West, Central America, North Africa, the Balkans, but also his native Germany. *Der Schatz im Silbersee* forms part of his best-known series of tales featuring figures who have achieved mythological status in German culture, such as the noble Native American Winnetou or the brave white hunters Old Shatterhand and Old Firehand. May became a writer after an unhappy childhood characterised by strict discipline and illness, unsuccessful attempts to become a teacher, and several scrapes with the law. He went to the North America he so fondly imagined only for a brief trip in later life.

I will begin by outlining what the three texts by such different authors have in common. Then I will highlight some strange contradictions that form part of their thematic configurations, contradictions that I will place in the context of debates that are contemporaneous with debates about Empire, but rarely related to them. These concern ideas of decadence, a cultural concept that came to prominence in the *fin de siècle,* but whose shadow falls over Western European cultures from the mid-nineteenth century onwards.

All three novels discussed here contain treasure hunts. All three hunts are triggered by maps which find their way into the hands of the protagonists by a chain of coincidences. In all three novels the hunters are faced with competitors or enemies, but only two of the novels grant their protagonists success. In Stevenson's tale, the treasure is the legacy of piracy, and was apparently deposited on a Caribbean island some time in the seventeenth century. The origin of the treasure is ultimately a multiple theft: it most probably consists of gold plundered by the Spaniards in Central or South America, which was then taken from them by English pirates. These pirates are clearly treated as criminals in the text (a position they did not always hold in history – Renaissance "privateers", for instance, frequently enjoyed the support of monarchs), so stealing from them apparently poses no legal or moral problems. The motley crew that sets out to retrieve the treasure consists of an interesting cross-section of English society, and the unlikely hero and narrator is effectively in the lowest position: Jim Hawkins, teenage son of a widowed innkeeper. The expedition is financed by an aristocrat, Squire Trelawney, but since he has more money than sense, its success ultimately depends on the solid middle-class characters Dr Livesey and Captain Smollett. Their most powerful antagonist is Long John Silver, a pirate who disguises himself as a cook in order to infiltrate the expedition.

In Rider Haggard's *King Solomon's Mines,* the origin of the treasure is even more fantastic: it is said to represent the mythical wealth of the biblical King Solomon, deposited – for whatever reason – in deepest, darkest Africa, where, conveniently, the

---

[6] One of the many biographical assessments of the novel is William H. Hardesty, III and David D. Mann, "Odds on *Treasure Island",* *Studies in Scottish Literature,* 25 (1996), 50-59.

natives are kept away from it by tales of evil forces. Besides characterising the natives as naive and superstitious (with very few significant exceptions), the text also implies that, ultimately, the treasure's biblical link justifies its plundering by those whom nineteenth-century English culture considered the heirs of the chosen people of the Old Testament: none other than the English themselves. The ingredients of this treasure are significant: diamonds and ivory, two colonial commodities associated with South Africa. Rider Haggard's treasure hunters again represent English culture. Although his tale is set in the late nineteenth century, it is remarkably close to Stevenson's story – not surprisingly, since Rider Haggard wrote his to prove that he could beat Stevenson at his own game. Once again, the expedition is financed by an aristocrat, Sir Henry Curtis, and he is supported by two solid middle-class characters, Captain John Good and the elephant hunter Allan Quatermain. The story contains no English underdog; instead, it gathers a devoted – and self-sacrificing – group of native servants around the English explorers. The most unusual and impressive of them, Umbopa, eventually turns out to be an African prince in disguise, whose mission is to regain his throne. The suave Sir Henry is a far cry from the foolish Squire in Stevenson's tale; it is not financial gain that motivates his expedition, either, but the attempt to find his brother, who has disappeared on the quest for the mythical treasure of King Solomon.

In Karl May's *Der Schatz im Silbersee,* the treasure is also associated with a vanished civilization. Information about it has been passed down the generations of one Native American family: it is hidden at the bottom of the "Silver Lake", protected not by magic, but by an intricate technology of tunnels and dams. Technology also determines the end of May's story, since the treasure itself is never found. Instead, silver ore is discovered. May's treasure hunters consist of a remarkable array of characters and are strikingly different from Stevenson's and Rider Haggard's. In keeping with the story's North American setting, but even more so with May's common device of making his heroes Germans in exile, the main protagonists include no aristocrat. Nobility of birth has been replaced by nobility of character: the story is full of praise for Old Firehand's noble and manly personality, but also his looks. Interestingly, this nobility is also attributed to the most important Native Americans in the tale, Little Bear, Great Bear and Winnetou. The middle class is represented by an American engineer, Patterson, and his daughter Ellen. Yet the story contains many more extraordinary characters who join the treasure hunters. The most formidable of them is called "Tante Droll" (Aunty Droll). With a high-pitched voice and dressed in what look like women's clothes, he is very much at odds with the conventions of tales of the Wild West (37-39). Yet, as it turns out, he is also a competent fighter and gunman who makes a living as a secret policeman, hunting and occasionally killing wanted criminals. He is by no means the only eccentric of the group, which furthermore includes a pair of very close friends, called "Langer Davy" (Tall Davy) and "Dicker Jemmy" (Fat Jemmy). Davy is American and Jemmy German, but their long friendship has resulted in a merging of speech characteristics (353).

There is also a character called "Hobble-Frank", whose real name is Heliogabalus Morpheus Franke (351). As if this was not eccentric enough, the story introduces a proper lord called Castlepool, who apparently hails from Scotland but is nonetheless called "Englishman" throughout (142ff.). The fact that he does not protest against this label is one of the many instances that show that May's accuracy regarding cultural contexts is not beyond reproof. Castlepool is an eccentric traveller in search of adventure, the typical aesthete incessantly seeking new impressions and sensations. Yet he also represents sound commercial thinking, since he buys adventures for between fifty and one hundred dollars from another two odd hunters called "Humply-Bill" and "Gunstick-Uncle" (146), and keeps a notebook for his calculations. The evil antagonists are a large group of outlaws: their leader, called "Cornel", is not only an arch-manipulator but also a master of disguise, and his most striking characteristic is his dyed red hair (122-124).

What already emerges from this brief survey of the stories' plots and main characters is that they largely conform to the standards of adventure stories: they contain no or only marginalised women, a clear distinction between good and evil, figures of identification who are wise, noble and strong, and no questioning of underlying ideologies. Yet they also display strange features: a transvestite character who calls himself "Tante" (a common German term for homosexuals until the 1920s, nowadays replaced by "Tunte"), or silly aristocrats.[7] Even Rider Haggard's tale, at first glance so affirmative with regard to colonial adventure, bases the success of the expedition not only on the manliness and courage of the aristocracy and decent middle class, but also on eccentricity. For the prototypical Englishman Captain John Good is also a dandy, who wanders through Africa in a monocle and rubber shirt collars (12ff.).[8] When the treasure hunters are suddenly surrounded by hostile natives, he is busy with his beauty routine and clad only in his undershirt. His pale white legs, "glass eye" (as they call it) and half-shaven face convince the attackers that he is a god and stop them from killing the white men and their black servants.

Yet eccentricity to the extent of decadence is not only found on the side of the "good" characters, where it might represent individuality although it still clashes with the ethos of muscular simplicity prevalent in empire narratives. The "evil" antagonists also display decadent patterns: Long John Silver is a competent actor, veering between sickly submissiveness and steely determination; the decadent (and for an outlaw rather impractical) dyed red hair of Karl May's "Cornel" has already been mentioned. In Rider Haggard the most powerful antagonist is a woman, the ageless witch Gagool, but her power is exerted through the corrupt usurper king Twala and his evil brother Scragga, who share the decadent habit of killing their subjects for pleasure. More important still, this decadent evil always manages to infiltrate the heart of the project: Long John Silver and several of his pirate mates are recruited by the treasure hunters; Gagool leads Rider Haggard's treasure hunters to King Solomon's mines; and Karl May's "Cornel" travels on the same river steamer at the start of the tale as the story's protagonists, prises their secret from them, and continues to haunt them. Evil is thus at the core of the enterprise,

---

[7] It is curious that the first serious ideological reading of the characters in May's novel fails or refuses to name Droll's gender-bending: Hans Wollschläger, "Karl Mays Schätze im Silbersee: Ein hundertjähriges Jugendbuch", *Jahrbuch der Karl May Gesellschaft,* 27 (1997), 272-274.
[8] For a detailed discussion of the links between colonialism and decadence, see my essay "Imperial Decadence/Postcolonial Decadence: Excess, Aesthetics, and Ideology in Late Nineteenth-Century and Postcolonial Twentieth-Century Writing", in: *Anglistentag 2000 Berlin: Proceedings,* ed. Peter Lucko and Jürgen Schlaeger (Trier: Wissenschaftlicher Verlag Trier, 2001), pp. 395-405.

where it needs to be contained and controlled. Yet this abjection of moral decay and decadence always also affects those in charge of the abjection: in May, but also Rider Haggard and even, to a certain extent, Stevenson, it is possible to detect decadence on the side of the more or less victorious treasure hunters, too.

Ultimately it is not surprising that Rider Haggard's story, which is most intimately entangled in the colonial and imperial project, presents the treasure hunt in a predominantly positive light. Yet its narrative of legitimisation displays cracks similar to those of the other two tales. These inconsistencies function through discourses of decadence, discourses that, according to the laws of the genre of boys' adventure studier, ought to be excluded and vilified. Yet, as just stated in connection with eccentric and decadent characters, the excluded Other has a habit of invading the space of the self, where it turns from alien into abject, an abject that recurs and returns with the force of the repressed. Within its description of the discovered treasure, *King Solomon's Mines* consequently contains the market-driven capitalism of its colonial project, a decadent fantasy of exquisite treasure as death, and even an illogical moment of guilt that turns honest treasure hunters into criminals:

> "We shall flood the market with diamonds," said Good.
> "Got to get them there first", suggested Sir Henry. And we stood with pale faces and stared at each other, with the lantern in the middle, and the glimmering gems below, as though we were conspirators about to commit a crime, instead of being, as we thought, the three most fortunate men on earth.
> "Hee! Hee! Hee!" went old Gagool behind us, as she flitted about like a vampire bat. "There are the bright stones that ye love, white men, as many as ye will; take them, run them through your fingers, *eat* of them, hee! Hee! *drink* of them, ha! Ha!" (278)

Treasure Island is even more ambivalent about the success of its expedition. It features no jubilation when the treasure is secured (it is not discovered as such, since it has been retrieved much earlier by a pirate, Ben Gunn, who – Crusoe-like – was left behind on the island by his comrades), nor is the prospect of wealth unambiguously welcomed:

> Therefore the work was pushed on briskly. Gray and Ben Gunn came and went with the boat, while the rest, during their absences, piled treasure on the beach. Two of the bars, slung in a rope's-end, made a good load for a grown man – one that he was glad to walk slowly with. For my part, as I was not much use at carrying, I was kept busy all day in the cave, packing the minted money into bread-bags. It was a strange collection [...] nearly every variety of money in the world must, I think, have found a place in that collection; and for number, I am sure they were like autumn leaves, so that my back ached with stooping and my fingers with sorting them out. (204)

> All of us had an ample share of the treasure, and used it wisely or foolishly, according to our natures. [...] The bar silver and the arms still lie, for all that I know, where Flint buried them; and certainly they shall lie there for me. Oxen and wain-ropes would not bring me back again to that accursed island; and the worst dreams that ever I have are when I hear the surf booming about its coasts, or start upright in bed, with the sharp voice of Captain Flint still ringing in my ears: "Pieces of eight! pieces of eight!" (208)

In Stevenson, treasure is work, in a very Protestant manner, and its effects depend on individual personality. The text's morality is its ambivalence, probably stemming from the position of an exiled Scot surveying the British imperial adventure from a multiple distance, that of geography and history.[9]

Karl May's *Der Schatz im Silbersee,* a German fantasy about the North American Wild West, lacks a clear colonial or imperial investment. Still, it can be regarded as an alternative version of an imperial text, taking its motivation from the mass emigration from Germany to the United States during the nineteenth century and perhaps also from the decision not to make German the official language of the USA, a snub that remained alive in the German imagination well into the twentieth century. May's wild and often culturally dubious ideas include natives that hold the moral high ground and tell the white treasure hunters to give up their futile quest. There is even a hint of romance between Little Bear and Ellen Patterson, a development that receives no criticism from the text, although it tries to contain it in unconvincing terms such as "beautiful sibling relationship" (643). And yet an alternative form of treasure hunt is very much condoned by the novel: the industrial exploitation of Native American land, after a thin veneer of legal bartering has been applied:

> "So you believe I have no right to discuss the issue?"
> "I cannot prevent you from doing so. [...] But you must refrain from making use of the secret; every other wish I will grant with pleasure."
> "Are you serious?" asked Old Firehand quickly.
> "Yes. My words always mean what they say."
> "Then I will ask a favour in the place of our comrade here." "Do so! If it is within my powers, it will be granted gladly." "Who owns the land on which we are standing right now?" (632)

Industrial exploitation and its long-term profits replace the hunt for treasure with its uncertain outcome and short-lived success.[10]

Even in their fantasies of return (like all good quest stories the three novels include a homecoming which is at least imagined), similarities as well as culturally specific differences become visible. *Treasure Island* is narrated by Jim Hawkins, who, one assumes, has returned home to his mother, although the story significantly remains silent about his use of his new-found wealth and thus his ultimate "nature". *King Solomon's Mines* concludes with Allan Quatermain receiving an invitation to return to Britain to join his son Harry as well as Sir Henry Curtis, who furthermore urges Quatermain to invest in property near his estate. Sir Henry also liberally relates how he

---

[9] For a similar view, see Naomi J. Wood, "Gold Standards and Silver Subversions: *Treasure Island* and the Romance of Money", *Children's Literature* 26 (1988), 61-85.

[10] Eckehard Koch outlines the historical background of May's tale, including the roles of the diverse Native American tribes and the crucial discovery of the "Comstock Lode", a rich silver mine, in Nevada in 1859 and its subsequent exploitation by the German engineer Philipp Deidesheimer: "'...den Roten gehörte alles Land; es ist ihnen von uns genommen worden...': Zum zeitgeschichtlichen Hintergrund von Mays *Schatz im Silbersee*", *Jahrbuch der Karl May-Gesellschaft* 27 (1997), 361-388 (375).

has decorated his stately home with the artefacts of their adventure, such as the tusks of elephants that had killed their servants and axes that had chopped off heads. Adventure becomes commodity, just as it does for the ironic figure of Lord Castlepool in Karl May. May's exiled Germans also dream of home: the unlikely figures of Tante Droll and Hobble-Frank fantasise about investing their riches in a farm in Saxony and a villa on the banks of the river Elbe (644). In dreams such as these, the intimate entanglement of morality and decadence becomes visible once more, when restored normality merges with – or indeed becomes – decadent fantasy.[11]

---

[11] Klaus Lüdersen's moral reading of May's tale in "Landschaften mit Moral: *Der Schatz im Silbersee* – eine erste Welt", *Jahrbuch der Karl May-Gesellschaft* 27 (1997), 389-406, overlooks the interesting contradictions that structure May's text.

Russell West-Pavlov

Treasure, Value and Signs in Conrad's *Nostromo*

Nostromo and Naming

Who is Nostromo? In the course of the novel of the same title,[1] Conrad's protagonist changes his name at frequent intervals: first Gian' Battista, then the Capataz de Cargadores, then Nostromo, and finally Captain Fidanza, which Conrad, rather ingenuously, calls "his rightful name" (527). Who is behind all these masks?

The answer is simple. "I am nothing!", Nostromo himself remarks (454); metonymically, he says to old Viola, "bring me out a cigar, but don't look for it in my room. There's nothing there" (125). Such emptiness is a recurring motif in Conrad's fiction. Marlow's paddle steamer in *Heart of Darkness* is as a hollow as an old biscuit tin; one of his colonising interlocutors in the jungle has nothing "inside but a little loose dirt". Axel Heyst in *Victory* is reputed to have "buried or put away on the island" his accumulated "plunder", but there is no treasure.[2] Again and again, the inner spaces of essence prove to be empty. Treasure, in its various forms, the object of desire, the goal of a quest, is not to be found there. And tales of treasure transpire to be no less hollow, buttressed by mendacious language: Kurz's name "was as true as everything else in his life", Marlow reflects ironically, and German speakers cannot but reflect upon the homonym "heisst".[3]

The link between emptiness and language resides in the demise of self-possession, one of pillars of Enlightenment selfhood. In *Nostromo*, this means that the eponymous protagonist is never his own man. As his name suggests, he belongs to others: he is "our man", not his own: "Clearly he was one of those invaluable subordinates whom to *possess* is a legitimate cause of boasting", and his superior, Captain Mitchell, is not above "*lending* you my Capataz de Cargadores" (44; emphasis added). Yet Nostromo's lack of self-possession is in part of his own choosing: "his prestige is his fortune", observes Dr Mongyham (320). Nostromo's identity is based upon reputation, and once out of the sight of others, he fades to insignificance. To his "I am nothing!" he adds, significantly, "Nothing to anyone" (454).

---

[1] Joseph Conrad, *Nostromo*, ed. Keith Carabine (Oxford: Oxford University Press, 1984 [1904]). All subsequent references are given parenthetically in the text.

[2] Joseph Conrad, *Heart of Darkness* [1899/1900], in: *Heart of Darkness and Other Tales*, ed. Cedric Watts (Oxford: Oxford University Press, 1990), p. 171; *Victory*, ed. John Batchelor (Oxford: Oxford University Press, 1986 [1915]), pp. 156, 158.

[3] Conrad, *Heart of Darkness*, p. 224.

90 Russell West-Pavlov

The narrator may be not entirely correct, then, when he highlights "Captain Mitchell's *mispronunciation*...calling [the Italian sailor] Nostromo" (43; my emphasis), or, five hundred pages later, upon reminding the reader that "Nostromo [is] the *miscalled* Capataz de Cargadores" (527; my emphasis). The narratorial insistence upon the error of this appellation is itself erroneous. For Nostromo's name has little to do with his professional identity as a sailor, as etymological speculations tend to suggest.[4] Rather, it conveys the infinitely more apposite fact of his entire dependence upon the eyes and tongues of others. "The only thing he seems to care for...is to be well spoken of" (246). Nostromo is hired by Captain Mitchell "simply on the strength of his looks", and even at the end of the novel, when Nostromo is rich, he still is "*seen*" – an aspect of his being so important and enduring that Conrad sets the word in italics (483, 527). Nostromo's name, then, to the extent that it is a misnomer, a mistranslation, accurately expresses his nature: "A nickname may be the best record of success. That's what I call putting the face of a joke upon the body of a truth", quips the mine's chief engineer (316). But while the name does indeed speak eloquently of Nostromo's entire career, the veritable truth of Nostromo is that his body is the least significant thing about him. It is the mythical body (Dr. Mongyham, for instance, is "under the spell of [Nostromo's] established reputation"; 432) as it exists for others which counts most. Nostromo's identity is based not upon inner being, but rather, upon the outward refraction of selfhood in the eyes of others.

The displacement tracked here also needs to be applied to the very notion of the literary character and its indebtedness to the linguistic fabric to which it owes its being. This displacement from inner being to outer construction says less about Nostromo the man or fictional figure than about a general theory of language. The character is less an entity in its own right than a synecdoche of the ambient culture: "Exceptional individualities always interest me, because they are true to the general formula expressing the moral state of humanity" (246). It is not the inner essence of the character which is named by the name, but the outer shell. Even the mode of naming does not faithfully express that which is named, but rather, names by mis-naming. Misrecognition and misreading, as in Lacan and Bloom,[5] lie at the heart of human knowledge of self and others. To the extent that Modernism reposes upon the scission of an essential link between word and thing expounded most cogently by de Saussure (signs are merely "associations which bear the stamp of collective approval"[6]), any name can *only* be a misnomer: in Calvino's formulation, "Non c'è linguaggio senza inganno" ["There is no language without deceit"].[7]

Naming, in *Nostromo*, resembles the "Custom House, whose strong room, *it was well known*, contained a large treasure of silver ingots" (15; my emphasis). Naming is a public, exterior matter, based upon convention, "custom" and commerce, whose

---

[4] See, for instance, Ian Watt, *Conrad: Nostromo* (Cambridge: Cambridge University Press, 1988), p. 6.

[5] Jacques Lacan, *Ecrits* (Paris: Seuil, 1966), p. 99; Harold Bloom, *A Map of Misreading* (New York: Oxford University Press, 1975).

[6] Ferdinand de Saussure, *Course in General Linguistics*, trans. Wade Baskin (London: Fontana, 1974 [1916]), p. 15.

[7] Italo Calvino, *Le Città invisibili* (Milan: Oscar Mondadori, 1993 [1972]), p. 48.

putative interior referent, its ostensibly true worth, is a matter of public knowledge, hearsay, reputation – but which, as we might suspect if we attend to Conrad's oblique irony, may be of dubious value. Here, then, is the heart of Conrad's theory of language: it does not reveal a "secret", an interior meaning hidden "within the shell of a cracked nut...like a kernel", but rather, constructs a significance "enveloping the tale which brought it out only as a glow brings out a haze", thereby highlighting an ambient valency which owes its currency to the social environment.[8] The "secret" narrative promises to divulge, its epistemological treasure, whose objective correlative in Conrad's tales is so often a treasure-trove (Lord Jim's girlfriend, for instance, is named Jewel), exists only in the moment of circulation in and by narrative itself.

I begin this essay not with the treasure, the central object of desire and avarice in Conrad's *Nostromo*, but with the eponymous protagonist, by no means out of respect for traditional categories of literary analysis such as character or plot. Rather, I do so because Nostromo embodies the theory of value and representation which Conrad elaborates in his great novel. In *Nostromo*, Conrad pursues a notion of language as naming in which it is the outward sheen of the thing named, its involvement in the public face of narration and reception, and not its inner essence, which determines identity. In what follows, I consider issues of naming in relation to the semiotic regime of superficiality and exteriority central to Modernist aesthetics; I then show how the treasure in *Nostromo* instantiates the economic theories cognate with such an aesthetics of exteriority; and finally I explore the ways in which the scepticism of Modernism may conceal, in Conrad's uneasy truce with disbelief, a residual optimistic idealism which may be the other treasure hidden in the novel.

Superficial Semiotics

In *Nostromo*, Conrad's theory of meaning as a superficial matter rather than a profundity is coupled with a theory of value. Fiduciary value is a question of fluctuating supply and demand, not of fixed worth. Value is attributed from outside, rather than inhering in an object's innermost being. Captain Mitchell may claim to have "discovered [Nostromo's] *value*" (13; my emphasis), but this value is established and maintained by talk, placing external claims upon the man that belie the ipseity implied by "discovery". What Conrad calls the "preciousness of inner worth" is demystified as an "illusion" which "acquired force, permanency, and authority" (431). "[T]hings seem to be worth nothing by what they are in themselves... the only solid thing about them is the spiritual value which everyone discovers in his own form of activity" (318) – this discovery, already alienating by its failure to lay bare anything essential ("things...in themselves"), is doubly alienating by virtue of the fact that any discovery about oneself must be refracted through the eyes of others: the phrase "everyone discovers in his own form of activity" already splits the self into object and subject of observation, the latter replicating the social world via synecdoche.

---

[8] Conrad, *Heart of Darkness*, p. 138.

In response to this fluctuation of value, money itself as a physical object has become increasingly fluid over the ages. It has become progressively more ephemeral, advancing from kind to coin, via paper notes, to ledger-book accounting and, finally, to contemporary electronic commerce. This successive dematerialisation has enhanced the fluidity of exchange ("BILETS, biglietti, as coin was too heavy for transport", wrote Pound[9]), but banished any residual illusion of an essential worth inhering in money itself. Residual traces of an old quintessence of value may be found here and there: pound sterling notes, for instance, once bore an inscription in copperplate hand promising to pay the bearer the equivalent in gold upon demand.

The latter example helpfully dramatises the double target of the Modernist assault evinced in *Nostromo*: on the one hand, inherent value, and on the other, a depth of subjective identity indexed by the individuality of handwriting; both are gathered up into a critique of the economics of representation. These two components of the Modernist project are central to Conrad's concerns in *Nostromo*. Literary Modernism was concerned not so much with turning from an empirically grounded outer world to a subjective inner world[10] (this hermeneutics-based version of Modernism clings to the very idea which it was most as pains to discard) as with turning from an inner essence towards a theory of surfaces, an aesthetic of exteriority.[11] This results in the deflection of the hermeneutic drive expressed by the question "What does it mean?" (202). What ensues, in the impossibility of extraction of an inner meaning, is a foregrounding of the outer casing of an entity: "The impenetrability of the embodied Gould Concession had its surface shades" (203). The fundamental paradigm shift from depth to surface meaning goes hand in hand with a concomitant paradigm shift from depth to surface value. Underlying these is the pursuit of an analogy between meaning and value. Thus, from Mallarmé via Pound to Gide, Modernist writers were concerned about the groundlessness of monetary value. Mallarmé lamented literature's degradation to "une fonction de numéraire facile et représentatif", construed by Pound as a symptom of the generalized "Price of life in the Occident"; Gide, by contrast, quoted Shakespeare's conceit of the counterfeit coin to explore a freedom from the restricting genealogies of filiative identity and their regimes of mimesis: "We are all bastards; | And that most venerable man which I | Did call my father, was I know not where | When I was stamped".[12] In Modernism, signs come to circulate like money, and the value of money comes to be understood as an economy of signs. Both are released from the strictures of a fixed value and loosed into the freedom of arbitrary meaning. Treasure, in Conrad's proto-Modernist *Nostromo*, stands on the cusp between sign and value, and also between older and newer regimes of fiduciary-semiotic economy.

---

[9] Ezra Pound, Canto LVI, *The Cantos* (London: Faber & Faber, 1986), p. 301.

[10] See, for instance, Randall Stevenson, *Modernist Fiction: An Introduction* (Hemel Hempstead: Harvester Wheatsheaf, 1992), p. 82.

[11] See, for instance, Gilles Deleuze, *Foucault* (Paris: Minuit, 1986), pp. 101-130.

[12] Pound, Canto XXII, *The Cantos*, p. 101; Stéphane Mallarmé, 'Crise de vers', *Œuvres*, ed. Yves Alain Favre (Paris: Garnier, 1985), p. 279; André Gide, *Les Faux-Monnayeurs*, *Romans* (Paris: Gallimard/Pléiade, 1958), p. 975, quoting Shakespeare's *Cymbeline* 2.5.1-4. See also Jean-Joseph Goux, *Les Monnayeurs du langage* (Paris: Galilée, 1984).

Treasure

Treasure occupies a threshold position in *Nostromo*. Just as Costaguana itself is a fictive country whose economic base reposes entirely upon peasant agriculture, but which is in the process of becoming the "Treasure House of the World" (489, 522), a centre of foreign investment (192), and focus of American economic and indeed military interests (an American warship comes to fire a salute to celebrate the founding of the new Occidental Republic; 487), so too the treasure stands at the cusp between old and new economies.

Treasure is an eminently transitional entity. It imposes its own imperative of translation. Almost every character in the novel comes in contact with the silver treasure produced by the San Tomé mine engages in this process. Mrs Gould, though she comes to hate the mine and its products, is entirely exemplary in this respect: "by her imaginative estimate of its power she endowed that lump of metal with a justificatory conception, as though it were not a mere fact, but something far-reaching and impalpable, like the true expression of an emotion" (106). Thus, from being pure materiality, the treasure becomes "emblem" and "symbol" (260). To this extent, it dispels older regimes of meaning structured around what Latour has called the "confusion of facts and value".[13] In the novel, this demystification of the universe by dint of pure (exchange) value is embodied in the manner in which the treasure overrides religious values in the Catholic world in which it takes place. Nostromo places more importance on saving the silver of the mine that fetching a priest for the dying Padrona, Teresa Viola. Even Nostromo is "uneasy at the impiety of his refusal" (255). It is significant that at the end of the novel, the Catholic church in the Occidental Republic is fighting a rear-guard action against the missionary work of North-American evangelicals, the latter funded by the same bodies which have underwritten the mine (507, 508-9).

Paradoxically, the dematerialisation of value in the treasure is intimately linked to its basal materiality. It is the patent materiality of the treasure, its sheer bulk (reflected perhaps in the corresponding bulk of Conrad's longest novel) which impedes the creation of value, "because of the difficulty of converting [the treasure] into a form in which it could become available" (523). Only via mobility, the transport out of the treasure out of Costaguana, does it become valuable. To gain in value, the treasure must become abstract, as Dr Mongyham, in a masterful act of understatement, makes clear: "the shadow of the treasure may serve as well as the substance" (410). Financial liquidity reposes upon the liquidity of the treasure itself: "This stream of silver must be kept flowing north to return in the form of financial backing from Holroyd. Up at the mountain in the strong room of the mine the silver bars were worth less…than so much lead, from which at least bullets may be run" (219). In the final analysis, it is the external circulation of the treasure, its centrifugal movement away from its source and away from its own material essence, which endows it with value. What emerges in the place of its material use value (virtually zero) is its exchange value. The silver must

---

[13] Bruno Latour, *Un Monde pluriel mais commun: Entretiens avec François Ewald* (Paris: L'Aube, 2005), p. 12.

"come down [from the mountain], so that it may go north, and return to us in the form of credit" (221). That credit is little different from Nostromo's prestige, a value residing in a conventionalised system of signs, whose fluctuating worth is assigned externally and circulates freely – that is, in a language.

If language is a form of fiduciary value, then the silver functions like a language: "There was no mistaking the growling mutter of the mountain pouring its stream of treasure under the stamps; and it came to [Gould's] heart with the peculiar force of a proclamation thundered forth over the land" (105). For Mrs Gould, the silver becomes "something far-reaching and impalpable, like the true expression of an emotion" (106). And like any system of signs, the functioning of the silver is at least in part not referential but self-referential. The ungrounded value of the treasure serves to underwrite the production of more ungrounded value: "The next north-going steamer would carry [the silver] off for the very salvation of the San Tomé mine, which has produced so much treasure" (219) – what the mine produces is its own perpetuation, which is merely there to produce more of itself. The silver is thus caught in a hollow cycle of self-referential autotelic circularity.

If the silver of the mine has no value outside of circulation and publicly assigned value, the mine itself, in a certain sense, is no more real. The mine, despite its geographical situation, its visibility (195), and its infrastructure, is merely an apparatus for the production of a raw material. From this point of view, the mine itself has no substance, except in order to produce a substance. From the outset it is conceived as a means of extortion, as a concession ceded to Henry Gould so as to legitimize demands for capital: "The third and most important clause stipulated that the concession-holder should pay at once to the Government five years' royalties on the estimated output of the mine" (53). The virtual character of the mine is underlined by the fact that from the outset, the principal guarantee of the mine's immunity from meddling, manipulation or damage is the latent threat of its utter destruction. Gould has had the entire San Tomé mountain seeded with charges of dynamite so that it can be blown up at any instant. Gould's threat of the definitive destruction of the mine is his "last card to play…Card only when it's played" (206), his ultimate threat (400). This semiotic token ("card") lays bare the virtual character of the mine, so that like any sign it is endowed with agency only for the duration of its activation within a sender-receiver relationship, thus constantly demanding performative iteration.

What keeps this virtual character at bay is the fact that so many people idealize the mine, denying the evidence of its brute materiality – not, paradoxically, so as to render its value ephemeral and unstable, but rather, to re-endow it with an essence which it clearly never possesses. Decoud asks Mrs Gould, "are you aware to what point he [Charles Gould] has idealized the existence, the worth, the meaning of the San Tomé mine? … He could not believe his own motives if he did not make them first part of some fairy tale" (214). Likewise, the mine's employees, the "harassed, half-wild Indians…were proud of, and attached to, the mine. It had secured their confidence and belief. They invested it with a protecting and invincible virtue as though it were a fetish made by their own hands, for they were ignorant, and in other respects did not differ appreciably from the rest of mankind which puts infinite trust in its own creations. It never entered the alcade's head that the mine could fail in its protection and force" (398). Even the cynical and pragmatic American financier who underwrites the mine,

Holroyd, idealises the project, feeding his "insatiable imagination of conquest" (76) on the idea of Costaguana become his private hobby (79-82).

The idealisation of the silver and of the mine is a compensation for the emptying of meaning which occurs under the conditions of high-capitalist incipient global finance. Paradoxically, the evacuation of physically present essence and use value goes hand in hand with a compensatory re-investment of the materiality of the silver and of the mine. Treasure itself is the most immediate manifestation of this return of the materiality of money – a materiality which Walter Benjamin explained by coining the concept of the aura. If the treasure has an auratic value, it is in part because that value is susceptible of imaginary inflation, but also because the aura, in Benjamin's usage of the term, implies the fetishising of a bygone materiality in a dematerialising age.[14] The treasure, in its mobility, embodies the purely symbolic value of signs. Yet its materiality, albeit removed to a distance once it is hidden on the island off Sulaco, by no means dwindles away. On the contrary, treasure indexes the stubbornly residual materiality at the heart of signification which was equally important to Modernism.

This materiality takes its revenge in Conrad's novel in an appropriately tragicomic manner. The boundless scepticism regarding all fixed meaning harboured by the young Decoud rapidly tumbles over into an utter lack of referential anchoring whose logical consequence is hallucination and finally something bordering on psychosis. The loss of referential grounding is already evinced as Decoud and Nostromo cast off in the treasure-laden lighter: "Martin Decoud called out from the lighter…it seemed to him that the wharf was floating away into the night…the effect was that of being launched into space" (260-1). Decoud then remains alone on the island with the treasure, succumbing to a sense of unreality whose only antidote is the gravity of the treasure itself – four ingots weigh down his pockets when he finally commits suicide out at sea (499-501). Ironically, however, the only signs of his end that he leaves behind are the empty metonymies indexing his death – the absence of four missing ingots from the treasure-trove hidden on the island, and a darkening blood-stain on the gunwale of the lighter's abandoned dinghy (492, 494). Like the treasure itself, they are so many empty signs, susceptible of fixity only in the act of interpretation.

Conrad – Sceptical Idealist?

Another impulse may motivate the idealisation of the mine by so many characters in the novel. In an unguarded moment, Conrad describes mining as "the sordid process of extracting metal from under the ground" (53). This turn of phrase echoes similar judgements upon economic exploitation such as his bitter memory of the Congo as "the vilest scramble for loot that ever disfigured the history of human conscience and geographical exploration".[15] The treasure, and the manner it enslaves various characters

---

[14] See Walter Benjamin, *Das Kunstwerk im Zeitalter seiner technischen Reproduzierbarkeit: Drei Studien zur Kunstsoziologie* (Frankfurt am Main: Suhrkamp, 1977), p. 15.

[15] Joseph Conrad, 'Geography and Some Explorers', *Tales of Hearsay and Last Essays* (London: Dent, 1955), p. 17.

(Nostromo "become[s] the slave of a treasure"; 523), may stand synecdochically for the manner in which the monetary and semiotic economies Conrad probes in the novel are simultaneously implicated in the New Imperialism so vociferously attacked by nineteenth-century opponents of colonialism.[16] The treasure functions in the narrative as an index for the munificent and maleficent facets of a US-driven economic imperialism (contrasting with the colonial imperialism pursued by the European powers) that prefigures the globalisation of the late twentieth century. The treasure is carried away from Sulaco, snatched from the hands of the insurgents, so as to bring it safely back to North America and Holroyd – with the intention of gaining his support for the secession of the Occidental Province from Costagunana. The hoisting of the new flag is saluted by an American cruiser, a sign of the benevolent presence of the Northern power guarding over the new state (487).[17] In the event, the treasure, hidden on the island and believed lost, proves to be irrelevant to the successful independence of the Occidental Republic. This form of wealth, then, stationary as it is, falls by the wayside of historical progress.

Conrad makes many remarks, always placed in the mouth of characters whose identity qualifies their statements, on the New Imperialism. The insurgents "[declare] the national honour sold to foreigners" (145), delivered up to the "sinister land-grabbing designs of European powers" (146), with "Sulaco...on the point of being invaded by all the world" (150). Decoud, rarely capable of speaking without irony, sardonically remarks that "the whole land is like a treasure house, and all these people [foreign investors] are breaking into it, whilst we are cutting each other's throats. The only thing that keeps them out is mutual jealousy" (174). When the well-meaning Don José proposes, "'We must cable encouraging extracts [from the newspaper *Porvenir*, edited by Decoud] to Europe and the United States to maintain a favourable impression abroad'", Decound ripostes, "'Oh yes, we must comfort our friends, the speculators'" (175). Conrad's narratorial commentator cautiously employs a marked ambivalence with regard to the inroads of Modernism. The line of telegraph poles, bearers of communication within the text, is portrayed as "a slender, vibrating feeler of that progress waiting outside for a moment of peace to enter and twine itself about the weary heart of the land" (166). Conrad's simile is ambivalent, with salutary repose undermined by a threatening sinuosity.

At the same time, however, does not the stability which economic development that comes to the Occidental Republic legitimise the idealism, albeit specious and mercantilist, which drives it? This has been Charles Gould's motivation from the outset. He idealises the mine as the bait that will draw foreign investment, bringing political stability in its wake: "I pin my faith in material interests. ... It is justified because the security it demands must be shared with an oppressed people. A better justice will come afterwards" (84). At the end of the novel, with prosperity and political stability assured for the newly independent republic, Gould's wager appears to be vindicated.

Yet the accusations against "colonization" (117, 392) placed in the mouths of the ruffianly, often grotesque insurgents, appear to be borne out by Holroyd's plan to "take

---

[16] See Robert J. C. Young, *Postcolonialism: An Historical Introduction* (Oxford: Blackwell, 2001), pp. 41-42.

[17] See Edward W. Said, "Under Gringo Eyes: With Conrad on Latin America", in: *Reflections on Exile & Other Literary and Cultural Essays* (London: Granta, 2000), pp. 276-281.

Treasure, Value and Signs in Conrad's *Nostromo* 97

in hand the outlying islands and continents of the earth. We shall run the world's business whether the world likes it or not" (77). The San Tomé mine and its silver are underwritten by American capital, in the service of an "undertaking which is to put money into the pockets of Englishmen, Frenchmen, Americans, Germans, and God knows who else", in the words of Decoud (231). Thus the mine saves the Occidental Province from the ongoing turbulences of Costaguana and guarantees stability, but also delivers the country up to a New Imperialism. Just as Conrad tracked the pitfalls inherent in an "ideal of conduct" in *Lord Jim* (Dr Mongyham is a similar case of a rigid ideal of conduct which fails its bearer; 375), and the excesses to which the idealism of the "civilising mission" could lead its "emissary[ies] of light" in *Heart of Darkness*,[18] so in *Nostromo* he documents the possible consequences of economic idealism. Decoud's sober assessment of idealism accurately summarises Conrad's reserves about the power attained by the dynamics of economic imperialism in *Nostromo*: "the picturesque extreme of wrongheadedness into which an honest, almost sacred, conviction may drive a man...every conviction, as soon as it became effective, turned into that form of dementia the gods sent upon those they wanted to destroy" (200).

However, it is precisely Decoud, whose premature end removes him abruptly from the novel's broad canvas, whom Conrad utilises to offer a quite contrary perspective on the tension between scepticism and idealism concretised in the treasure. Decoud and Nostromo are entrusted with the task of "saving the silver" (232), in its double meanings (the sense of "holding in reserve", rather than "rescue", prevails, to the advantage of Nostromo). Decoud's motivation for accepting the mission is the possibility of guaranteeing the emergence of a new independent republic where he can remain with his lover Antonia (240). Decoud is left alone on the island with the treasure, and in the solitude and silence "[b]oth his intelligence and his passion were swallowed up easily in this great unbroken solitude of waiting without faith" (498); he "died from solitude and from want of faith in himself and others" (496). Conrad, generally so ironical in his treatment of ideals, so sceptical about their power to do good, abruptly does an about-turn, disparaging scepticism and implicitly promoting the salutary power of an ideal: "Solitude...becomes very swiftly a state of soul in which the affectations of irony and scepticism have no place" (497).

Decoud, like Mrs Gould or Dr Mongyham, is one of the few characters whose idealism is directed first and foremost at another character, taking the form of a "passionate desire...clothed in the fair robes of an idea" (239). Conrad's use of this phrase, initially to describe the self-deluding abstraction of a Charles Gould, is now reversed to explore the intersubjective engagement of these less egotistical figures. All of them, in a sense, fail to realise their desires, and for each of them, the treasure has a fatal role to play in that failure. For Decoud, the treasure is supposed to enable but finally prevents his return to Antonia. For Mrs Gould, the mine begins as a shared idealistic project with her husband, but eventually separates him from her. For Dr Mongyham, the treasure is the means to save Mrs Gould from the fanaticism of her husband and the consequent neglect of his wife, though, ironically, the success of the doctor's goals merely vindicates Gould's own enterprise (245, 376). But in the case of

---

[18] Joseph Conrad, *Lord Jim*, ed. Jacques Berthoud (Oxford University Press, 2002 [1900]), p. 88; *Heart of Darkness*, p. 149.

Decoud, of whom we are once told "now and then a tender inflection crept into the flow of his ironic murmurs" (188), it is not idealism which scuppers his plans. It is an excess of scepticism, and meagre resources of idealism to carry him through the solitude of the island, which is at fault.

Here Conrad, always a reluctant Modernist despite the evidence of his own aesthetic presuppositions, makes space for an idealism which he almost without exception in every other respect cannot but discredit. If in *Heart of Darkness* we are justified in wondering if there is not a degree of bad faith in the declaration, "What redeems it is the idea only. An idea at the back of it; not a sentimental pretence but an idea; and an unselfish belief in the idea",[19] in *Nostromo* there may be a few instances where idealism displays an untarnished axiological valency.

These double, paradoxical aspects of the Modernist project of a "revolution of the word"[20] are connected to Conrad's critique of idealism as a treasure-house of belief, but also his sense that without idealism, the modern subject would tumble into solipsism and bleak nihilism. Idealism is the target of his scepticism, but at the same time, idealism may be harnessed to temper the excesses of scepticism. *Nostromo* begins with blank denunciation of a hoard of treasure said to be hidden at Punta Mala on the barren peninsula of Azuera: "The poor, associating by an obscure instinct of consolation evil and wealth, will tell you that it is deadly because of its forbidden treasures" (4). This wealth, in its inorganic half-life, does not produce anything. Yet, like Stevens' jar that "did not give of bird or bush, | Like nothing else in Tennessee", the treasure generates meanings, rippling out here in the form of rumour.[21] Treasure's hiddenness, like the absence of the referent to which the linguistic signifier none the less gestures, guarantees its existence in discourse, and instantiates thereby the release of the virtual values upon which capitalism's generation of surplus value reposes. Such generation of *meaning*, like Lévinas' "language",[22] may however also evince a basal ethical relationship concealed, like Nostromo's treasure on the island, amongst the rough scrub of Modernism.

---

[19] Conrad, *Heart of Darkness*, p. 141.
[20] See Colin MacCabe, *James Joyce and the Revolution of the Word* (London and Basingstoke: Macmillan, 1979), p. 27.
[21] Wallace Stevens, 'Anecdote of the Jar', *Selected Poems* (London: Faber & Faber, 1965), p. 36. On rumour, see Kai Wiegandt, 'Partial Truth: Rumour in Conrad's *Heart of Darkness*', *Poetica* 40: 3-4 (2008), 397-424.
[22] See, for instance, Emmanuel Lévinas, *Humanisme de l'autre homme* (1972; Paris: Livre de poche/Biblio essais, 1987), pp. 105-106.

Marcin Stawiarski

Treasure and the Desire to Know:
Richard Wagner's *Der Ring des Nibelungen*
and Anthony Burgess's *The Worm and the Ring*

"But Error is the mother of Knowledge; and the history of the birth of Knowledge out of Error is the history of the human race, from the myths of primal ages down to the present day."[1] With these words, Wagner begins *The Art-Work of the Future*, written in 1849, about the time he produced the first drafts of his masterwork, *Der Ring des Nibelungen*. In 1961, Anthony Burgess drew on the *Ring* to write *The Worm and the Ring*,[2] recasting the Wagnerian *Gesamtkunstwerk* within the context of an English grammar school. On reading Burgess's novel, one cannot help reconsidering Wagner's opera and viewing it first and foremost as a symbolic network of multifarious epistemological itineraries. As a *milieu* of scientific thought and scholarly knowledge, the setting of the school allows Burgess to reinterpret the meaning of the treasure in Wagner.

Obviously enough, treasure primarily calls to mind pecuniary symbols – the quest for riches itself evoking the quest for power. The idea of treasure also implies burial or interment. And even though treasure conjures up a whole array of connotations pertaining to natural resources – ore, lode or even the myth of cornucopia – treasure is rarely of purely natural provenance. It is more of a human construct, either because a natural deposit has been transformed by the human (remodelled or hidden) or because it has been culturally determined to be valuable. Thus, treasure seems to be an intrinsically anthropological object – and doubly so. One the one hand, it calls for a particular craftsmanship and a specific action operated on a natural object. On the other, as a human construct, treasure becomes an intellectual entity, which may be evidenced by its arbitrary nature. That is to say, an object may possess considerable value in one cultural situation and be totally valueless in another.

The idea of human transformation is extremely important in the context of this study. Wagnerian metals take their full value only after they have been turned into a ring or a sword. But the idea of a hidden hoard also implies a code, secret or something else that renders access to the desired object difficult or impossible – yet another human intervention. Consequently, often enough treasure narratives deal with illegibility and the need to decipher a code or uncover a mystery. Because the access to the precious

---

[1] Richard Wagner, *The Art-Work of the Future* (Whitefish: Kessinger, 2004), p. 3.
[2] Anthony Burgess, *The Worm and the Ring*, 2nd ed. (London: Heinemann, 1970). All references to this text are given parenthetically in the text.

object is barred, encoded or conditioned by magical formulae or specific predispositions on the part of its seeker, the quest for treasure is on par with rites of passage.

Etymologically speaking, the word treasure (from Lat. *thesaurus*, Gr. Θησαυρός) indicates the act of putting aside, accumulating wealth or amassing. This meaning is still preserved in French where the verb *thésauriser* means "to pile up". But the idea of accumulation of riches goes together with the notion of hidden wealth. In Russian, for instance, there are two words for treasure – one, *клад* (klad) is probably akin to the verb "to put" (*класть*), hence suggesting accumulation or collection; the other, *сокровище* (sokrovistche) is related to the verb "to hide" (*сокрыть*), thus closer to the English "hoard" or German *hort*. There is a distinction between a hidden, accumulated hoard, and a stolen or fought-for hoard (English "booty", "loot", or "plunder", French *butin*). In Polish, there exists only one word – *skarb* – which seems to derive from the word *skrb* ("woe" or "sorrow"). This astonishing origin seems to indicate that, besides the common associations related to treasure and implying a hidden trove, an accumulated pile of precious objects, or a hard-earned trophy, there exists a negative value, perhaps resulting from myths of malediction or curses.

Hidden, engulfed, stolen, or lost, treasures imply complex networks of relationships between those who are initiated and those who are not. The first group is separated from the second by sophisticated itineraries and rites of passage with oracles, spells, curses and maledictions. The initiates must resort to cunning and guile to outwit opponents and persevere through traps, transgressions and dangerous expeditions. I argue that such networks may be interpreted as symbolical epistemological itineraries, often as allegories of quests for knowledge, and that the treasure in both Wagner's *Ring* and Burgess's *The Worm and the Ring* may be considered to carry such a meaning.

First, I will consider the ways in which Burgess transposes Wagner's *Ring* into fiction. I will argue that Burgess's text is predicated on a multi-layered intertextuality whose strata build up a clockwork of references to the Wagnerian *oeuvre*. Second, I will demonstrate that the *Ring* may be interpreted as an epistemological itinerary and that *The Worm and the Ring* follows suit, presenting a polysemous symbolism related to knowledge.

Burgess's Subversive Orthodoxy

Because of its musico-literary and intertextual aspects, Burgess's novel may be considered a case of *musicalization of fiction*: a work of literature drawing on a given musical form or borrowing musical techniques. Werner Wolf explained the theory of musicalisation in his critical work *The Musicalization of Fiction*.[3] *The Worm and the Ring* does show some structural features akin to musical techniques, and it may thus be compared to at least two other novels Burgess wrote in close relation to musical

---

[3] Werner Wolf, *The Musicalization of Fiction: A Study in the Theory and History of Intermediality* (Amsterdam and Atlanta, Georgia: Rodopi, 1999).

structures, *Napoleon Symphony* (1974) and *Mozart and the Wolf Gang* (1991).[4] Nevertheless, the relationship between Burgess's work and Wagner's work seems to be particularly intricate, relying on a multilayered mechanism of interartistic and intertextual relationships that must be considered. *The Worm and the Ring* does not simply borrow a structure or transform a plot. It is a complex literary work in which music and text intermingle. Moreover, Wagner's *Ring* is already a musico-literary work, a *Gesamtkunstwerk*, because Wagner himself borrowed and forged different sources into one. Therefore, Burgess's novel is an interdisciplinary text drawing on an already interdisciplinary project.

Hence, theoretically, it should be possible to recognise different cases of borrowing. Burgess's novel may well relate to the libretto itself, thus showing intertextuality proper – a relationship between two texts. But it may also relate to music, a relationship that belongs to *intermediality*, i.e., a work of art implying different media in its creation. It is possible to draw a typology of different ways in which Wagnerian inspiration permeates Burgess's text. I prefer to speak of *undertexts* to signify that each layer is not necessarily immediately recognisable, that it is not independent of other layers, and, finally, that some of the elements are mock borrowings or subversions that undermine the Wagnerian undertext in some way.

Topical or Symbolic Undertexts

This type of intertextuality is at work from the very start of the novel. The *Ring* opens on the Rhine scene. The work begins with one note, E flat extending through several bars and symbolising the beginning of the universe. The genesis starts with *pianissimo* dynamics and an extremely static and almost inaudible sonorous mass:[5]

Example I

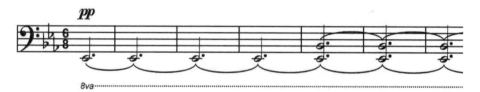

Several leitmotivs spring from this initial sound – Nature, the waves, the Rhine. Similarly, the opening scene of the novel presents many-faceted watery symbols in the school cloakrooms:

---

[4] Anthony Burgess, *Napoleon Symphony*, 2nd ed. (New York: Bantam Books, 1975); *Mozart and the Wolf Gang*, 2nd ed. (London: Vintage, 1992).
[5] Richard Wagner, *Das Rheingold*, trans. Frederick Jameson (Mainz: Schott's, 1899).

In the caverns of the cloakrooms there was treble laughter and guffaws rang under the showers. The whole building seemed to turn to water – flushing cisterns, hissing taps, elementary games in the urinals. (3)

Water thus pervades the internal world of the school, but it is also present outside ("and outside was rain"; 3). The perception zeroes in on sound, and music is mentioned so that, from the very start, the allusion to the Wagnerian motifs and a certain sound-perception informs readers of the novel's intermedial nature.

This static beginning evolves. With the motif of waves or the Rhine, the music becomes increasingly dynamic. Sticking with the 6/8-measure, the music grows from a single E flat into the characteristic motif of the Rhine/Nature:

Example 2

And then into the more vivid motif of waves:

Example 3

Although Wagner's incipit remains within the nuance of *piano*, it presents an accretion of dynamism – the gradual awakening of the nascent universe. Mimetically,

Burgess's novel begins with the end of a music class and propels the scene into the bustling school yard.

From the very beginning, it seems clear that the novel draws on thematic or symbolical fragments of the *Ring*. Most frequently, the fragmentary nature of the intermedial relationship comes to the foreground in the form of clues or allusions to Wagner's work. The following table presents only some of the allusions and their possible correspondence with the *Ring*:[6]

Burgess	Wagner
"Above the easing rain a shining bow stretched, the colours neatly filed as on some garish cosmetic chart, arched and shameless, a covenant." (78) "Ennis played, on the new Bechstein, a kind of limping march of his own composition. The staff hoods gave them a certain transient rainbow dignity." (79)	In *Das Rheingold*, Wotan, creates a rainbow to access his new abode, the castle Valhalla. In the *Worm and the Ring*, Woolton, the headmaster, celebrates the opening of a new school. In both cases, the rainbow accompanies the inauguration of the new building.
"Lodge, pipe still going lovely, dipped into the gap between Rich's jacket and more worn pullover and pulled out like a chestnut from the fire, a little book in blue leatherette." (54)	In *Das Rheingold*, the god of fire, Loge, gives Wotan advice. Wotan has promised to give Freia to the giants who built Valhalla. Loge will go to the underworld in order to get back the stolen gold and use it against the giants and Alberich. In *The Worm and the Ring*, Lodge is associated with chemistry. In the passage, the simile alludes to fire.
"The bells now inaugurated a brief mad period of noise. Into this solid cacophony masters' voices tried to pierce like hammered nails." (58) "The world of disease, really an underground world, went on alive and bright and bustling under the lamps." (157)	In *Das Rheingold*, Wagner makes use of anvils symbolising the slavery of the Nibelungen. The passage seems to allude to the dichotomy of slaves/masters as well as to the Wagnerian anvil leitmotif.

[6] Richard Wagner, *Die Walküre*, trans. Frederick Jameson (Mainz: Schott's, 1899); *Siegfried*, trans. Frederick Jameson (Mainz: Schott's, 1899); *Götterdämmerung*, trans. Frederick Jameson (Mainz: Schott's, 1899).

"In the cosy smoke of the fashionable bar of the Dragon, Dr Gardner stood with comfortable business-men, men of his own class." (73)	In *Siegfried*, the dragon, the transmogrified giant Fafner, keeps the treasure. In *The Worm and the Ring*, Gardner relates to Fafner, and the bar stands for the dragon. (The word *bar* is itself closely related to Wagner's *oeuvre* because it signifies the ancient musical form Wagner uses in his operas.)
"'When birds sing, Dad, is it meant to be really a kind of music?' 'Well', said Howarth cautiously, 'it's a kind of self-expression, I suppose. But human music's meaningless, isn't it? Bird song always means something. It means things like 'Come here, I'm waiting for you,' or 'I've just had a very good feed of worms,' or it means sexual desire.'" (104)	In the third part of the *Ring*, having wounded the dragon, Siegfried drinks some of its blood and gets to understand the language of birds, which warn him. Burgess alludes to that episode, turning it into an overall meditation on language and musical meaning.
"rubbish wallah" (218) "there's no smoke without fire" (223) "Fire sprang" (225)	*Twilight of the Gods* (*Götterdämmerung*) finishes with Valhalla engulfed by fire and the treasure returning to the Rhine. The end of *The Worm and the Ring* gradually prepares this cyclical turn through different puns on fire or on the decline of gods.

The reader is thus presented with a web of scattered references, puns and allusions. There appears an underlying text – an intermedial and intertextual 'undertext' – whose first manifestation is a network woven from more or less explicit hints. The mechanism of rewriting takes the form of punctual or local references that build up the first type of undertext. The novel turns intertextuality into a symbolical and allusive codification.

Narrative Undertexts

It is difficult to draw a net wedge between what belongs to the dispersive network of references and what may be qualified as a 'narrative undertext'. This second technique of rewriting in *The Worm and the Ring* takes up and rewrites entire chunks of the Wagnerian plot. The main difference between the 'thematic undertext' and the 'narrative undertext' in Burgess is quantitative – the former is limited to scattered intertextual elements, whereas the latter makes use of extended rewriting of the plot. Both types naturally dovetail and intermingle.

In this sense, the novel builds a network of correspondences with the characters of the *Ring*. The young girls in the school yard at the beginning of the novel tally with the young naiads who keep the treasure of the Rhine and enchant those who get close to it in order to distract their attention from the gold. Their names – Woglinde, Wellgunde, Flosshilde – are transformed but still recognizable – Linda, Thelma, and Flossie. Alberich, the king of the dwarves, the Nibelungen, is incarnated in the novel as Albert Rich. The headmaster of the school, Woolton, reminds us of Wotan, the god of gods, and Veronica Woolton represents Wotan's spouse, Fricka. The parallelisms between the works thus operate through onomastics (mostly hypocoristic transformation), and, more precisely, through paronomasia (as in the case of Lodge, the chemistry teacher who incarnates Loge, the god of fire, or Miss Fry whose name echoes that of Freia, the goddess of youth).

Moreover, it is also possible to find parallels between the plot of the *Ring* and the novel. For example, Christopher Howarth has some traits of Siegfried; his adultery with Hilda recalls Siegfried's love for Brünhilde. Adulterous bonds create a rich echo with the manifold Wagnerian transgressions. Thus, intertextual elements go far beyond sheer symbolical correspondences and become plot transferrals. Numerous plot chunks borrowed from the *Ring* can thus be found in *The Worm and the Ring*. Some of them have already been mentioned as allusions, but they can be extended to entire episodes.

The key event in the *Ring* – Alberich outwitting the naiads and stealing the gold – may be reconstructed from the scattered network of allusions. In *Das Rheingold*, the theft is first associated with eroticism: the opening sequence is a play of seduction between Alberich and the naiads. But the naiads poke fun at Alberich; he slips and stumbles, and he finally forfeits love. In Burgess, Albert Rich first envisages the sexual potential of the young girls:

> By God, he would have one of them, which one didn't matter. His little pug-face was flushed with a boy's lust. It wasn't right, it wasn't fair, the whole system was wrong in allowing them to flaunt their country-girl breasts [...]. And it was sex all day long, damn it, wasn't it, whichever way you looked at it. (4)

The girls make fun of him ("Your legs aren't long enough, Rich!"; 4), and the dance-like chasing and fleeing between them soon stops being merely "concupiscent" and "modulate[s] swiftly to the vengeful" (4). As to cursing itself, some of it appears as early as the incipit: "the raincoated dwarfs screamed their valedictions of insult" (4); "Everybody, damn it" (4). It becomes possible to reconstruct parts of the Wagnerian narrative within Burgess's novel out of isolated fragments.

Structural Undertexts

The third correspondence between the works occurs on the level of structural elements. Like the *Ring*, *The Worm and the Ring* is organised into four parts. Otherwise, however, the number of divisions in every part of Burgess's work seems to diverge from Wagner's. The intermedial comparison of the macrostructure between the works is less relevant than some internal, microstructural elements.

Burgess's novel unfolds two other types of structural undertexts: a) a motivic undertext and b) a phonetic or prosodic undertext. Both appertain to the microstructure, and both have something to do with the Wagnerian leitmotiv.

At first sight, it seems rather difficult to single out specific motives in Burgess that could be at one with those in Wagner. If defined as a recurring musical phrase, as mere repetition, the leitmotif is scant in Burgess. Perhaps, one may point to the recurring phrase, taken from a poem by Martin Luther: "Ich kann nicht anders." But that takes into account only the signifier-part of the motivic function.

If one focuses on the signified-part of motifs, the novel seems more pregnant with structural parallels. The importance of the signified is precisely the basis of the Wagnerian leitmotif, which is supposed to denote objects, characters or ideas. Added to that is the crucial role played by the temporal nature of the Wagnerian leitmotif. In my opinion, the way Wagner deals with time through the leitmotif is more significant than mere repetition or denotation. Indeed, the literary or linguistic nature of the sign in Wagner results in a specific time-treatment whose main consequence is the capacity of a motif to refer simultaneously to the past and the future. Often enough, a motif tells the listener what is on the point of happening before it happens or, conversely, reminds the spectator of what has already happened. Thus, the leitmotif seems to imply, at least partially, the literary dynamics of anachronies (prolepsis, analepsis). In *Das Rheingold*, to take an instance, Loge comes and discusses possible solutions to free Freia, and listeners suddenly hear the motif related to the Rhine. The answer to the dilemma is clear: it is the gold that will be used to liberate Freia. The motif foreshadows what is to come and reminds us of what has already happened.

In much the same way, Burgess builds up a motivic undertext closely related to puns and allusions to the *Ring*. The difference between the sheer pun and the motivic one is that the latter carries a precise meaning related to what is actually taking place. It thus becomes a commentary on what is happening. The above-mentioned fire motif at the end of the novel demonstrates this mechanism. Another example may be that of water. In *The Worm and the Ring*, just as in Wagner, the substantial cause and origin keeps reappearing in the underlayers of the text. When Lodge asks Rich questions about the stolen treasure, puns on liquids are provided in the interstices on the text, so that the undertext becomes an intermedial leitmotif, referring both to Wagner's use of temporality in the leitmotif and to the textual temporality itself: "Rich heard the waters of inspiration lapping again" (51); "In the w.c. next door water sang explosively" (55).

Similarly, when, on coming home, Howarth finds his wife, Veronica, in the company of Dr Leary and suspects adultery, readers are once again reminded of the original transgression: "Glass in hand, he went to make water, the lavatory-bathroom being on the ground floor" (90); "Heracliteans. You know, *Panta* rhei. They like to see things flowing" (92).

It is noteworthy that the leitmotif in Wagner and Burgess carries a temporal meaning before denoting anything else. It is also important to remark that in constructing his leitmotif in the footsteps of Wagner, Burgess makes use of an eminently literary technique. In other words, in keeping with intermediality and the musicalisation of fiction, the technique resorts to literary and linguistic means. It thus undergoes a detour of sorts – what Wagner strived to introduce in music (the specificity of Wagnerian meaning) is restored in this literary text through music.

This becomes even more obvious with leitmotifs related to intertextuality proper. Indeed, some of the quotations in Burgess's novel tend to recur, as though they were leitmotifs themselves. Howarth keeps referring to Rilke, and Lodge is a staunch admirer of Elizabethan poetry. And because it may be considered both as a commentary on the action and as a proleptic or analeptic temporal mechanism, the cited text becomes akin to the specificity of the Wagnerian leitmotif. Lodge's recall of a line from Shakespeare's *The Tempest*,[7] for example, is not simply a quotation – it preserves a link with Wagner through water and fire: "Light bubbled down, full fathom five. Thy father lies. Of his bones are phosphor made" (48). Some intertextual citations are thus portent of a) their meaning proper b) the meaning from their context and from their (re)occurrence and c) the implicit intermedial meaning linked to Wagner.

The final mechanism of the undertext in *The Worm and the Ring* is at one with phonetic sublayers of the text. As in his other novels, Burgess resorts not only to puns toying with meaning, but also to a certain musicality of the word, playing with the acoustic potential of language. Sound-repetition, alliteration, assonance and paronomasia are the tools of Burgess's technique. Here the sonorous aspect of words takes on a specific dimension, contributing to the construction of a phonetic intermedial undertext. One example is the recurrence of the sound [ɔ:], naturally linked to the Latin *aurum*, gold. Puns on this sound are galore, echoing the English "or" (gold in heraldics), "orb" (as in a king's orb), "ore" (as metal ore), or even the French *or* (gold). The main idea of both works – the stolen treasure – is thus constantly recalled to the reader through a phonetic undertext. Quite frequently, it is possible to recognise a specific unfolding of such a *phonetic signature*: 1) some music or sound is mentioned in the vicinity of the phonetic undertext (musical allusion); 2) the phonetic undertext is reinforced by aid of a pun on Wagner or the *Ring*; 3) so that the phonetic undertext becomes easily recognizable (often underlined through alliteration as well). The following examples illustrate this underlying structure (Wagner, *Rheingold*, 3):

| "Albert Rich and his rain reflection sloshed through the puddles after the three giggling fourth-form girls." (3) |
| "She was Veronica's sole luxury, her strip-lighted cocktail cabinet, her Dior original." (13) |
| "His ears drumming to the corncorncorning." (172) |
| "Howarth moved on to a café where billiard-balls clacked and an accordion on the radio wheezed a fast waltz." (172) |
| "a thorn of ice hit a tooth like a tuning-fork" (175) |

---

[7] It is a pun on Ariel's Song from *The Tempest*: "Full fathom five thy Father lies, | Of his bones are coral made: | Those are pearls that were his eyes, | Nothing of him that doth fade, | But doth suffer a sea change | Into something rich and strange | Sea nymphs hourly ring his knell"; William Shakespeare, *The Tempest*, ed. G. B. Harrison, *Shakespeare Major Plays and the Sonnets* (New York: Harcourt, Brace & World, 1948), I.2.397-403, p. 1011.

Once again, the technique carries multiple meanings. Once again, it is closely linked to Wagner. On the one hand, the phonetic undertext becomes motivic in itself. On the other hand, it so happens that Wagner himself attached great importance to alliteration in his libretto (*Rheingold*, 4), so that the numerous sound-repetitive devices in Burgess seem to hint at Wagner's technique as well ("the tiny tinny triangles of tin tabernacles of ten or more different sects tintinnabulated" (Burgess, 190), not merely as a prosodic technique, but as a means of inserting a secondary meaning – another undertext.

Intermediality and Subversion

With its close relationship to Wagner, Burgess's novel subverts the apparent orthodoxy of the intermedial link. A number of transferrals from Wagner to Burgess seem to reveal a mechanism of false correspondences. The girls wound Albert Rich in the eye, whereas it is Wotan who has lost his left eye in Wagner. If Albert Rich stumbles in the incipit just as Alberich does in *Das Rheingold*, it is also Woolton's mother who stumbles and is hurt at the opening of the new school. In this way, the metamorphosed archetypes are unstable. The archetype becomes a floating attribute that may well pass from one character to another. Such seems to be the case with the role played by Siegfried: Howarth seems to incarnate some of Siegfried's traits, but so does his son, Peter. Through such subversive elements, the novel keeps a number of Wagnerian elements at bay, but it also plays with the comic and the ludic for which Burgess is renowned.

It seems essential that the novel be considered in terms of the multi-faceted metamorphosis of Wagner's work. Firstly, it should be remembered that it is not entirely a project of the musicalisation of fiction. Burgess seems to have abandoned the systematic *rapprochement* between music and literature (Wagner, *Rheingold*, 5). Secondly, there exists a degree of ambiguity between the musical and the literary. And such ambivalence is already present in Wagner's work. The most obvious token of the blurred frontier between the arts appears with the leitmotiv, which functions both as a musical object, predicated on repetition, and as a literary object, closely related to linguistic signification. Finally, the nature of the transformation of Wagnerian elements in *The Worm and the Ring* may be understood in different ways: the notion of dispersal is essential, but also those of subversion, condensation or even miniaturization. This casts a different, modern light on the *Ring*, and gives the most crucial symbol of the work – the gold, the treasure, and its cognates – a new meaning in Burgess's novel.

The Treasure as Knowledge

To approach a modern meaning of the *Ring*, Burgess highlights the symbolism linked to knowledge. If it is to be interpreted in this way, treasure becomes a symbol of a usurped but easy path to information, reminiscent of the biblical apple. In that case, *The Worm*

Treasure and the Desire to Know: Wagner and Burgess   109

and the Ring appears to be an enhanced mode of the epistemological meaning of the *Ring*.

The Epistemological Itinerary of the *Ring*

The Rhine maidens – Woglinde, Wellgunde and Flosshilde – protect the Rhinegold. The opening of *Das Rheingold* shows the first, natural state of the treasure that, symbolically enough, emits a luminous aura. If interpreted as a source of knowledge sheltered by Nature, the scene unveils the first stage of the epistemological itinerary of the *Ring*. But the secret is uncovered, bringing about the first epistemological transgression. Alberich, the dwarf, is intrigued by the glow and asks the Rhine maidens about it. Heedless of danger, the Rhine maidens tell him the hoard can be turned into a ring which will give its owner the power to rule the universe on condition that he forswears love.

The first stage of the epistemological itinerary of *The Ring* consists in the discovery of the treasure, the breach of secrecy, the theft, the forsworn love and the malediction. The association of gold and light (vision) seems to justify the epistemological interpretation of the treasure: "Nicht weiß der Alb von des Goldes Auge [...]?" (Wagner, *Rheingold*, 6).

The second scene reveals the second stage of the epistemological itinerary. Valhalla, the new castle, is finished, and Wotan, the ruler of the gods, has to pay the giants (Fasolt and Fafner) who have built it. Wotan promised to give them Freia, Fricka's sister and goddess of eternal youth. The giants remind Wotan of his promise. It must be kept because it has been engraved in Wotan's spear along with other laws and contracts, the runes. It stands for written, official, and compelling knowledge that has to be obeyed. Nonetheless, Wotan tries to circumvent the document, which suggests the second epistemological transgression – Wotan's knowledge and might are cursed:

> "Lichtsohn du, | leicht gefügter! | hör und hüte dich: | Verträgen halte Treu'! | Was du bist, | bist du nur durch Verträge: | bedungen ist, | wohl bedacht deine Macht | bist weiser du | als witzig wir sind, | bandest uns Freie zum Frieden du: | all deinem Wissen fluch' ich, | fliehe weit deinen Frieden, | weißt du nicht offen, | ehrlich und frei | Verträgen zu wahren die Treu'!" (7)

The scene also constitutes the second revelation of the treasure – Loge tells Wotan about the stolen gold and its power. The power the ring can bring seems to be inscribed on it as though it were a text of law: "Beute-Runen berge sein roter Glanz" (8). The hoard is thus likened to the treaties of law. The metamorphosis needs a magic formula, a text: "Ein Runenzauber | Zwingt das Gold zum Reif. | Keiner kennt ihn; | doch einer übt ihn leicht, | der sel'ger Lieb' entsagt" (9). To *activate* the treasure, an unknown text is necessary unless love be foresworn. The gods begin to covet the hoard themselves, and the treasure becomes a potential way of freeing Freia. But theft must be committed: "Durch Raub!" (10). Therefore, the treasure and the knowledge or the skill guaranteeing its power begin to undergo a series of thefts and transgressions: "Was ein Dieb stahl, | das stiehlst du dem Dieb" (11).

The next step of the itinerary is Alberich's brother's complaint. Mime tells Wotan and Loge about the toil and slavery of the Nibelungen. The stolen treasure, associated with slavery, turns into a theft of knowledge and skill. Mime has forged the Tarnhelm, the invisible cloak. Once again a symbolical object tells us something about knowledge itself – how power is wielded more efficaciously when knowledge is narrowed down to one possessor only and how it operates better when it is kept secret. Knowledge appertains to wit and guile. Wotan and Loge outwit Mime and Alberich.

Next, when the ring has been cursed by Alberich, the gods engage in commerce with giants to get Freia back. The hoard acquires a commercial value. So does the goddess. The giants want as much gold as will cover Freia entirely, but when she is covered with gold, one of the giants spots an empty space (*Ritze*), and the ring must be used to fill it up. The crack within the whole symbolises the incompleteness of the treasure unless it be returned to the Rhine. This idea of incompleteness accompanies many valuable objects in the *Ring* and casts a singular light on knowledge. At this stage, two truths become obvious: Fafner kills Fasolt, proving that the curse on the ring is unavoidable, and Loge knows that the twilight of the gods has begun: "Ihrem Ende eilen sie zu" (12).

In the first act of *Die Walküre*, the epistemological itinerary is predicated on identity discoveries. Siegmund and Sieglinde gradually become aware of their kinship – they are both Wälsungs. Through mirroring effects, mere intuition turns into certainty. This discovery is brought about through light, just as the treasure was discovered because of its light: "Was gleißt dort hell | im Glimmerschein?" (Wagner, *Walküre*, 13). The light uncovers the sword in the ash tree that was left there for Siegmund by the Wanderer (Wotan). The sword is above all a token of recognition and a final proof of Siegmund's identity because he is the first to withdraw it from the tree's trunk without difficulty. It has a symbolical epistemological value. Their names are revealed only at the very end of the first act.

The next epistemological stage also revolves around the opposition between knowledge and ignorance. Fricka wants Wotan to punish Siegmund and Sieglinde for their incestuous love. Fricka knows that Wotan betrothed them (disguised as Wälse, a mortal). Wotan needs a free hero, ignorant of his own destiny and Wotan's plans: "Not tut ein Held | der, ledig göttlichen Schutzes | sich löse vom Göttergesetz" (Walküre, 14), but he decides to obey Fricka's order. This stage is fraught with transgressions and punishments: Siegmund will have to die; Brünhilde will be put to sleep encircled by flames; Sieglinde will have to flee, impregnated with the new hero, Siegfried.

In *Siegfried*, the opposition between knowledge and ignorance is at its utmost. Siegfried lives with Mime, Alberich's brother, and knows nothing of his own forefathers. Nor does he suspect Mime's plans to get the ring. But Siegfried has observed Nature and has understood there are fathers and mothers, so he questions Mime about it and puts Mime's knowledge to the test. Mime eludes the questions ("Müßige Frage!"; Wagner, *Siegfried*, 15), but Siegfried strives for knowledge: "So muß ich dich fassen | um was zu wissen" (16). Knowledge is thus gained through lies and by force, but truth finally prevails.

In the second scene, the Wanderer meets Mime. Knowledge is at the centre of the scene: "Mancher wähnte | weise zu sein, | nur was ihm not tat, | wußte er nicht; | was ihm frommte | ließ ich erfragen: | lohnend lehrt' ihn mein Wort" (17). It is put to the test through three riddles. Knowledge is thus set within an agonistic context. Wotan promises his head if he does not answer Mime's questions. The first question relates to the Nibelungen and is correctly answered; the second deals with the giants and is rightly answered as well; finally, the third one refers to the gods, which gives the Wanderer the opportunity to speak of his past. It, too, reveals epistemological symbols. Wotan had shaped himself a shaft from the world-ash-tree's branches. It is with this spear that he rules the world. He engraved treatises in the spear. The ash-tree is thus a symbol of original order and timeless knowledge – the tree's roots go down into the past, its branches go up into the future.

It is noteworthy that the ash-tree dies away with Wotan's transgression and that etymologically the word *runes* should be linked to the word *branch*. In his turn, Mime is put to the test. The first question deals with the Wälsungs and is answered, the second with Nothung and is also answered, but the third one is left unanswered – how should the Nothung be recreated? Mime has been unable to discover the mystery of creation: "Der weiseste Schmied | weiß sich nicht Rat!" (18). His quest is thus branded as "eitlen fernen" (19).

An epistemological agonistics is shown. It is crucial that questions about cosmogony and the order of the world be raised, as though the scene were a metadiscursive sequence about the *Ring* itself. Siegfried forges the sword. Only the one who does not know fear can do that; only through letting the shards and re-forging the whole can Nothung be cast again. The sword is thus a telltale symbol of creation as recasting everything anew, almost from scratch. Here again, the idea of wholeness comes to the foreground – the sword is broken into shards and splinters, and only after being reduced to nothingness can it be wholly reconstructed.

In the next stage, knowledge is closely linked to warnings and new discoveries. When Siegfried stabs the dragon, the beast warns the hero. When Siegfried drinks some of the dragon's blood, he comes to understand the language of the birds, which give him council. The dragon's blood also allows Siegfried to read in Mime's thoughts, and it leads him to kill Mime. Finally, the birds sing about Brünhilde.

The next part, *Götterdämmerung*, begins with an important allegory of knowledge – the three Norns are spinning the rope of destiny. The scene opens once again with light. Once again, Wagner presents the world-ash-tree, the symbol of (fore)knowledge. We also learn about the spring that used to flow under the tree – another symbol of wisdom – and that it is tarnished now. When Wotan drank of its water, he lost his left eye – the symbol of intuition that confirms the association of vision and knowledge (insight) and thus the one between the hoard and wisdom: "seiner Augen eines zahlt' er als ewigen Zoll" (Wagner, *Götterdämmerung*, 20). All these symbols have been destroyed, and now the rope of Destiny breaks, putting paid to all foreknowledge.

The final epistemological stage reveals the manipulation of knowledge and ignorance. Gunther, at the head of the Gibichungs, the people living by the Rhine, wants Brünhilde as his wife and Siegfried as his sister Gutrune's husband. Siegfried is made to drink a magic potion to forget Brünhilde and fall in love with Gutrune. A series of warnings (Brünhilde's sister), betrayed secrets (Siegfried's weakness), plots and manipulations follows, at whose very core lies knowledge, memory and ignorance, with numerous symbolic elements, such as the magic potion or Wotan's ravens (his messengers).

This scheme of the epistemological itinerary of the *Ring* allows listeners to draw one important conclusion: Wagner's work is predicated on a multifarious network of symbols related to knowledge, to foreknowledge, to doom and to destiny; the itinerary is fraught with multiple transgressions, and it seems possible to interpret the entire work in relation to epistemology and to relate the latter to power. Such a viewpoint is particularly relevant in relation to Burgess's novel because *The Worm and the Ring* revolves around the scholarly universe where the stolen treasure is first and foremost knowledge itself.

The Value of the Written Word: The Stolen Treasure and its Cognates
in Burgess's *The Worm and the Ring*

The key idea of Burgess's novel is a confrontation between two temporalities: that of the Wagnerian cyclical and mythical time and that of an English grammar school of the early 1950s. The simple transferral of the treasure's value from Wagnerian gold to a girl's diary bears testimony to a specific interpretation linked to epistemology, hermeneutics or exegesis. Burgess seems to single out the epistemological approach to the *Ring*, underlining the idea of knowledge and other, derivative questions: the question of reliability, the valour of evidence, and the nature of fiction as opposed to reality or faith.

Thus, it is interesting to note that Burgess constantly brings readers' attention to the written word – letters, postcards, documents, research papers, forms, books or quotations loom large. The concept of fiction, of extreme importance in Burgess's creative *oeuvre*, is once again under investigation. It is the value attached to the written word that is under question. Ironically enough, the book has been withdrawn from sale and is still out of stock today because of a libel threat issued by a person whose identity was used in the novel.

Consequently, the written word lies in the opposition between reality and fiction. It seems plausible enough that parts of *The Worm and the Ring* should have been rewritten by the author for the second edition: clues about libel and the theme of naïve reading of fictitious events are thick on the ground and more than obvious. It was would be fascinating to conduct research work on the genesis of this novel. In this work, I limit my analysis to the second edition text only, and I focus on the value of the written word as a token of the relationship between the epistemological nature of Wagner's *Ring* and the metaphorical aspect of the treasure as a vehicle of epistemological questions.

Because the stolen gold and the ring are metamorphosed by Burgess into a stolen diary, the symbolical meaning of the treasure seems to be metamorphosed from sheer power to intimate knowledge. But it is more accurate to speak of the symbol's contiguous gliding from the idea of power to the notion of epistemology over and over again. Indeed, at first sight, the stolen treasure in Burgess gives way to a discovery that will play a major part in the plot – secret, private information is revealed about a pupil's life. The diary describes alleged sexual intercourse the girl has had with the headmaster: "*...He had me in his study today. He has ever such lovely hands. He stroked my hair* *and then he kissed me. And then...*" (6). The treasure thus becomes the source of erotic secrets.

Nevertheless, as a precious symbol, the diary swiftly takes on new threads of meaning. No sooner is it discovered than it becomes an object of speculation. It is Christopher Howarth who joins the argument between the girl and the thief, but he makes light of the contents of the diary, judging it certain to be only a naïve piece of adolescent writing: "*Went to tea with Myrtle, pictures afterwards, will have to do homework on bus tomorrow morning, telly gone to be repaired, row between mum and dad*" (8). The treasure of intimacy thus appears as a projection of one's desires and has something to do with psychoanalytical interpretations of the *Ring* that see the treasure as a projection of hidden, unconscious contents.

Moreover, the diary *does* carry a symbolical meaning related to power, since several characters will speculate on how it could be used to overthrow the headmaster. Woolton represents humanist and Hellenic ideals, believes in goodness hidden in every one, and as the head of the school, is unable to assert his power and desperately tries to combat his own leniency.

The diary becomes an ambivalent object, related to both power and knowledge. It is possible to compare the treasure's development throughout the novel with the Wagnerian epistemological itinerary. The precious object goes through a series of stages. Soon after its discovery, Lodge is told by the headmaster to retrieve the stolen diary from Rich, who denies having stolen it: "I didn't steal anything [...] She lent it to me" (49). The diary also becomes a powerful weapon, namely in erotic matters:

> Power. With that book he would have her where he wanted, when he wanted. And as for him... He had lain awake last night dreaming of blackmail. But how much better to be the only one in the school who could, with a wrist-flick, send packing the man at the top. If he wanted to. (50)

Lodge takes Rich to the Headmaster, and even though Rich tries to manipulate the teacher by telling him how indecent it is and that he has burnt the diary, the treasure ends up being retrieved: "Lodge, pipe still going lovely, dipped into the gap between Rich's jacket and more worn pullover and pulled out like a chestnut from the fire, a little book in blue leatherette" (54). Once again, the contents of the diary are read out:

> *Mr Woolton had me in his study to tell me off about being late. But he didn't tell me of. He asked me to sit down in his chair. He said don't be frightened I am not going to punish you. He said you have awfully nice hair and he started to stroke it. Then he said do you mind if I put my hand down there. And then he said will you give me a kiss. So I did and he said come again tomorrow. And at the door before he opened it he did it again.* (63)

This time the question of interpretation is at stake. Whereas Howarth analyses it as an erotic fantasy resulting from an overabundant imagination, Gardner is keen to take it at its face value. The question of exegesis soon takes on a forensic value because the written word is to serve as evidence. This gives way to sophistry – all that is written, and because it is written, must be believed: "there it is, in black and white" (64). The debate upon the treasure is thus not about to whom it belongs but what it represents. The stake of the written word reminds us of the ancient debates about the Scriptures, which is justified by the underlying conflict between the Catholics and the Protestants in the novel, but it also echoes more general questions, such as the dialectic between fiction and reality or the one between truth and lies. Howarth wants to annihilate the diary, but Gardner is opposed to the idea and willing to bring *truth* to the daylight. He thus becomes the treasure-keeper, like Fafner, but unlike the latter his aim is more ambiguous. On the surface, he may be perceived as the patron of a cultural, sacrosanct value, but, of course, his pertinacity feeds less on the desire to know than on the desire to govern.

The diary as treasure takes on an interesting secondary meaning with religious overtones – as a teenager, Howarth kept a diary himself and it got confiscated and destroyed: "His own diary of religious doubts, found by the headmaster, burnt in the boiler-room, *auto-da-fé*" (67). Thereby related to religious beliefs, to inquisition, confiscation, censorship or *auto da fé*, from now on the treasure will stand for both knowledge (secret or forbidden truth) and the exertion of power over knowledge (censorship, confiscation).

Investigation is under way. Dr Gardner interviews the diary writer, Linda. The question of treasure turns to the question of privacy or intimacy: "nobody should have taken it, sir. It's private" (107). What is the difference between the public and private written word? When does a written work become public domain and be considered out of copyright? What reliability does any written word carry? All these questions related to literature and fiction are answered by Gardner with sophistries:

> "when a person lets a diary out of his or her possession, Linda, it ceases to be private, it becomes public property. [...] many diaries have been published. Some are famous – Pepys, Evelyn, oh, lots of them. Similarly, a diary needs a really *safe* hiding-place." (107)

And much as Linda tries to persuade Gardner that it is all a made-up story, Gardner denounces the improbability of fiction-writing:

> I don't believe it, Linda! A young girl like you imagining things like that with a man old enough to be your grandfather. [...] "If," he said, "you had made up these fantasies about a fictitious person, then you would have had something like a story, a genuine – if improper – work of the imagination. But you have introduced, deliberately and quite unmistakeably, someone who actually exists – two people who actually exist. It's far, far worse, of course, than if these events had really taken place. Don't you see that? You've committed lie after lie to paper. You've published these lies – that means, in law, that you've allowed other people to see them. In other words, my poor Linda, you're guilty of a libel. A libel. A libel is a publication of lies intended to *harm* a person." (109)

Burgess thus seems to highlight a certain process of fiction writing. It all happens as though the suspension of disbelief in reading fiction suddenly turned into enforced belief, as though fiction turned into Holy Scripture. Consequently, the epistemological stake is not only the opposition between the stable and unreliable word, but also between the written and the oral word and between religious and lay documents.

The diary becomes a powerful weapon. Ironically enough, the mighty treasure has nothing to do with gold but is only a leatherette notebook. The act of reading, which

Treasure and the Desire to Know: Wagner and Burgess

usually gives vent to fiction, imagination, fancy, individual liberty, and ambiguous, sometimes contradictory statements, is baffled, giving place to tyrannical univocity and unique, biased interpretations.

Linda is blackmailed. Howarth tries to get the diary back and persuade Gardner not to use the foul weapon against the headmaster. But the contents have already been discovered by the staff, who assume it to be truthful. The treasure is said to have been stolen or destroyed, and the headmaster is accused of having caused its disappearance. The school advisory board demands Woolton's resignation, which he refuses to present. And although the *truth* will never be known, the question of fiction remains syllogistically intermingled with stable knowledge, indubitable truth, certainty and reality: "Diary usually is that. Write down what happened. As in the battalion war diary. Day by day. No point otherwise" (223).

The key ideas revolving around the main object of treasure permeate other types of written word in the novel. But they are too numerous to examine within the context of this paper. All of them together present a multifarious epistemological character; all of them somehow refer to the religious conflict; all of them revolve around power on the whole – the idea of manipulation appears quite clearly even in the religious context (echoes of inquisition and *auto da fé*). All of them, too, raise questions about fiction, legend, myth, reality, history and education. Importantly, as well, all major cognates of the main symbol of the written word seem to be related to the symbol of treasure.

The Wagnerian cloak of invisibility turns out to be embedded in a comic read by Mimms. Rich confiscates the comic under the pretext of "corruption of the young" (46). Howarth's research work gets plagiarised by Gardner. Knowledge thus appears to carry a specific price or value; like the treasure, it gets stolen, tapped, exploited, but also forbidden or confiscated. In any case, it becomes an instrument of power and manipulation.

Both Wagner's *Ring* and Burgess's *The Ring and the Worm* present complex epistemological systems, itineraries, and rites of passage. The treasure is a vehicle of the quest for power, but it is first a symbol of knowledge and initiation. Wagner's epistemological evolution is also a springboard for Burgess's questions about fictionality, literariness and the status of the written word in culture.

The treasure in Burgess's novel becomes a token of epistemological itineraries and a wellspring of questions related to literature and fiction. *The Worm and the Ring* may be considered a musicalised novel, predicated on a multilayered clockwork of intertextual and intermedial undertexts. To an extent, it echoes Wagner's composition itself – Wagner drew on multiple sources, such as *Edda*, *Nibelungenlied*, *Völsunga Saga* and *Thidriks Saga*. The creative process is one of condensed re-forging and re-creation. But whereas Wagner lifts, as it were, the precise temporal background of the legends to create an atemporal setting for his *oeuvre*, Burgess brings the myth and the legend back to a historical context. That enables Burgess to introduce epistemological questions within the context of multiple tensions between fiction and reality, deconstruction and re-creation, belief and disbelief. Through the symbol of a treasure's itinerary, both works meditate on epistemological mechanisms through art, and, to take up Wagner's own words again: "science, therefore, can only gain her perfect confirmation in the work of Art."[8]

[8] Wagner, *Art-Work of the Future*, p. 21.

Carl Plasa

"The Object of His Craving":
Loss and Compensation in Toni Morrison's *Song of Solomon*

> If mourning is the opposite of melancholy then, in the realm of capital transactions, so is insurance. Which is to say that insurance is the form that mourning takes when it equips itself for the market. For what else is mourning – upon the completion of its "work" – but the determination to exchange some lost thing for a viable substitute; and what else is insurance but that determination monetarized?[1]

> What better illustration of the degradation of gold than its capacity to turn persons into things; what better example of its offensive character than the excremental conditions of the barracoon; what better sign of its mutability than the "black gold" of the slave trade.[2]

> They say the people could fly. Say that long ago in Africa, some of the people knew magic. And they would walk up on the air like climbin up on a gate. And they flew like blackbirds over the fields. Black, shiny wings flappin against the blue up there.
> Then, many of the people were captured for Slavery. The ones that could fly shed their wings. They couldn't take their wings across the water on the slave ships. Too crowded, don't you know.
> . . . .
> [But they] kept their power, although they shed their wings. They kept their secret magic in the land of slavery.[3]

The resemblance between the pages of an open book and the wings of a bird in flight is no doubt fortuitous and perhaps even fanciful. In the context of Toni Morrison's *Song of Solomon* (1977), however, such a correspondence seems weirdly and immediately appropriate. After all, no sooner does the novel begin than it is aflutter with a deranged ornithological intent:

---

[1] Ian Baucom, *Specters of the Atlantic: Finance Capital, Slavery, and the Philosophy of History.* (Durham, North Carolina: Duke University Press, 2005), p. 135.
[2] Saidiya Hartman, *Lose Your Mother: A Journey Along the Atlantic Slave Route* (New York: Farrar, 2007), p. 47.
[3] Virginia Hamilton, *The People Could Fly: American Black Folktales*, illus. Leo and Diane Dillon (New York: Knopf, 1985), pp. 166-167.

118   Carl Plasa

The North Carolina Mutual Life Insurance agent promised to fly from Mercy to the other side of Lake Superior at three o'clock. Two days before the event was to take place he tacked a note on the door of his little yellow house:

At 3:00 p.m. on Wednesday the 18th of February, 1931, I will take off from Mercy and fly away on my own wings. Please forgive me. I loved you all.

(signed) Robert Smith,

Ins. agent[4]

This psychotic venture into the afternoon skies ends, of course, in failure. The diminishing font and drifting signature of the indented text might create the illusion of a body gradually receding from view, but Robert Smith's "wide blue silk wings" (5) do not help him "fly away" as he plans: when Morrison's would-be birdman launches himself from the roof of the Michigan infirmary to which his promissory "note" refers, it is not to reach "the other side of Lake Superior" but simply to crash to the pavements of Not Doctor Street. This downward career is rendered all the more ironic when it is remembered that the insurance agent's appearance atop the all-white "charity hospital" (4) is mistaken by those who witness it for "one of those things that racial-uplift groups were always organizing" (6).

Smith plays only a cameo role in *Song of Solomon*, but his bathetic leap "into the air" (9) remains a significant event in terms of the novel's overall design, inaugurating a concern with the possibilities and problems of flight which becomes increasingly prominent as the text progresses. His action also provides an early indication of the novel's rich literary and cultural inheritance, evoking the fate of Icarus, another doomed aviator,[5] and thus linking Morrison's imaginative enterprise to the archive of Greek myth. Yet Smith's significance is not reducible to what he suggests about the novel's thematic preoccupations and Hellenic debts, but extends to include his public identity as an employee of the North Carolina Mutual Life Insurance Company – the first African American institution of its kind, established in 1898 and numbering the ex-slave, John Merrick, among its founders.[61] In this capacity, Smith serves an organization not only specifically formed to protect black families against the "illness and death" (8) with which they associate him, but also more generally predicated upon the calculation of human life in terms of money and the principle that the loss of the one can somehow be

---

[4] Toni Morrison, *Song of Solomon* (New York: Vintage, 2004), p. 3. All further references are given parenthetically in the text.

[5] Thomas Bulfinch, *The Age of Fable: Or, Stories of Gods and Heroes*, rev. and enlarged ed. (New York: Crowell, 1913), pp. 156-157.

[6] For an enthralling account of the socio-historical context and cultural significance of this business, see Walter B. Weare, *Black Business in the New South: A Social History of the North Carolina Mutual Life Insurance Company*, updated ed. (Durham, North Carolina: Duke University Press, 1993). Merrick's status as "the son of a dark-skinned slave woman and a white man" (Weare, *Black Business*, p. 51) is particularly notable given the symbiotic relationship between the history of slavery and the history of insurance, with each institution fortifying and enabling the growth of the other, from the early eighteenth century onwards. As Baucom glosses this relationship: "The cowrie may have fed the slave trade, but the slave trade fed the insurance industry which in its turn nourished the financial revolution . . . inaugurat[ing] an Atlantic cycle of accumulation"; *Specters of the Atlantic*, p. 99.

offset by the provision of the other. While this logic of loss and compensation would necessarily not pertain in Smith's own suicidal case, it nonetheless offers a framework within which to locate the multiple and interlocking stories of African American masculinity the novel articulates.

Like the Icarus fable, these stories place the father-son relationship at their centre, even as they reverse the dramatic emphasis of Morrison's classical pretext: in *Song of Solomon*, it is not fathers who lose sons but sons who lose fathers, whether through death or other forms of absence. As it explores these losses and the strategies of recompense they engender, Morrison's novel elaborates a broad if resolutely non-linear historical vision, stretching back from the turbulent Civil Rights era of the early 1960s to the understatedly "bad times" (324) of American slavery.

Like Father, Like Son: Macon Dead, Mourning and Repetition

Song of Solomon is patterned according to an opposition between two sets of values, whose conflict is most strikingly played out in the antagonism between Macon Dead and his sister, Pilate: while the one cultivates a future-orientated and self-seeking materialism, the other privileges familial bonds, community and, above all, a profound connection to the past.[7] Although there is no doubt that the novel affirms the sister's position rather than the brother's, Morrison's representation of Macon is less straightforward and more sympathetic than it might appear, not least because it bears the traces of the very values he seems to have rejected.

At first glance, it is true, Macon gives the impression of being the perfect apologist for capitalism. He fully embraces the arts of ownership and exploitation intrinsic to his role as local slumlord and is eager to co-opt others to his way, especially his late-born only son, Milkman. Proselytizing to the twelve-year-old boy at the end of Chapter 2, Macon declares: "'Let me tell you right now the one important thing you'll ever need to know: Own things. And let the things you own own other things. Then you'll own yourself and other people too'" (55). This doctrinaire credo, in which the distinction between "things" and "people" is all too blithely finessed, is understandably a source of anxiety for Macon's working-class black tenants, leading Guitar Bains's grandmother to her own reifying reflection that "A nigger in business is a terrible thing to see" (22) and Guitar himself to the more outspoken and racially damning conclusion that Macon "behaves [and] thinks like a white man" (223). The fundamental problem with Macon's materialism, in other words "is that it repeats the . . . structures of plantation oppression"[8] to which African Americans were subject under slavery.

---

[7] Valerie Smith, "The Quest for and Discovery of Identity in Toni Morrison's *Song of Solomon*", *Southern Review* 21 (1985), 721-732. Rpt. in *Toni Morrison's "Song of Solomon": A Casebook* ed. Jan Furman (Oxford: Oxford University Press, 2003), pp. 27-41 (pp. 33-37).

[8] Valérie Loichot, *Orphan Narratives: The Postplantation Literature of Faulkner, Glissant, Morrison, and Saint-John Perse* (Charlottesville, Virginia: University of Virginia Press, 2007), p. 168.

As is often the case in Morrison, though, the oppressor can also be a victim, or, more precisely, in this instance, a victim who is at the same time a mourner, struggling with the psychic wounds inflicted upon him by the murder of his father, the unlettered ex-slave, Jake, and it is in this light that Macon's "drive for wealth" (28) needs to be set. The formation of the link between Macon's material and affective investments is illustrated in Chapter 7, in the sustained flashback to the events which follow the murder. As the text later reveals, the murder itself occurs at the covetous hands of the Butler family, who swindle Jake out of Lincoln's Heaven – the Pennsylvania farm he so nurtures and cherishes–and subsequently blow him "Five feet into the air" (52) when he contests their claim to ownership. These crimes are partially reprised some six days later, as the grieving sixteen-year-old Macon, fresh from the spectacle of "his father's body . . . twitch[ing] and danc[ing] for whole minutes in the dirt" (169), kills a white hunter and then endeavours to steal the "gold nuggets" (170) the latter has been hoarding in a cave close to the farm. Although Macon's robbery is thwarted by the intervention of the wiser Pilate, it is clear that he desires the hunter's treasure not merely because of the visions of affluence and security it excites in him, but because the act of its appropriation would constitute a symbolic reversal of the original theft of Jake's homestead – figured as a promised land of physical and emotional closeness, in which father and son work "right alongside" (51) one another. When, at the end of the chapter, Macon commissions Milkman to retrieve the gold Pilate has denied him (and which he wrongly thinks she has confiscated for her own advantage), he does so not simply to service a "bottomless greed" (220) or settle a score with a meddlesome sibling, but to heal a grief.

That Macon's love of property should turn out to be the expression of love for his dead father is fitting, since property functions in a similarly symptomatic manner for the father himself, another of the novel's abandoned sons. Just as the gold Macon desires to steal is intended to redress the loss of Lincoln's Heaven and the father-son intimacies it nourishes, so Jake values the farm as a place which fills the gap left by the impromptu departure of his own father, the eponymous Solomon, who quite literally rises above his station as a slave in 1850s Virginia by magically flying back to Africa.[9] Nor is it any accident that Jake should gravitate towards land as his most prized possession, since the earth he cultivates – gradually transforming it into "one of the best farms in Montour County" (235) – stands as a symbolic rebuke to the celestial domains into which Solomon withdraws. As Milkman learns from the local elders who nostalgically recall it, Lincoln's Heaven is indeed a place radically grounded (despite the otherworldly connotations of its name) in a sense of its own worth as *terra firma*, its attractions speaking for themselves:

> [The] farm . . . colored their lives like a paintbrush and spoke to them like a sermon. "You see?" the farm said to them. "See? See what you can do? Never mind you can't tell one letter from another, never mind you born a slave, never mind you lose your name, never

---

[9] Although critics rarely mention it, the dating of Solomon's flight to this decade is clear from internal evidence. If Jake was a "baby" when Solomon attempts to fly off with him, this would have to be sometime between 1850 and 1856, because, as Macon tells Milkman, "Papa was in his teens" when he comes to "register" (53) at the Freedmen's Bureau in 1869.

Loss and Compensation in Toni Morrison's *Song of Solomon*   121

mind your daddy dead, never mind nothing. Here, this here, is what a man can do if he
puts his mind to it and his back in it. . . . We live here. On this planet, in this nation, in this
county right here. *No*where else! We got a home in this rock, don't you see!
. . . Grab it. Grab this land! Take it, hold it, my brothers . . . and pass it on–can you hear
me? Pass it on!" (235; italics in original)

With its call to ex-slaves to "Grab" and "hold" the "land" they inhabit, the
postbellum earth evoked in this passage elaborates a language of prehension whose
ironies become especially poignant when set against the account of Solomon's
attempted homeward flight with the young Jake cradled in his arms. As the
appropriately named Susan Byrd informs Milkman, "'[Solomon] brushed too close to a
tree and the baby slipped . . . and fell through the branches to the ground. He was
unconscious, but the trees saved him from dying'" (324).

There is certainly something mortifying about Macon's business empire, which
alienates him from family and neighbourhood alike: the various houses Macon owns
seem, even to him, "like squat ghosts with hooded eyes" (27), while the slow-rolling
"wide green Packard" (32), in which he ritualistically rides out with his wife and three
children "on Sunday afternoons" (31), both functions to showcase his wealth and status
and is simultaneously known locally as "Macon Dead's hearse" (33). One way of
viewing this kind of commerce between the world of the possession and the world of
death is as a Morrisonian comment upon the potentially destructive nature of bourgeois
accumulation, but it can also be seen as a reminder of the murderous family history out
of which the identity of this "propertied Negro" (20) is coined. As Milkman comes to
realize towards the end of the novel, at a juncture when his father is "An old man":

> [Macon] paid homage to his own father's life and death by loving what that father had
> loved: property, good solid property, the bountifulness of life. He loved these things to
> excess because he loved his father to excess. Owning, building, acquiring – that was his
> life, his future, his present, and all the history he knew. That he distorted life, bent it, for
> the sake of gain, was a measure of his loss at his father's death. (300)

Jake may be unable to "pass . . . on" his land to his son, but, as these reflections
indicate, what he transmits in its stead is a way of dealing with "loss" whereby "good
solid property" is imbued with an affective "excess" which is also the ground of its
value.

"The Sunday Man": Guitar and the Mathematics of Revenge

Early on in *Song of Solomon*, Guitar's eyes are figured as "gashes of gold" (22), an
image associating the spectral treasure Milkman is deputed to recover–tracking its
supposed flight from Pilate's Michigan home back to the Pennsylvania cave and thence
Virginia – with a certain bodily violence. The image is in this respect an apt one, since
Guitar's interest in the gold has less to do with the acquisition of material trinkets and
personal pleasures – "televisions, and brass beds, and week-long card games" (181) –

than with how the commodity might be used to fund and facilitate his political activities. These are carried out under the aegis of the Seven Days, a secret brotherhood (also once including Smith) committed to racial counter-violence within an outrageously nonchalant environment where "White people" are free to "Kill a nigger and comb their hair at the same time" (52). What is perhaps most distinctive about the *modus operandi* adopted by the Days is not so much its reactive quality (as Guitar observes, "They don't initiate anything"; 154), as its obsession with revenge as a kind of arbitrary but fastidious mimicry, designed to reproduce as nearly as possible the multifarious forms of an originary white aggression. As Guitar confides to Milkman, his closest if also disapproving friend:

> "when a Negro child, Negro woman, or Negro man is killed by whites and nothing is done about it by *their* law and *their* courts, this society selects a similar victim at random, and they execute him or her in a similar manner if they can. If the Negro was hanged, they hang; if a Negro was burnt, they burn; raped and murdered, they rape and murder. If they can." (154-155; italics in original)

The acts of counter-violence Guitar describes are determined by a philosophy of race resting upon the assumption that a black life is of equal value to a white one. This philosophy is in turn bodied forth in the macabre symmetries in which Guitar and his fellow-agents specialize.

Like Henry Porter, another of the Days (and indeed like Smith as well) Guitar rationalizes his political convictions by appealing to their aetiology in a burdensome love for his people, rather than a hatred for his oppressors (159). Yet the novel itself suggests that Guitar's identity as political assassin springs from a different and more personal kind of love, whose object is, once again, a dead paternal figure. In contrast to the deceased Jake, who sporadically appears in the novel in ghostly form, Guitar's unnamed father does not return from the dead in any literal sense, but is certainly a figure haunting his son metaphorically, his presence reemerging in unexpected contexts. One of these is a fragmentary exchange with Milkman in Chapter 3, in which Guitar descants upon his aversion to sugar, relating his distaste for this seemingly innocent everyday item to memories of "dead people" and "white people" which make him "want to throw up." Guitar's nausea might be explained easily enough as a gut-reaction to the tumultuous cocktails of the transatlantic slave trade (within which sugar, death and whiteness are routinely mixed), but his allusion is to a local rather than global catastrophe, occurring in the form of the industrial accident which befalls his father, "sliced up in a sawmill" (61) during Guitar's childhood. Tragic though it be, it is not this event itself which so disturbs Guitar as its farcical obsequies: instead of receiving the "life insurance" she is due, Guitar's racially submissive mother is given just "forty dollars" by the mill owner, gratefully using some of the money to buy each of her three bereaved children "a big peppermint stick on the very day of the funeral" (225). Like the "big sack of divinity" (61) donated by the "foreman's wife" (224), these candies do nothing to assuage Guitar's sense of dispossession, but simply embitter him: "bone-white and blood-red" (225), they function as cannibalistic mementos of the inadequate regard in which the white world holds black men.

Loss and Compensation in Toni Morrison's *Song of Solomon*   123

From this perspective, it is not difficult to see why Guitar should find the micro-society of the Days so welcoming, since it accords him a perversely utopian space in which the worth of a black life is fully embraced – precisely as it is not in the frivolously coiffured dystopias of America at large. It might even be argued that the murderous symmetries beloved of the Days themselves recollect and mirror the symmetrical disposition of Guitar's father's corpse as it is readied for burial:

> [He] was sliced in half and boxed backward. [Guitar had] heard the mill men tell how the two halves, not even fitted together, were placed cut side down, skin side up, in the coffin. Facing each other. Each eye looking deep into its mate. Each nostril inhaling the breath the other nostril had expelled. The right cheek facing the left. The right elbow crossed over the left elbow. (224)

Nor is it surprising, equally, that Guitar should in the end train his killer's gaze upon Milkman, wrongly believing him (in a paranoid echo of Macon's erroneous suspicion of Pilate) to have taken the treasure for himself. In Guitar's "golden eyes" (106), this phantom theft is not just a betrayal of a long-term friendship already seriously compromised, but, more urgently, an act which jeopardizes both the retaliatory project of the Days and, by implication, the complex strategies of psychological compensation the project supports.

Different Directions: From Treasure to Flight

Unlike Macon and Guitar, Milkman does not lose a father to a violent death but to an emotional distance generated, amongst other things, by Macon's exorbitant appetite for property. Milkman eventually comes to reappraise such avarice along the lines already suggested, but, for most of the novel, is animated by the desire to be free not just of his father and the plantation consciousness he seems so shamelessly to promote, but of interpersonal relationships altogether. It is in this fiercely independent spirit that he answers his father's instruction to "Get the gold" (172), embarking, in the novel's second half, upon a quest which loosely parallels the tale of Jason's search for the Golden Fleece and thus discloses another aspect of the text's classical inheritance.[10] Yet

---

[10] As well as echoing Jason's morally ambiguous quest in terms of broad narrative trajectory, *Song of Solomon* makes a specific allusion to this mythic tale in Chapter 9. At this point, First Corinthians overhears Macon and Milkman clashing at night about the failed raid on Pilate's home (where they first believe the gold to be hidden) and wonders whether she has entered "a secret hour in which men rose like giants from dragon's teeth" (202). This oddly recondite speculation recalls the episode in the classical source in which, in order to win the Fleece, Jason is required by the King of the Colchians to use two bronze-hooved fire-breathing bulls "to plough a field four measures great" and then plant it with "seed from a dragon's jaws which . . . send[s] up earth-born warriors with bronze weapons"; Apollonius of Rhodes, *Jason and the Golden Fleece (The Argonautica)*, trans. and intro. Richard Hunter (Oxford: Oxford University Press, 1993), p. 77. Morrison, of course, is not the first African American writer to have refashioned this particular myth from a contemporary perspective, her main precursor being Du Bois, who invokes

even as Milkman's adventure resonates with Jason's, his pursuit is slowly alchemized into something else, becoming a higher and more abstract search for the secrets of a family history leading back, finally, to slavery – and the superhuman retreat from it carried out by Solomon. This shift in the direction of Milkman's quest – he sets out looking for material riches but ends up possessing a plentiful historical knowledge instead – simultaneously marks a shift in the matrix of the novel's influences, revealing a debt not to Greek myth but African American oral tradition, from which the ancestral story of Solomon's flight takes wing.

As if to emphasize the difficulty of pinning him down, Solomon goes by two other names in the novel (Sugarman and Shalimar), making his textual debut under the former alias in the riddlesome blues raised up by Pilate as she watches Smith's desperate avian charade and awaits Milkman's birth:

> *O Sugarman done fly away*
> *Sugarman done gone*
> *Sugarman cut across the sky*
> *Sugarman gone home.* (6; italics in original)

This elusive figure is attractive to Milkman for a number of reasons, including the fact that he practises a mode of resistance not bound to the ceaseless replication of white violence which seduces and entraps Guitar, but distinguished by the ability simply to transcend it. As Milkman puts it, marvelling at the superior exploits of his "great-granddaddy": "'He didn't need no airplane. He just took off; got fed up. *All the way up!* No more cotton! No more bales! No more orders! No more shit!'" (328; italics in original). Yet Solomon's appeal additionally entails a compensatory dimension, since, as "one of those flying African children" (321), he possesses the very "gift" whose lack has dismayed and perplexed Milkman ever since his own childhood, during which he "discover[s], at four, the same thing Mr. Smith had learned earlier – that only birds and airplanes could fly" (9). In this sense, he is a kind of ecstatic double or idealized self for Milkman, a mirroring also evident in terms of the consequences directly arising out of Solomon's self-removal from the field of slavery: leaving both the infant Jake and a further twenty sons to the care of his wife, the similarly abandoned Ryna, Solomon effects a radical severance of family ties not unlike that to which Milkman himself aspires. The critical difference between the two situations, however, is that Milkman actively desires familial freedom, while Solomon presumably does not.

As is widely recognized, Milkman's celebration of the slave who arcs his way across the heavens in a triumphant flight from oppression is not fully upheld by the text itself, which offers a more down-to-earth and ambivalent assessment of Solomon's apparent heroics.[11] One place where such debunking occurs is in Chapter 11, at a point when

---

it both in Chapter 8 of *The Souls of Black Folk*, intro. Donald B. Gibson (Harmondsworth: Penguin, 1989 [1903]) and his first fictional work, complete with its boldly contrary title, *The Quest of the Silver Fleece: A Novel*, intro. Arnold Rampersad (New York: Harlem Moon, 2004 [1911]).

[11] Michael Awkward, "'Unruly and Let Loose': Myth, Ideology, and Gender in *Song of Solomon*", *Callaloo* 13 (1990), 482-498 (482-485); Marianne Hirsch, "Knowing Their Names:

Loss and Compensation in Toni Morrison's *Song of Solomon* 125

Milkman has become increasingly distracted from his increasingly frustrating search for the missing gold and finds himself drawn into a rather more mundane sort of quest, hunting raccoon with a company of locals in Virginia. As the hunters traverse a night-time landscape quite alien to their citified new recruit, the dislocated Milkman seems repeatedly to hear a human voice:

> He heard the sound of the sobbing woman again and asked Calvin, "What the hell is that?"
> "Echo," he said. "Ryna's Gulch is up ahead. It makes that sound when the wind hits a certain way."
> "Sounds like a woman crying," said Milkman.
> "Ryna. Folks say a woman name Ryna is cryin in there. That's how it got the name." (274)

Whether the folktale is taken at face value or discounted as a superstitious freak of nature is of secondary importance to the doubling of female figures occurring here, as Morrison once again rewrites Greek myth for her own purposes. This doubling not only identifies Milkman's "sobbing woman" with the classical figure of Echo, but also sets up an unflattering, if unobtrusive, parallel between Solomon and Narcissus, by whom Echo's love is so cruelly spurned.[12]

Solomon is also placed in a less than heroic light by the broader and more sustained parallel the novel elaborates between his relationship with Ryna and Milkman's own relationship with Pilate's granddaughter, Hagar, with both women figured as fatally maddened, if overdependent, victims of male neglect. Hagar is unhinged by the "flat-out coldness" (99) of the letter in which, "after more than a dozen years" (91), Milkman ends their love, eventually dying of a fever and a broken heart, while Ryna is said, for her part, to have "screamed and screamed [and] lost her mind completely" following her husband's desertion. Equally, though, the predicaments of the two women should not be conflated. While the "gossip, stories, legends [and] speculations" (323) Milkman garners from Susan construct Ryna in the romanticized terms just outlined, "the Byrd woman's" (326) own surmise is that it is not so much lost love which destroys the sanity of Solomon's wife, as the tribulation of "trying to take care of [her] children" (323) on her own. Similarly, in a second disparity from the childless Hagar, Ryna does not suffer merely at the hands of a black man who refuses to settle down, but must also confront the sexual threat embodied in the white, as suggested, in the euphemistic protest of the song Pilate sings in Chapter 2:

> *O Sugarman don't leave me here*
> *Cotton balls to choke me*
> *O Sugarman don't leave me here*
> *Buckra's arms to yoke me.* (49; italics in original)

Toni Morrison's *Song of Solomon*", in: *New Essays on "Song of Solomon"*, ed. Valerie Smith (Cambridge: Cambridge University Press, 1995), pp. 69-92 (pp. 77-78); Wendy W. Walters, "'One of Dese Mornings, Bright and Fair, / Take My Wings and Cleave De Air': The Legend of the Flying Africans and Diasporic Consciousness", MELUS 22.3 (1997), 3-29 (18-19).
[12] Bulfinch, *The Age of Fable*, pp. 101-102.

Throughout *Song of Solomon*, the value of gold is surplus to the value ascribed to it, having less to do with either a rabid materialism and wrong-headed vendetta, in Macon's case, or a deathly racial accountancy, in Guitar's, than a shared struggle to come to terms with the void left by paternal loss. In Milkman's case, conversely, it is not that the gold provides its baffled quester with the means to counterbalance such loss (though the traveller's tale he brings back to Macon in the novel's final chapter does produce a filial rapprochement of a sort). Rather it is that the absence of the commodity is outweighed by the discovery of the fabulous if troubling Solomon. As he pursues this fugitive figure to the very brink of the text, Milkman turns gradually from a literal to a metaphorical treasure-hunter, before finally honouring his quarry in the perfect way:

> Milkman stopped waving and narrowed his eyes. He could just make out Guitar's head and shoulders in the dark. "You want my life?" Milkman was not shouting now. "You need it? Here." Without wiping away the tears, taking a deep breath, or even bending his knees – he leaped. As fleet and bright as a lodestar he wheeled toward Guitar and it did not matter which one of them would give up his ghost in the killing arms of his brother. For now he knew what Shalimar knew: If you surrendered to the air, you could *ride* it. (337; italics in original)

As Milkman "wheel[s] toward Guitar" in this climactic moment, so the novel circles back to its beginning. Although the outcome of the impending fraternal combat remains unclear – it is indeed left up in the air, so to speak – what is certain is that the novel's ending contains its own kind of compensation, rewriting Smith's Icarus-like fall in the elevated, if equivocal, language of black legend.

Following Milkman: Reading, Questing and Catching Slaves

The comparison of Milkman to a "lodestar" in the passage above is in one sense curious, since it is he who is attracted to his so-called "brother" at this terminal point in the novel rather than the reverse. In another sense, though, the simile is well-chosen, serving as a reminder of how the mistrustful Guitar has been furtively tracking Milkman on his travels ever since the latter leaves Michigan for Pennsylvania at the beginning of Part II. Yet if Guitar anxiously follows in Milkman's footsteps (and even attempts to strangle him amid the darkness of the Virginia raccoon-hunt), the novel's reader is invited by the text to shadow Milkman too, paralleling his double quest – for a secret treasure supplanted by a secret history – by becoming his questing double. Milkman and the reader are further compounded by their shared resemblance to the figure of the slave-catcher, a conflation of identities which is as disturbing as it is surprising.

Considered in relation to the original "object of [Milkman's] craving" (219), it could be said that the reader in fact succeeds where Morrison's protagonist fails, for one of the ironies of *Song of Solomon* is that the gold Milkman vainly seeks is to be found in abundance on the novel's surfaces, as if hidden in plain sight. This pattern is initiated in Morrison's allusion to the minor figure of Freddie the janitor, the "gold-toothed man" (6) who is one of the witnesses at the scene of Smith's suicide and also works as

Macon's informant cum "flunky" (14). It is subsequently developed in a profusion of images which glint across the narrative for the reader to scoop up and sift. Along with Guitar's "golden eyes," these include the "peeling gold letters" on "the plate-glass window" of Macon's "office," which irreverently proclaim it still to be "Sonny's Shop" (17); the "bit of gold wire" soldered to "the little brass box" (167) Pilate wears as an earring and which contains her name (copied from the Bible by Jake); and the "compact trimmed in a goldlike metal" (308) owned by Hagar. Taken together, these and the countless other images which might be adduced constitute a textual embarrassment of riches, whose presence in the novel is once again compensatory, offering repeated refractions of the commodity for which Milkman initially searches.

Of all the novel's golden moments, perhaps the most complex occurs in Chapter 1, in the episode in which the ubiquitous Freddie catches Milkman's mother, Ruth, breastfeeding her son some years after the period sanctioned by convention:

> She felt him. His restraint, his courtesy, his indifference, all of which pushed her into fantasy. She had the distinct impression that his lips were pulling from her a thread of light. It was as though she were a cauldron issuing spinning gold. Like the miller's daughter – the one who sat at night in a straw-filled room, thrilled with the secret power Rumpelstiltskin had given her: to see golden thread stream from her very own shuttle. (13-14)

Although Milkman is "old enough to be bored by the flat taste of mother's milk" and comes to her breast "reluctantly, as to a chore," Ruth draws "pleasure" from the clandestine rituals she has evolved, using them as a means of consoling herself for the loss of emotional and sexual intimacy which rapidly overtakes her marriage to Macon. Indeed the ironic implication is that it is Milkman's very disinterest which encourages Ruth to value her deviant practices all the more, extravagantly imagining the "thin" liquid he "pull[s]" from her "flesh" (13) as "golden thread." In this way, in another irony, Ruth carries out a specifically female version of the compensatory strategies deployed by the husband from whom she has become estranged, with one of the differences between her rituals and his being that the "spinning gold" she celebrates is the product of "fantasy" rather than a material object to be sought and grasped. Another difference is that this delicate substance is associated not with the storytelling traditions of classical myth but European fairy-tale, a genre always tugging at the hem of Morrison's novel in playful allusions not only to "Rumplestiltskin," but also "Goldilocks" (135 and 314), "Jack and the Beanstalk" (180 and 183) and "Hansel and Gretel" (219).

The invocation of the first of these stories at this juncture in *Song of Solomon* is certainly to the point in terms of the two texts' concern with the amassment of gold, even as, in another sense, Morrison's allusion precipitates a third and final irony. In the most popular version of the fairy-tale told by the Brothers Grimm, Rumplestiltskin threatens the "miller's daughter" (to whom Ruth compares herself) with the loss of her child unless she can guess his unguessable name aright (54), whereas in the later narrative it is precisely an act of correct naming – or rather definitive nicknaming – which brings Ruth's indulgences to a sudden end and hence further loosens her already questionable hold over her son. This act is performed by Freddie, who first revels in the salacious *mot juste* on which he alights, before broadcasting it both to "the homes in Ruth's neighborhood [and] to Southside, where he live[s]": "'A milkman. That's what you got here, Miss Rufie. A natural milkman if ever I seen one. Look out, womens. Here he come. Huh!'" (15).

The reader also emerges as a double to Milkman in relation to the latter's pursuit of Solomon, the recusant slave whose allure finally outshines that possessed by gold. In a similar way to how Milkman gradually searches out and puts together the missing details in Solomon's story, particularly during his detective-like investigations in Virginia, so the reader recurrently encounters textual clues to Solomon's existence and, especially, the capacity for flight which is his most charismatic feature. These clues combine to form a network of images which at once complements and is just as systematic as that created by the novel's images of gold. At times, the images are writ large, as in the self-destructive spectacle at the novel's outset, but, more often than not, are both more oblique and more ordinary, as if woven into the fabric of Morrison's narrative as a matter of course. They appear far too frequently to be inventoried here, but examples might range from the figurine of the "silver winged woman poised at the tip of [Macon's] Packard" (32) and Hospital Tommy's "pinfeather toothpick" (60), to the "feathery kiss" (201) First Corinthians bestows upon Porter after their love-making and "the wings of . . . other people's nightmares" (220) which Milkman finds so blinding. At times, indeed, the avian terms in which the novel is so well-grounded can even be used to figure the quest for gold itself. For instance, the "little gray bags" containing the treasure Macon originally discovers in Pennsylvania are "arranged like nest eggs," triggering dreams of "Life, safety, and luxury" which open up "like the tail-spread of a peacock" (170), just as, when Milkman returns to the scene in the hope of refinding these precious items, he imagines them as "pigeon-breasted" (252). But whether conspicuous or covert, the bird-images populating the novel all have the same effect, working to create a fictional world everywhere abuzz with memories and traces of Morrison's flyaway slave.

One of the paradoxes of Morrison's novel is that although Solomon is revered by Milkman as a figure of freedom, Milkman himself can seem oddly like a slave-catcher, drawing his renegade African back from the realms of an apparent historical oblivion by carefully reconstructing his narrative. Central to the success of Solomon's recapture is the hermeneutic pressure Milkman exerts upon the words of the cryptic song which gives the novel its title. As if struggling towards its own verbal flight, this song makes a series of fragmentary appearances throughout the text, before at last becoming fully-fledged at the end of Chapter 12. At this expansive point in the novel, it is performed as part of a circle-game played among a group of "About eight or nine boys and girls" (264) in Virginia, as Milkman listens and "memorize[s] all of what they sang," closing his "eyes" (303) the better to concentrate:

> *Jake the only son of Solomon*
> *Come booba yalle, come booba tambee*
> *Whirled about and touched the sun*
> *Come konka yalle, come konka tambee*
>
> *Left that baby in a white man's house*

Loss and Compensation in Toni Morrison's *Song of Solomon* 129

Come booba yalle, come booba tambee
Heddy took him to a red man's house
Come konka yalle, come konka tambee

Black lady fell down on the ground
Come booba yalle, come booba tambee
Threw her body all around
Come konka yalle, come konka tambee

Solomon and Ryna Belali Shalut
Yaruba Medina Muhammet too.
Nestor Kalina Saraka cake.
Twenty-one children, the last one Jake!

O Solomon don't leave me here
Cotton balls to choke me
O Solomon don't leave me here
Buckra's arms to yoke me

Solomon done fly, Solomon done gone
Solomon cut across the sky, Solomon gone home. (303; italics in original)

Even as Milkman commits the children's "round" (303) to memory, he is strangely familiar with it already, or at least its last six lines, which both echo the "old blues . . . Pilate sang all the time" and change her "Sugarman" into a less sweet-sounding "Solomon" (300). Yet when he first hears the preceding four verses, he dismisses them as nothing more than "a meaningless rhyme" composed of "nonsense words": "'Solomon rye balaly *shoo*; yaraba medina hamlet *too*'" (264; italics in original). More concerted audition and analysis lead him, however, to a sharper understanding of the song's secrets and, crucially, the recognition that "These children were singing a story about his own people!" (304). Nonetheless, as Milkman realizes, the "story" in question still has many gaps which it is Susan's task to fill. This she accomplishes by telling him, for example, that when Solomon flies off, he does so in a literal rather than metaphorical sense (322-23) and that Jake was not in fact Solomon's "*only son*," but rather "the only one [he] tried to take with him" (323) at the start of his voyage.

While Milkman is thus able to achieve a certain interpretative mastery over Solomon and the song which remembers him, the song itself harbours other mysteries whose resolution this time casts the reader in the role of slave-catcher. This becomes apparent when the critical gaze moves beyond the frame of Morrison's fiction and towards the text which provides it with some of its most vital raw materials. As several critics have observed, that text is *Drums and Shadows: Survival Studies among the Georgia Coastal Negroes* (1940), a collection of interviews with ex-slaves and descendants of slaves compiled by the Savannah Unit of the Georgia Writers' Project, under the supervision of Mary Granger. In Keith Cartwright's comprehensive summation, this ethnographic

130   Carl Plasa

work yields up an "epic catalogue of folk facts" which "finds coherent reassembly" in *Song of Solomon*:[13]

> stories of flight back to Africa, tales of wings for sale, workings of conjure and birth cauls, the presence of ghostly figures and voices, communication with spirits (including a woman transformed into a bull), and retransmitted names – Coupers and Butlers (repeated as the Reverend Cooper and the Butler family), day names (informing the vigilante Seven Days) . . . even the name of Solomon himself.[14]

As Cartwright notes, however, the presence of *Drums and Shadows* in Morrison's text is evident in other ways too, including the echoes of Mende funeral song in the refrains to the first three verses of the Virginia children's chant, the allusion to saraka cake and, in particular, the sudden glut of "Fulbe Muslim names" appearing in verse four.[15] The most historically resonant of these undoubtedly belongs to Bilali Mohammed (Morrison's "*Belali*"), the African Muslim who worked for Thomas Spalding as a slave-driver on Georgia's Sapelo Island from the early to mid-nineteenth century. Despite the problematic nature of his office, Bilali remains a celebrated if fundamentally enigmatic figure in Gullah folk memory, distinguished, *inter alia*, for a range of gifts – literacy, erudition, religious integrity, forceful character and, significantly, a technical knowledge of long-staple cotton production.[16] He is recollected affectionately in *Drums and Shadows* by his descendants, one of whom is his great-granddaughter, Katie Brown. Described by the Southern white commentary which surrounds and connects the book's various "field reports" as one of Sapelo's "oldest inhabitants",[17] Katie responds graciously to the inquiries of her interviewers:

> Knowing that Katie was a descendant of Belali, we asked her if she knew anything of him. She nodded and answered, "Belali Mohomet? Yes'm, I knows bout Belali. He wife Phoebe. He hab plenty daughtuhs, Margret, Bentoo, Chaalut, Medina, Yaruba, Fatima, an Hestuh."[18]

---

[13] Keith Cartwright, *Reading Africa into American Literature: Epics, Fables, and Gothic Tales* (Lexington: University Press of Kentucky, 2002), p. 81.

[14] Cartwright, *Reading Africa into American Literature*, pp. 81-82. In addition to Cartwright's own analysis, a particularly detailed exploration of the role of *Drums and Shadows* as one of the key sources for Morrison's novel is to be found in Nada Elia, "'Kum Buba Yali Kum Buba Tambe, Ameen, Ameen, Ameen': Did Some Flying Africans Bow Down to Allah?", *Callaloo* 26 (2003), 182-202 (182-186). Both critics are ultimately indebted to Susan L. Blake, who was the first to point out the link between the two texts in "Folklore and Community in *Song of Solomon*", MELUS 7.3 (1980), 77-82. See also Walters, "'One of Dese Mornings'", 9 and 16.

[15] Cartwright, *Reading Africa into American Literature*, p. 82.

[16] Allan D. Austin, *African Muslims in Antebellum America: Transatlantic Stories and Spiritual Struggles*, rev. and updated ed. (New York: Routledge, 1997), pp. 85-99; William S. McFeely, *Sapelo's People: A Long Walk into Freedom* (New York: Norton, 1994), pp. 32-43.

[17] McFeely, *Sapelo's People*, pp. xxiii and 152.

[18] McFeely, *Sapelo's People*, p. 154.

Loss and Compensation in Toni Morrison's *Song of Solomon*

As the stealthy intertextual migration of these names suggests, there is, in the end, more than just one legendary slave to be extrapolated from Morrison's novel, with the fictional Solomon complemented by the historically real Bilali. While Solomon evidently possesses the greater procreative power – siring a "slew" (322) of some twenty-one sons to Bilali's more modest crop of seven "daughtuhs"[19] – he also differs from his counterpart in his negotiation of the slavery which is their mutual bane, taking flight from a regime within which Bilali remains grounded.

Despite such differences, though, the two slaves whose identities become visible at the end of *Song of Solomon* have at least one thing in common and that is that their respective presences are adumbrated in its opening sequence. If it is possible, as Pilate does, to hear the faint sound of Solomon's wings beating beneath Smith's, it is also possible to pick up the merest prospective trace of Bilali in the sentence which launches the novel's second paragraph. This contrasts the hometown fame gained by Smith with the international celebrity lavished upon a rather more fortunate aviator, Charles A. Lindbergh:

> Mr. Smith didn't draw as big a crowd as Lindbergh had four years earlier – not more than forty or fifty people showed up – because it was already eleven o'clock in the morning, on the very Wednesday he had chosen for his flight, before anybody read [his] note. (3)

Here the allusion is to Lindbergh's pioneering non-stop solo transatlantic flight from New York to Paris on 20-21 May 1927, an exploit which, on the face of it, would seem to align its perpetrator more closely to Solomon than Bilali. Yet as well as flying the Atlantic, Lindbergh, like several other famous people of his era, briefly visited Sapelo, where he was a guest of the island's owner, Howard Earle Coffin, on 15 February 1929 and stayed at the Spalding residence Coffin had renovated.[20] In this covert manner, *Song of Solomon* brings Lindbergh and Bilali into a fleeting if improbable liaison, with the itinerary pursued by the one looking back to the path taken by the other.[21]

In the "Foreword" to the 2004 edition of *Song of Solomon*, Morrison demystifies artists' conventional celebration of their "muses," exposing it as a tactic by which they

---

[19] It should be noted, however, that Katie's account of Bilali's progeny is a partial one, making no mention of the dozen male children whom he also fathered. Although nothing is known of these sons, their existence expands the number of Bilali's offspring to respectably Solomonesque proportions. Cf. Austin, *African Muslims in Antebellum America*, p. 99; Michael A. Gomez, *Black Crescent: The Experience and Legacy of African Muslims in the Americas* (Cambridge: Cambridge University Press, 2005), p. 156.

[20] McFeely, *Sapelo's People*, p. 147; Buddy Sullivan, *Sapelo Island* (Charleston, South Carolina: Arcadia, 2000), pp. 96-97.

[21] If Lindbergh is obliquely connected to Bilali, he is also linked, more firmly, to Milkman. This is so both in terms of their shared Michigan provenance and Milkman's expensive jewellery, especially the "gold Longines" (226) which is given him by Ruth and stolen by Grace Long in Virginia (291-92). Longines timed Lindbergh's transatlantic journey (at 33 hours, 30 minutes and 29.8 seconds), while Lindbergh in his turn designed for them a navigational watch, intended to assist pilots in the calculation of longitude and manufactured by the company shortly after his flight. The flight itself gained Lindbergh precisely the sort of material wealth (the $25,000 Orteig Prize) whose value Milkman finally unlearns.

can conceal the origins of their work and "avoid articulating, analyzing, or even knowing the details of their creative process – for fear it would fade away" (xi). Ironically, though, Morrison practises a version of the very ruse she challenges, attributing the birth of her novel to the death of her father and, in particular, the conversations she holds with him even after his passing: these, she claims, provide sufficient insights into the *terra incognita* of masculine identity for her to effect "a radical shift in imagination from [the] female locus" of her first two fictions – *The Bluest Eye* (1970) and *Sula* (1973) – to the male-centred realms of her third work. Yet even as this touching tale of posthumous instruction might be said, at the very least, to lead the reader away from the novel's sources, it simultaneously points back towards them, since the inquiry Morrison makes of her lost father – "'What are the men you have known really like?'" (xii) – is not only reminiscent of the sorts of "set-ups" (153) with the dead described in *Drums and Shadows*, but also strangely akin to the questions the book's interviewers ask of their informants. At the same time, the "Foreword" performs another operation, actively participating in and prefiguring the narrative dynamics of the novel it so belatedly introduces. This it does by implicitly figuring Morrison's text as a compensatory creation or work of mourning in its own right, standing in, as best it can, for the "Daddy" to whom it is dedicated.

Oliver Lindner

Broken Future, Broken Narrative:
Risk and the Threatened Treasure of the Environment in David Mitchell's *Cloud Atlas* (2004) and Margaret Atwood's *The Year of the Flood* (2009)

Introduction

Literature and film are the primary media that shape our perception of what it means to live in a post-apocalyptic world in which all the certainties of modernity have vanished and in which the survivors are forced to cope with a radically different environment. Environmental dystopias, one can argue, are nowadays the most crucial branch of this category of future histories, since they are thought experiments which extrapolate from present ecological developments and related risks.[1] As a subgenre, they can be placed within the broad category of Science Fiction, which Damien Broderick defines as "that species of storytelling native to a culture undergoing the epistemic changes implicated in the rise and supersession of technical-industrial modes of production, distribution, consumption and disposal".[2] The eminent British author J.G. Ballard once called Science Fiction the "only true literature of the twentieth century".[3]

Science fiction is a genre which, due to its flexibility and its portrayal of possible futures, can contribute more to raising an awareness of impending ecological catastrophe than any other established literary genre, thereby highlighting the position of the environment as a threatened treasure.[4] Due to their speculative nature, these literary worlds mediate current trends and have the power to turn our diffuse anxieties about the future into representations of full-scale, fleshed-out future worlds that, because of the reader's immersion in this fictive world and its characters, perhaps manage to impress the reader as much as public discussions on climate change or the

---

[1] Cf. Adam Roberts, *Science Fiction*, The New Critical Idiom (London and New York: Routledge, 2000), p. 10.

[2] Damien Broderick quoted in Roberts, *Science Fiction*, p. 8.

[3] See http://www.ballardian.com/sterling-on-ballard (16 December 2011).

[4] Brian Stableford provides an interesting introduction to aspects of ecology in Science Fiction in "Science Fiction and Ecology", in: *A Companion to Science Fiction*, ed. David Seed David (Malden, Massachusetts: Blackwell, 2008), pp. 127-141. See also Timothy Clark, *The Cambridge Introduction to Literature and the Environment* (Cambridge: Cambridge University Press, 2011), p. 10.

dangers of genetic engineering. Or, in other words, it is through fictitious environmental catastrophe that the treasure at risk becomes the more visible to the reader.

Recent environmental dystopias display a wide variety of sinister future developments. They examine the boundaries between the natural and the artificial, focus on the manipulation of both human and non-human biology, explore the results of nuclear catastrophe or climate change, and they also address issues of authority and gender. Indeed, both the prophetic quality of Science Fiction and the concept of environmental risk are bound up with the idea of futurity, since they are likewise not about "that it is happening, but that it might be happening".[5]

Since the turn of the millennium, Anglophone literature has dwelt extensively on the topic of environmental disaster and global breakdown, with some prominent examples being Margaret Atwood's novels *Oryx and Crake* (2003) and *The Year of the Flood* (2009), Maggie Gee's *The Flood* (2004), David Mitchell's *Cloud Atlas* (2004), Cormac McCarthy's *The Road* (2006), Jim Crace's *The Pesthouse* (2007), Suzanne Collins's young adult novel *The Hunger Games* (2008) and Tama Janowitz's *They is Us* (2009).

Contemporary discourse on the environment is to a large extent influenced by notions of risk. For this reason, examining the environment as a threatened treasure in Mitchell's and Atwood's texts will employ some broad lines of thought from risk theory. Of course, treasure and risk are intertwined: it is the defining characteristic of a treasure that it is at risk; otherwise it would lose its status. Sociological research has extensively focused on the 'culture of risk' as a determining feature of contemporary Western societies and has thereby provided productive approaches that have also become increasingly influential in the field of cultural and literary studies.[6] Anthony Giddens characterizes our age as being defined by a "climate of risk", in which we face "high-consequence risks" and in which "precise risk assessment is virtually impossible."[7] In his books *World Risk Society* (1999) and *World at Risk* (2009), the renowned sociologist Ulrich Beck has carved out a theory of the 'world risk society'.[8]

Beck describes the semantics of risk as "the present thematization of future threats that are often a product of the success of civilization" and further specifies risk as "the perceptual and cognitive schema in accordance with which a society mobilizes itself when it is confronted with the openness, uncertainties and obstructions of a self-created future [...]".[9] The world risk society, according to Beck, is defined by the fact that humanity is turning into a "global community of threats" that are no longer restricted to

---

[5] Barbara Adam and Joost van Loon, quoted in Gabe Mythen, *Ulrich Beck: A Critical Introduction to the Risk Society* (London: Pluto Press, 2004), p. 14.

[6] See Mythen, *Ulrich Beck*, p. 12. A recent overview of the representation of risk in the contemporary American novel is provided by Susan Mizruchi's "Risk Theory and the Contemporary American Novel", *American Literary History* 22 (2010), 119-135.

[7] Anthony Giddens, *Modernity and Self-Identity: Self and Society in the Late Modern Age* (Cambridge: Polity Press, 1991), pp. 123 and 137.

[8] It is of course impossible to give a comprehensive survey of Beck's concept of the world risk society in this paper. I will therefore restrict myself to highlighting those aspects of his risk theory that allow particularly meaningful insights into the representation of environmental risk in dystopian fiction.

[9] Ulrich Beck, *World at Risk* (Cambridge: Polity Press, 2009), p. 4.

the internal affairs of single countries, but cut across national, ethnic, cultural and social boundaries.[10] The status of the individual in this society, however, is precarious, since, as Beck accentuates, "he is severed from the decision contexts which escape his influence", and it is also increasingly difficult for the lay person to calculate risk in a world of rapid technological progress.[11] Beck further points out that risk as the anticipation of catastrophe is mediated to the public through a process of 'staging' that illustrates scenarios of possible catastrophes and thus makes risk 'tangible'.[12]

Beck's approach to risk offers fruitful perspectives on recent dystopian fiction which, like other forms of mediation, also participates in the process of the staging of environmental risk. Revealing the results of what could await humanity in a "'post-secure' world", environmental dystopias are essential texts that can engage the reader in a profound reflection on risks our societies face in a globalized world.[13] This essay will examine the representation of the treasure of the environment and its fragile or even doomed future in David Mitchell's *Cloud Atlas* and in Margaret Atwood's *The Year of the Flood*. It aims at showing how the prevailing imagery, but also the narrative structure and the place of Mitchell's and Atwood's novels within the generic boundaries of literary dystopias can be linked to the discourse of risk perception and Beck's concept of the world risk society. It will therefore investigate how the novels, in Beck's terminology, 'stage' environmental risk, providing the reader with a scenario of environmental apocalypse and possible forms of prevention.

David Mitchell, *Cloud Atlas* (2004)

Containing six separate, but loosely related narratives, the British author David Mitchell's novel *Cloud Atlas* is set on a 19th century Pacific island, a 1930s Belgian estate, in a 1970s Californian power plant and its vicinity, a contemporary retirement home in Hull, a futuristic eatery in Korea and, finally, a post-apocalyptic Hawaiian island. Despite its distinctly postmodern narrative structure which includes a variety of genres, narrative modes and media, the novel tells nothing less than the 'grand narrative' of humanity over a period of roughly eight centuries.[14] With its wide chronological and spatial scope, *Cloud Atlas* can be regarded as contributing to what Berthold Schoene views as the emerging genre of the 'cosmopolitan novel' where "nothing less, in fact, than the world as a whole will do as the imaginative reference

[10] Beck, *World at Risk*, p. 8.
[11] Beck, *World at Risk*, p. 170. See also Giddens, *Modernity and Self-Identity*, p. 138.
[12] See Beck, *World at Risk*, p. 10: "The distinction between risk as anticipated catastrophe and the actual catastrophe forces us instead to take the role of staging seriously. For only by imagining and staging world risk does the future catastrophe become present – often with the goal of averting it by influencing present decisions."
[13] Mythen, *Ulrich Beck*, p. 2.
[14] A detailed analysis of Mitchell's narrative inventiveness is provided in Courtney Hopf, "The Stories We Tell: Discursive Identity through Narrative Form in *Cloud Atlas*", in *David Mitchell: Critical Essays*, ed. Sarah Dillon (Canterbury: Gylphi, 2011), pp. 105-126.

point, catchment area and addressee [...]".[15] In what follows I will investigate how environmental risk is depicted in three of the five narratives of *Cloud Atlas* that foreground environmental issues: "Half-Lives", "An Orison of Sonmi ~ 451" and "Sloosha's Crossin'". It will be investigated how the narratives mediate risk and how the threatened treasure of the environment is represented both on a thematic and structural level.

In "Half Lives", whose title borrows a term from nuclear physics, humanity's experiment with radioactivity is at the very heart of the narrative. It delineates the successful investigation of an ambitious female journalist, Luisa Rey, into the dealings of an American corporation and its introduction of a new reactor at a nuclear plant in a fictional district in 1970s California. Mitchell constructs a scenario here which also holds a crucial place in the general discourse on environmental risk, since it is clearly the media which in the last decades "has been recognized as a primary source of public information about risk".[16] Thus, narrating a fictitious media investigation into the realm of nuclear technology offers the opportunity to explore meanings, functions and also metaphors of environmental risk in contemporary Western society.

Indeed, risk is omnipresent in this part of Mitchell's text and mainly operates on two levels, the personal and the collective. Firstly, due to their investigation into environmental risks, the protagonist and her helpers are permanently in danger of being prosecuted and even killed by the corporation's hitman. Secondly, the risk of impending nuclear catastrophe as a result of a defective nuclear plant continually looms in the background of the text. Risk is thus mediated as a part of individual biographies as well as a threat to the whole population of California. The characters themselves discuss risk as an option. When Luisa confronts her former boss with the fact that he has sacked her because of pressure from the board of the corporation, he replies:

> We all make choices about levels of risk. If I can protect my wife in return for playing a bit part in the *chance* of an accident at Swanneke, well, I'll have to live with that. I sure as hell wish you'd think a little more about the risk you're exposing *your*self to by taking these people on.[17]

The passage clearly divulges the two levels of risk within the text. The reporter's employer avoids risk and, by choosing individual well-being over collective safety, risks the possibility of radioactive fallout. Luisa's position is exactly the opposite of that of her employer. In another passage, Luisa considers her investigation an "acceptable degree of risk" (412). Within the narrative the high personal risk of those fighting for the truth reduces collective risk of nuclear breakdown.

Apart from Luisa's individual commitment, the narrative also depicts two other agents of resistance. Firstly, there is the scientist Dr Rufus Sixsmith who hands his report on the environmental risk of the nuclear plant to Luisa and thereby initiates her

---

[15] Berthold Schoene, *The Cosmopolitan Novel* (Edinburgh: Edinburgh University Press, 2009), p. 13.

[16] Mythen, *Ulrich Beck*, p. 74.

[17] David Mitchell, *Cloud Atlas* (London: Hodder and Stoughton, 2004), p. 433. Further references are given parenthetically in the text.

Risk and the Threatened Treasure of the Environment 137

interest in the case. He represents the scientific authority on risk assessment and has worked inside the corporation. In fact, his actions of resisting to cover up the environmental risk brought about by the new nuclear plant correspond to Beck's notion that "[t]he most influential opponent of the threat industry is the threat industry itself".[18]

Moreover, there is a group of activists who protest near the site of the nuclear plant and whose "tatty rents, rainbow-sprayed camper vans, and trailer-homes look like unwanted gifts the Pacific dumped here" (124). However, their demonstrations do not get sufficient public support (cf. 124ff.). It also becomes apparent here that the preservation of the threatened treasure through the elimination of risk falls primarily to a woman, the investigative journalist, which echoes the traditional link between femininity and nature in the patriarchal Western cultural tradition.

On the final pages of the story, the investigation into the life-threatening activities of the corporation is made public due to Luisa's individual research. The nuclear reactor is shut down as a result of extensive media coverage. With this, the narrative underlines the fundamental role of the media in the communication of risk, and it also corresponds to Beck's verdict that "daily newspaper reading becomes an exercise in technology critique".[19] Thus, within the boundaries of this single story, environmental risk is averted. However, from a broader perspective that includes the whole novel, the risk of not taking action that is embodied in Luisa's boss' decision to keep quiet about environmental danger appears programmatic. Due to its interlocking narrative structure, the reader already knows that the future will result in an uninhabitable radioactive world and thus in the loss of the treasure, so that the courage of individuals like Luisa Rey is meaningless against the overwhelming passivity or ignorance of the public. The victory over rapacious capitalism in 1970s California in "Half-Lives: The First Luisa Rey Mystery" is neutralized and dwarfed by the detailed depiction of ecological disaster in the following stories. Knowing the doom of the future world, the reader is not relieved at Luisa's success: individual effort ultimately appears futile in the larger context of human development.

Mitchell's novel also reflects on the treasure of the environment in relation to the post-human. "An Orison of Sonmi ~ 451" is the first narrative of the future which is set in 22nd-century 'Nea So Copros' (former Korea) and whose protagonist Sonmi is a genetically-engineered clone who performs lowly service tasks. The narrative consists of an interview in which Sonmi, imprisoned for fighting against the government, is questioned by an archivist who records their dialogue for posterity. In this highly polluted future world, clones are employed for tasks which cannot be performed by humans any longer, as Sonmi realizes in a conversation with one of her fellow fabricants, Wing ~ 027:

> "We operate in deadlands so infected or radioactive that purebloods perish there like bacteria in bleach." [...] I didn't even know what a deadland was. Wing ~ 027 xplained how these irradiated or toxic swathes force the Consumer and Production Zones to retrench, mile by mile. [...] The day when all Nea So Copros is deadlanded, he told me, will be the day of the fabricants. (215)

---

[18] Beck, *World at Risk*, p. 43.
[19] Beck, *World Risk Society*, p. 68.

The passage indicates a reversal in the assessment of 'treasures', since, in contrast to humans, it is the radioactive wasteland that is of value to the fabricants and will ensure their victory. The narrative here also returns to the theme of environmental risk introduced in "Half-Lives". Whereas "Half-Lives" shows the reduction of environmental risk in the United States in the 1970s, humanity's future in "An Orison of Sonmi ~ 451" is characterized by a high degree of environmental risk that not only threatens a particular region but the whole globe, thereby echoing Beck's description of the world risk society. The comparison of humanity to "bacteria in bleach" reduces humans to the status of objects and relegates power to the post-human. Humans are perceived by the post-human individual primarily in terms of economic exchange as producers and consumers, highlighting the impending environmental catastrophe as a consequence of ubiquitous consumption. The 'staging' of environmental risk is here undertaken by the clone Sonmi, who recalls her conversation with Wing ~ 027 in her interview with the archivist. Within the narrative it is the post-human replicant who is aware of global environmental risk and its danger to the treasure and who relates these to the human 'purebloods' kept in ignorance by the totalitarian government of Nea So Copros. As in "Half-Lives", it is again a female being, this time a replicant, who enlightens a largely ignorant public about the dangers of environmental pollution. With this, the nature-woman dyad in *Cloud Atlas* is even extended to a post-human level.

Applying Beck's concept of the world risk society to "An Orison of Sonmi ~ 451", it becomes clear that in Mitchell's portrayal of the hypercapitalist future the factors to which Beck ascribes a counterbalance to economic decision makers have not evolved. Whereas Beck proposes the development of a 'cosmopolitan democracy' with a "politically strong consciousness" and with "corresponding institutions of global civil society and public opinion", the future in *Cloud Atlas* does not provide an agency that has the power to combat rapacious capitalism.[20] Thus, risks have become bigger whereas society has become 'smaller'. Although the narrative centers on the fight of underground resistance groups, their concerns are primarily based on class and the distinction between artificial and human agents, but not on developing a consciousness of environmental risks and their implications. Humanity has not developed the strategies necessary to safeguard the treasure of an intact environment.

The climactic chapter of *Cloud Atlas*, "Sloosha's Crossin' an' Evry'thin After", is set in a post-apocalyptic future and deals with the adventures of a member of a Hawaiian tribe, Zachry. This final narrative contains, one can argue, the end of civilization and also the end of the creation of environmental risk as a man-made category. Nuclear disaster, genetic engineering and ecological catastrophe – all three "icons of destruction",[21] to use Ulrich Beck's terminology, have become reality and have produced their worst-case effects. Only the risk of further damage is effectively neutralized by humanity's return to primitivism. Without technology, society finds itself back again in a 'pre-industrial' (and at the same time post-industrial) phase in which,

---

[20] Beck, *World Risk Society*, p. 14.
[21] Beck, in Mythen, *Ulrich Beck*, p. 19.

according to Beck, risk is largely defined by natural hazards instead of the 'manufactured risk' of more technologically advanced societies.[22]

However, although the primitive tribes of the far future have no power to create environmental risks any longer, the legacy of industrialized society is still prevalent, as, for example, in the depiction of the baby born to the protagonist Zachry and his partner Jayjo: "The babbit'd got no mouth, nay, no nose holes neither, so it cudn't breath an' was dyin' from when Jayjo's ma skissored the cord, poor little buggah" (254). The harm of environmental catastrophe remains a burden on forthcoming generations which, as the narrative shows, continues long after the extinction of industrialized society. This is also perhaps the novel's most drastic illustration of 'risk antagonism', described by Beck as "a world of difference between the decision-makers [...] and the involuntary consumers of dangers, [...] unto whom the dangers are shifted as 'unintentional, unseen side-effects'".[23] "Sloosha's Crossin'" also upholds the importance of women as the keepers of the treasure. Firstly, Zachry's tribe is led by a woman. More importantly, the tribe itself comes under close scrutiny from foreign visitors, the last beacon of modernity, who still command digital technologies and who roam the oceans on a ship in search of surviving communities. As their messenger Meronym, a woman, explains, the tribe is regarded as precious, since it comprises the most civilised community that has survived the catastrophe. Thus, it can be argued that in a world where a (contaminated) wilderness reigns supreme again, it is civilisation itself that acquires the status of a threatened treasure.

The thematic representation of conflicts and environmental catastrophe in *Cloud Atlas* is augmented by the structure of the text. With its Russian doll structure of narrative composition, the disruption of each of the first five narratives by another one disturbs the reader's sense of narrative sequentiality. However, because of its 'broken' structure, the narrative powerfully supports the rising sense of humanity on its way to destruction, something that gradually unfolds in the course of the text. It also shows the interconnectedness of past, present and future, while simultaneously negating traditional Western perceptions of a teleological development towards a better future. This abandoning of narrative linearity, it can be argued, reflects the complexity of the postmodern and futuristic world, and it also emphasizes environmental risk as a diverse yet also global scenario.

Besides the novel's narrative structure, the outlook on the future of mankind in "Sloosha's Crossin' an' Evry'thin After" is augmented on the linguistic level by Mitchell's creation of a fictive future language that forces the reader to see the world even more through the eyes of the narrator, and that emphasizes the radical alterity of his world.[24] With its broken-down syntax, reduced vocabulary and oral nature, the

---

[22] Beck, *World at Risk*, p. 25.

[23] Beck, *World Risk Society*, pp. 75 and 195; see also Beck, *World at Risk*, p. 142.

[24] This technique of explicating the characteristics of future worlds through a radically different language is generally used in Science Fiction as a significant means of elaborating on the future and heightening the credibility of the alternative world model. See Dunja Mohr, "'The Tower of Babble'? The Role and Function of Fictive Languages in Utopian and Dystopian Fiction", in: *Futurescapes. Space in Utopian and Science Fiction Discourses*, ed. Ralph Pordzik (Amsterdam and New York: Rodopi, 2009), pp. 225-248 (p. 226).

dialect in Mitchell's chapter is the key to understanding the protagonist's world view. As well as this, it plays a role in illuminating humanity's post-apocalyptic condition. To conclude, the narrative structure together with the invention of a fictive language in *Cloud Atlas* represent structural defamiliarisations that correspond to the thematic direction of portraying an unknown future and thereby increase the power of Mitchell's staging of environmental risk.

As this exemplary investigation into the three narratives shows, environmental risk in *Cloud Atlas* is only reduced or eliminated by subsequent catastrophe. Technological development coupled with free-wheeling capitalism brings forth environmental risks that spiral out of control and end in a worst-case scenario, the destruction of the treasure. The novel thus defies the conventions of much of classical Science Fiction and of general storytelling: it is not the hero or the heroine whose risk-taking manages to eschew collective catastrophe and thus confirms the myth of individual sacrifice for the successful restoration of order. Whereas "Half-Lives" focuses on the local by depicting the struggle against the possibility of nuclear catastrophe in a specific region, the Sonmi chapter takes a global perspective, albeit a bleak one, since here the cosmopolitan impetus of a global society is absent. The post-apocalyptic scenario of "Sloosha's Crossin'", on the other hand, displays the end of environmental risk and industrial society alike. Thus, one could argue that *Cloud Atlas* sketches the expansion of the global risk society without the accompanying cosmopolitan consciousness necessary for the containment of environmental destruction.

Margaret Atwood, *The Year of the Flood* (2009)

Margaret Atwood's *The Year of the Flood* is set somewhere on the north-east coast of the United States in a future when nearly all humanity has died from a pandemic, man-made plague. It also contains some characters from Atwood's earlier novel *Oryx and Crake* (2003). As Hannes Bergthaller has pointed out, both novels suggest that "society is collapsing because it has failed to produce workable strategies for taming the human animal".[25] *The Year of the Flood* narrates the events before and after the catastrophe from the perspective of Toby and Ren, two members of an eco-religious sect, "God's Gardeners".[26] The philosophy of this group, who are generally despised by the public, centres on animal rights, ecological issues and veganism, and they can be regarded as 'treasure keepers' with respect to the environment. In the following, I will focus on how different groups in the text respond to environmental risk and the destruction of the natural world. I will also examine how the text's narrative structure and generic characteristics tie in with the thematic aspects of the novel.

---

[25] Hannes Bergthaller, "Housebreaking the Human Animal: Humanism and the Problem of Sustainability in Margaret Atwood's *Oryx and Crake* and *The Year of the Flood*", *English Studies: A Journal of English Language and Literature* 91:7 (2010), 728-743 (732).

[26] Margaret Atwood, *The Year of the Flood* (New York: Doubleday, 2009), p. ix. Further references are given parenthetically in the text.

The text can be divided into the chapters that deal with society shortly before the pandemic and the period after the pandemic when the two protagonists and narrators Toby and Ren struggle for survival – information that is given in separate, alternating narratives. Although the leader of the sect is a man, the fact that the world is depicted through the eyes of two female members of God's Gardeners, Toby and Ren, can again be linked to the nature-woman dyad, opposed to the male-dominated world of science as represented by Crake.

It seems that the pre-catastrophic world Atwood depicts is Ulrich Beck's risk society running wild, with the environmental risks becoming so tangible that the upcoming catastrophe looms large. Gene-spliced life forms like a lion-lamb hybrid are created, environmental pollution is endemic, and powerful corporations have replaced democratically elected governments. The threats of environmental catastrophe or genetic engineering are augmented by signs of imminent social collapse. Since the Gardeners have to struggle in a hostile urban environment, tension in the novel largely centres on the conflicts between their lifestyle and that of mainstream society.

One of the most striking features of Atwood's dystopian future is the clear-cut separation between what can be regarded as 'high-risk' and 'low-risk' zones. The wealthy have erected their own compounds, which are hermetically sealed off from the public and serve as an autonomous microcosm in which all the commodities of advanced technology are available to residents. These compounds, it can be argued, represent the attempt to minimize risk for the risk-generators, selling the idea that global risk can be averted if you live in the right area. In sharp opposition, the urban areas, called 'pleeblands', are virtually lawless zones where rampant consumption goes hand in hand with crime, poverty and gang warfare. When some characters in the novel manage to transcend the boundaries between high-risk and low-risk zones, it involves a complete change of lifestyle.

This erection of low-risk zones in *The Year of the Flood* can be described with Andrew Szasz's concept of 'inverted quarantine', which captures "the ability of the privileged to create a protected zone to keep them safe from the escalating environmental and human destruction caused by rampant economic exploitation of the earth and life on it".[27] Szasz further points out that this attitude shows that "people act not as political subjects, not as citizens, but as consumers who seem interested only in individual acts of self-protection".[28] The strict spatial separation of the rich from the poor has been a common feature of dystopian literature, neatly detaching the seemingly intact bourgeois world from its sinister underbelly, and thereby extrapolating contemporary urban processes of both gentrification and slumification.[29] In Atwood's novel, the elite as the most powerful group among potential treasure keepers has shunned its ecological responsibilities by a strict spatial separation.

---

[27] Andrew Szasz, "The Dangerous Delusions of Inverted Quarantine", *Chronicle of Higher Education* (25 January 2008), B12.

[28] Szasz, "Dangerous Delusions", B12.

[29] H.G. Wells's genre-defining narrative *The Time Machine* (1895) can be regarded as a powerful model of the literary depiction of a class-based separation of the population. Recent novels that employ this scenario are, for example, Mitchell's *Cloud Atlas* and Jeanette Winterson's *The Stone Gods* (2007).

142   Oliver Lindner

However, the state of inverted quarantine with its effort to exclude risk is finally exposed as an illusion, since the pandemic manages to enter even the most fiercely guarded compounds. It illustrates Beck's notion of the world risk society and the 'democratic' nature of global risk.[30] After the plague has left only few survivors, the protagonists are confronted with the risks of pre-industrial society: hunger, dangerous animals, storms or human predators. Nature, in particular, regains its status as a primary threat, but it is nature shaped by genetic engineering, with new, lab-generated animal organisms, and it can therefore be regarded as a 'spoiled treasure' that stands in stark contrast to the ecological convictions of the God's Gardeners.

Resistance to the rapacious nature of unlimited capitalism and thus the destruction of the treasure in *The Year of the Flood* rests in two main groups, the Gardeners as well as the individual Crake, the hyperintelligent scientist.[31] The lifestyle of 'God's Gardeners' themselves, with its technophobia and its praise of primitivism, comprises an attempt to minimize environmental risk, an alternative version of living that erases the 'manufactured risk' of human origin. It is only by a deliberate return to nature that, as the sect claims, all man-made dangers can be averted, although, as Bergthaller argues, "their efforts to minimize their own ecological footprint are utterly insufficient to ward off the larger environmental collapse".[32] Even more extreme than what Beck has described as the condition of uncertainty and not-knowing that the individual faces in the world risk society, the Gardeners as well as mainstream society have nearly no access to information about environmental risk. This is apparent in the sect's excessive use of sermons and liturgy and their blurry expectation of an upcoming "Waterless Flood" (312), but also in Toby's reflections on the almighty corporations and her claim that "nobody knows what they're doing. They're locked into those Compounds of theirs, nothing gets out..." (105). All in all, despite their effort to revive an ecological balance in pockets of the cities, their power as treasure keepers is marginal.

The more powerful threat to the society and its destructive consumption in the novel is located in the scientist, who is part of an elite that, bereft of ethical considerations, constructs hybrid species. Crake manages to create a group of genetically modified humans who are specifically trained to establish themselves in a post-apocalyptic world and to replace humanity. After finishing the production of the 'new man', the scientist initiates a lab-generated pandemic that leads to the near-extinction of humanity and the end of modern society. From the perspective of environmental risk, Crake's vision suggests that the destruction of the environment can only be stopped by changing the genetic disposition of humanity to suppress violence, greed and the lust for power altogether. Regarding the perception of the environment as a threatened treasure, Crakes vision aims to restore the treasure while at the same time it eliminates its perception. His lab-generated humans, unaware of mankind's cultural and economic history, will not grant the quality of a treasure to the environment.

---

[30] Cf. Beck, *World at Risk*, p. 8; cf. also Giddens, *Modernity and Self-Identity*, p. 142.

[31] Crake's actions as a scientist are more properly explored in Atwood's earlier novel *Oryx and Crake*, which narrates the breakdown of society as a result of the self-induced pandemic through the eyes of a different protagonist.

[32] Bergthaller, "Housebreaking the Human Animal", 738.

Resembling Mitchell's depiction of the hypercapitalist future in the narrative "An Orison of Sonmi ~ 451", with whom the world of *The Year of the Flood* shares many characteristics, society in Atwood's novel lacks a widespread and organized movement that acts against the imposition of environmental risk by the corporations and the government. Indeed, Beck's notion of the 'cosmopolitan democracy' as a form of resistance against the decision makers and producers of environmental risk is replaced by a highly stratified society, in which public discourse is dominated by shallow entertainment and rampant consumerism. The fight of the "urban green-guerilla scene" (267) and the eco-warriors among the more radical followers of the Gardeners appears as a form of underground activity that fails to catch the attention of a broader public.

The theme of environmental dystopia in Atwood's novel is mediated through a strategy of narrative fragmentation and generic hybridity so that the reader enters a fictional universe only accessible in pieces, resembling the precarious status of the treasure of the environment.[33] The novel opens with a song text out of "The God's Gardener's Oral Hymnbook". These song texts occur throughout the novel as part of the sermons by Adam One, the leader of the sect, which punctuate the narrative and can be regarded as a form of staging a new master-narrative of humanity. With their mixture of religious contemplations, everyday instructions and an all-too-benevolent interpretation of community life, the sermons display naivety and are a major source of irony in the novel. The frequent flashbacks and the switch between the different time levels, tenses and between the voices of Ren, Toby and Adam One also fracture the narrative. These narrative voices show competing discourses, presenting three different versions of the catastrophe from which the reader has to extract meaning, and they continually break up linearity and narrative authority. In particular, the construction of the God's Gardener's own calendar with days assigned to innumerable Saints defamiliarises the reader's notions of time. Atwood's postmodern, experimental writing is, one could argue, particularly suitable for a dystopian representation of environmental risk in the twenty-first century, since its rejection of narrative authority as well as its focus on multiple perspectives and its open ending mirror the fragmented nature of knowledge and the 'staging of reality' that Beck has characterized as a major feature of the world risk society.[34]

Conclusion

Margaret Atwood considers her novel fiction, but, as she claims, "the general tendencies and many of the details are alarmingly close to fact" (433). It is this proximity to facts that make literary environmental dystopias vital contributors to the contemporary discourse on risk perception. Both Mitchell and Atwood have staged environmental risks and created a future world where the manufactured risks of genetic engineering

---

[33] See Bouson J. Brooks, "'We're Using Up the Earth. It's Almost Gone': A Return to the Post-Apocalyptic Future in Margaret Atwood's *The Year of the Flood*", *The Journal of Commonwealth Literature* 46:1 (2011), 9-26 (11).

[34] Beck, *World at Risk*, p. 10; see also Beck, *World Risk Society*, pp. 14 and 70.

144   Oliver Lindner

and environmental pollution have resulted in the end of modern society and ushered in a new pre-industrial age in which risk once again resides primarily in natural hazards. With this, they offer gloomy versions of the future of technological society: its environmental risks are portrayed as ultimately unmanageable. Both novels delineate the rapacious nature of capitalism without the necessary accompaniment of a global culture of responsibility towards the threatened treasure of the environment.

Along with many other literary environmental dystopias published in the last decade, *Cloud Atlas* and *The Year of the Flood* comprise, as readers' opinions on the internet testify, important cultural texts that can contribute to bringing environmental issues to the very core of public opinion.[35] They mediate what Beck has described as "the anthropological shock experience of the vulnerability of the foundations of the civilized world".[36] Moreover, in displaying the self-induced downfall of technological societies, both authors' extrapolations also correspond to what some historians define as the great dilemma of progress: social development nourishes the very forces that undermine it.[37]

As literary texts, the novels are, as Steven Rosendale claims, "primary locations where human relationship to the environment can be understood and perhaps altered".[38] Reflecting on the general attractiveness of environmentalism as a mobilizing force, Richard Kerridge has argued that

> [u]nlike feminism, with which it otherwise has points in common, environmentalism has difficulty in being a politics of personal liberation or social mobility. [...] Environmentalism has a political weakness in comparison with feminism: it is much harder for environmentalist to make the connection between global threats and individual lives.[39]

Novels like David Mitchell's *Cloud Atlas* and Margaret Atwood's *The Year of the Flood* could be answers to this dilemma, despite their debatable gender constellations. Their linking of universal themes with individual lives offers a way of illustrating the hazards of environmental disaster on the level of individual biographies. Perhaps more importantly, the texts' narrative and thematic structure, in which many narrative fragments present a comprehensive commentary of humanity's sinister future, manages to incorporate a challenging global vision. It also echoes the overall condition of the world risk society, in which the certainties of absolute knowledge as well as absolute safety have evaporated.

Finally, beyond raising the reader's awareness of the risks of global environmental destruction, the novels emphasize that our age requires a rethinking of concepts such as

---

[35] For example, amazon provides many commentaries by customers on Mitchell's and Atwood's novels, many of which stress the role of the novels as warning voices.

[36] Beck, *World at Risk*, p. 70.

[37] See, for example, Ian Morris, *Why the West Rules – For Now: The Patterns of History and What They Reveal about the Future* (New York: Farrar, Straus and Giroux, 2011), p. 195.

[38] Steven Rosendale, "Introduction", in: *The Greening of Literary Scholarship*, ed. Steven Rosendale (Iowa City: Iowa University Press, 2002), pp. xv-xxix (p. xxviii).

[39] Richard Kerridge, "Introduction", in: *Writing the Environment: Ecocriticism and Literature*, ed. Richard Kerridge and Neil Sammels (London: Zed Books, 1998), pp. 1-9 (p. 6).

'state' or 'nation' whose geographically and politically limited sphere seems inadequate when it comes to dealing with the challenges of the global risk society. It can be argued, then, that texts like *Cloud Atlas* and *The Year of the Flood* can be regarded as a contribution to Beck's cautiously optimistic notion of the 'cosmopolitan moment' of the world risk society.[40] This, as Beck explains, entails an increasing consciousness of global responsibilities, mutual interdependence, global citizenship and "the irreversible non-excludability of those who are culturally different".[41] With their bleak scenarios, the contemporary literary dystopias of Mitchell, Atwood and many others show what the price we have to pay could be if this movement towards global responsibility fails to come into being and potent treasure keepers remain absent.

[40] Beck, *World Risk Society*, p. 47.
[41] Beck, *World at Risk*, p. 56; see also Beck, *World Risk Society*, p. 70.

Ellen Grünkemeier

Antiretroviral AIDS Medication in South(ern) Africa – a Treasure?

Introduction

While it might seem unusual to discuss HIV/AIDS and antiretroviral medication in terms of a 'treasure', the concept can still be made productive as an analytical category in this context. Yet, to meet the cultural and historical specificities of the epidemic in South(ern) Africa, the notion of a 'treasure' needs to be negotiated and redefined. Exploring further connotations of treasures from a postcolonial and cultural studies perspective, this article shall approach the issue from an angle that adds to the other contributions in this volume.

Although neither cure nor vaccine is available, HIV/AIDS need no longer be a death sentence because the syndrome can be medically managed and thus turned into a chronic condition. Antiretroviral medication helps to halt the advent of AIDS and to reduce the frequency and severity of AIDS-defining illnesses such as pneumonia (*pneumocystis carinii*), a rare cancer called Kaposi's sarcoma, encephalitis, lymphoma, oesophageal thrush or other fungal infections.[1] In order to minimise the replication of the virus and to reduce the risk of drug resistance, different drugs, commonly referred to as highly active antiretroviral therapy (HAART), are usually taken in combination rather than as a monotherapy. Since the 1990s, the biomedical standardised care of HIV/AIDS has come to comprise life-long antiretroviral therapy and additional pharmaceutical drugs to treat opportunistic diseases. In 1995, HAART was shown to be effective; in 1997, the first antiretroviral programme was introduced in Africa, in Kampala, Uganda; and in 2004 a public rollout was initiated in South Africa after much political controversy.[2]

Despite the treatment's obvious benefits, there are some major drawbacks to antiretrovirals, especially their costs, side effects and interactions with other drugs. To make the drugs most effective, people have to adhere to a strict regimen and have to schedule their eating habits accordingly, which is why the therapy easily interferes with their social and professional lives. Nonetheless, as antiretroviral mediation is 'life-

---

[1] Theresa McGovern and Raymond A. Smith, "AIDS, Case Definition of", in: *Encyclopedia of AIDS*, ed. Raymond A. Smith (New York: Penguin, 2001), pp. 32-36; George Manos, Leonardo Negron and Tim Horn, "Antiviral Drugs", in: *Encyclopedia of AIDS*, pp. 51-53.
[2] Nicoli Nattrass, *Mortal Combat: AIDS Denialism and the Struggle for Antiretrovirals in South Africa* (Scottsville: University of KwaZulu-Natal Press, 2007), p. 17.

148   Ellen Grünkemeier

saving', it can metaphorically be considered a 'treasure'. While the drugs are widely
available in North America and Europe, antiretrovirals are of yet greater 'value' in other
and less privileged parts of the world such as Sub-Saharan Africa where HIV
prevalence is high[3] but where access to medication is – for a number of reasons – still
limited. Not only is the AIDS medication 'valuable' for those who take the medicine but
also – in monetary terms – for the multinational pharmaceutical companies that develop,
manufacture and sell antiretrovirals. Focussing particularly on South Africa, I will use
the treasure metaphor as an analytical category to explore different perspectives on the
'value' of AIDS medication. In so doing, I will take into consideration global
imbalances of power and capital. To set the ground for the analysis of literary texts, I
will first sketch relevant statistical figures as well as political and social responses to the
HIV/AIDS epidemic.

Statistics

Recent statistics make apparent why sub-Saharan Africa is an appropriate centre of
attention. The region has been most heavily affected by the virus: an estimated 22.9
million people live here with HIV/AIDS and the countries with the highest HIV
prevalence worldwide are all located in this area.[4] The area "accounted for 67% of HIV
infections worldwide, 68% of new HIV infections among adults and 91% of new HIV
infections among children. The region also accounted for 72% of the world's AIDS-
related deaths in 2008."[5] These figures indicate the impact HIV/AIDS has had on sub-
Saharan Africa; and yet, wide variations within and between the countries are not to be
disregarded.

According to the UNAIDS World AIDS Day Report 2011, out of South Africa's
total population of about 49 million, approximately 5.2 million South Africans of all age
groups are HIV positive.[6] Comparing the findings of national health surveys from 2002,
2005 and 2008, it becomes evident that the overall prevalence has stabilised at

[3] In Sub-Saharan Africa, HIV prevalence is high not only among men but also among women and
children. In Europe and North America, by comparison, homosexual men, prostitutes, drug users
and other marginalised social groups are considered to be 'at risk'; they are set apart from 'the
general population' and blamed for the spread of the virus. For a discussion of the power implied
in this terminology, see Jan Zita Grover, "AIDS: Keywords", in: *AIDS: Cultural Analysis,
Cultural Activism*, ed. Douglas Crimp (Cambridge, Massachusetts: MIT Press, 1988), pp. 17-30.
In analogy to Raymond Williams's *Keywords: A Vocabulary of Culture and Society* (London:
Croom Helm, 1976), Grover identifies and scrutinises recurrent terms used across medical,
political and media discourses to discuss HIV/AIDS.
[4] UNAIDS, World AIDS Day Report 2011 (Geneva: UNAIDS, 2011), p. 10. <http://
www.unaids.org/en/media/unaids/contentassets/documents/unaidspublication/2011/JC2216_Worl
dAIDSday_report_2011_en.pdf> (20 November 2012).
[5] UNAIDS, AIDS Epidemic Update: November 2009 (Geneva: UNAIDS, 2009), p. 27.
<http://data.unaids.org/pub/Report/2009/JC1700_Epi_Update_2009_en.pdf> (1 June 2010).
[6] Fußnote: UNAIDS, World AIDS Day Report, p. 7.

approximately 11%.[7] Although variation between men and women is notable particularly in younger age cohorts, women still face a higher risk of infection in almost all age groups. The results of the three surveys show persistently high levels of HIV prevalence among women, increasing rapidly with age, reaching 6.7% among 15–19-year-olds, 21.1% among 20–24-year olds and peaking at 32.7% among 25–29-year-old women.[8] For males, by comparison, the epidemic curve peaks at 25.8% among 30–34-year olds. Not only does the epidemic vary in its impact on men and women but also on South Africa's nine provinces. As for regional estimates, HIV prevalence is lowest in Western Cape (3.8%), Northern Cape (5.9%) and Limpopo (8.8%), followed by Eastern Cape (9%), Gauteng (10.3%), North West (11.3%) and Free State (12.6%) and highest in Mpumalanga (15.4%) and KwaZulu-Natal (15.8%).[9]

In spite of scientific achievements and the medical progress of antiretroviral treatment, AIDS is still one of the leading causes of death in South Africa. In 2011, an estimated 43% of deaths were related to HIV/AIDS.[10] This high mortality rate can only be explained by the fact that of those people in need of medication, only about 40% received antiretrovirals.[11] In absolute numbers, about 568,000 South Africans received treatment by mid-2008, almost 80% of whom obtained their medication through the public sector.[12] By comparison with figures for previous years, the constant and considerable progress in the accessibility of treatment becomes evident. National coverage in adults was estimated to be less than 5% in 2004, prior to the rollout of medication through the public health care system, and achieved about 10% in 2005, 19% in 2006, 28% in 2007 and 40% in 2008.[13] The percentage of AIDS-related deaths decreased between 2005 and 2011 from about 52% to 43%, suggesting a positive trend which can be attributed to antiretroviral therapy.[14] Access to medication has also had a positive impact on life expectancy estimates. Between 2001 and 2005, life expectancy had declined but has since increased due to the rollout of medication so that for 2011, life expectancy at birth is estimated at approximately 55 years for men and 59 years for women.[15] These figures underscore the notion of antiretrovirals as a 'treasure'.

To understand the comparatively late and insufficient provision of AIDS medication through the public health care system, it is necessary to scrutinise governmental AIDS policies.

---

[7] Olive Shisana et al., eds, *South African National HIV Prevalence, Incidence, Behaviour and Communication Survey, 2008: A Turning Tide among Teenagers?* (Cape Town: Human Sciences Research Council, 2009), p. 30.

[8] Shisana et al., *South African National HIV Prevalence*, pp. 30-31.

[9] Shisana et al., *South African National HIV Prevalence*, p. 32.

[10] Statistics South Africa, "Mid-Year Population Estimates 2009" (Pretoria: Statistics South Africa, 2009). 8.
<http://www.statssa.gov.za./Publication/ statsdownload.asp?PPN=P0302&SCH=4437> (1 June 2010)

[11] Muhammad A. Adam and Leigh F. Johnson, "Estimation of Adult Antiretroviral Treatment Coverage in South Africa", *South African Medical Journal* 99.9 (2009), 661-667 (665).

[12] Adam and Johnson, "Estimation of Adult Antiretroviral Treatment Coverage", 663-64.

[13] Adam and Johnson, "Estimation of Adult Antiretroviral Treatment Coverage", 665.

[14] Statistics South Africa, "Mid-Year Population Estimates 2009", 8.

[15] Statistics South Africa, "Mid-Year Population Estimates 2009", 7.

Political Responses to the HIV/AIDS Epidemic

The first democratically elected South African government under Nelson Mandela (1994-1999) did not make HIV/AIDS a priority as it attended to more immediate challenges of the political transition in an attempt to construct a 'New South Africa'.[16] Compared to the Mandela administration, the spread of the virus could no longer be overlooked during Thabo Mbeki's presidency. The government under Mbeki was therefore expected to develop and implement effective strategies to monitor and curb the epidemic. However, especially in his first term as President (1999-2004), Mbeki's stance on HIV/AIDS caused major political controversy. Although he has meanwhile distanced himself from his earlier denialist views, Mbeki's past connections, decisions, pronouncements and silences have continued to shape the ambiguous public perception of HIV/AIDS in South Africa. "Views that had previously existed as 'fringe notions' in the global AIDS debate were brought into mainstream South African AIDS policy deliberations."[17] Although Mbeki has never publicly denied a possible link between HIV and AIDS, his distrust of mainstream AIDS sciences became obvious when he sided with dissident scientists who called into question that HIV causes AIDS.[18]

Controversies about the virology of AIDS also resulted in debates about medication and in questions of whether antiretrovirals are the best possible therapy. The repercussions of this dispute are not to be underestimated because treatment is a key issue with consequences for the social stigmatisation of the virus and of people living with HIV/AIDS. "The availability of treatment would sever the link between AIDS and death and begin to undo the fear and shame that prevent open discussion."[19] The government under Thabo Mbeki regarded antiretrovirals as toxic and questioned whether the benefits of this treatment would really outweigh its risks and side effects. Manto Tshabalala-Msimang, the Minister of Health in Mbeki's administration, sustained this argument. Sceptical of drug-based strategies for managing the epidemic, she supported alternative dietary interventions. While nutritionally rich and balanced food is, of course, beneficial for all people regardless of their HIV status, Tshabalala-Msimang focussed on particular dietary components: she advocated a healthy nutrition of beetroot, lemon, garlic and African potato, which is why she was nicknamed 'Dr Beetroot'.[20] Following the logic of this argument, antiretrovirals are not a 'treasure' but

---

[16] Helen Schneider, "On the Fault-Line: the Politics of AIDS Policy in Contemporary South Africa", *African Studies* 61.1 (2002), 145-167 (146). John Iliffe, *The African Aids Epidemic: A History* (Oxford: James Currey, 2006), pp. 142-143. Nattrass, *Mortal Combat*, p. 40.

[17] Suzanne Leclerc-Madlala, "Popular Responses to HIV/AIDS and Policy", *Journal of Southern African Studies* 31.4 (2005), 845-855 (849).

[18] For example, Peter Duesberg and David Rasnick, two internationally renowned dissidents, were included in Mbeki's Presidential Advisory Panel on AIDS which they used as a forum to circulate their opinions that there is no connection between HIV and AIDS, that antiretrovirals are toxic and blood tests inaccurate (Leclerc-Madlala, "Popular Responses", 849).

[19] Liz Walker, Graeme Reid and Morna Cornell, *Waiting to Happen: HIV/AIDS in South Africa – the Bigger Picture* (Cape Town: Double Storey, 2004), p. 127.

[20] Some of these nutritional interventions may even be harmful to people living with HIV/AIDS. The African potato was, for example, shown to weaken the immune system and to cause bone-

merely one treatment option. She thus prefers local alternative remedies to internationally accepted biochemical interventions. As evident in this debate, defining medical interventions as a 'treasure' is an act of power and thus likely to generate conflict. The idea of 'choosing' treatment has been highly controversial in the context of the South African HIV/AIDS epidemic as it implies different but equally effective and safe options. Nicoli Nattrass strongly disapproves of this "confusing discourse of 'choice'".[21] What she evaluates as 'confusing' are the false promises of the alleged 'choice' which result from simplified and limited descriptions.[22] Stressing that antiretrovirals do not heal HIV/AIDS and that they have unwanted side effects unlike a healthy diet, the Minister of Health presents them as inferior to the alternatives. As her statements are informed by unreflected assumptions about 'good' medicine, she can be said to confuse patients as to the most appropriate and reliable treatment option. This unbalanced presentation is not in keeping with the concept of 'choice' because people living with HIV/AIDS are not provided with all the research results and information necessary to weigh up different options.

Doubts about the safety and effectiveness of antiretrovirals are a major reason why the provision of medication through the public health care system was delayed. Nonetheless, the government's scepticism is not the sole reason. Bearing in mind the legacies of apartheid and South African socioeconomic realities, equitable access to treatment has posed major challenges that range from establishing, improving and maintaining health care facilities to meeting people's basic needs concerning, among others, nutrition, water, housing and social security.[23] Similar to these resource constraints, the costs of antiretroviral therapy were a crucial factor. As the prices for HAART fell considerably, however, the investment was no longer "an insurmountable obstacle. The decision not to provide them [antiretrovirals] is a social and political one, rather than economic."[24] In 2000, the costs of 4000 Rand per person and month had been too high for a universal rollout, but by 2003 they were down to 1000 Rand so that public-sector medication programmes were no longer unaffordable for South Africa's health care system.[25] Arguing that antiretroviral therapy had become "cost-effective if not cost-saving",[26] economists emphasise that government's resistance against antiretrovirals was not based on purely economic reasons but had, after all, clearly political overtones. Furthering this idea about the government's central motives, Iliffe speaks of "an insecure regime's anxiety to maintain control over a situation perceived as threatening".[27] He argues that government under Mbeki was apprehensive of political

---

marrow suppression in HIV-positive people; and both the African potato and garlic can interact with antiretrovirals, which is why they are not recommended for people who receive treatment (Nattrass, *Mortal Combat*, p. 143).

[21] Nattrass, *Mortal Combat*, p. 143.

[22] Nattrass, *Mortal Combat*, p. 143.

[23] Alex de Waal, *AIDS and Power: Why There Is No Political Crisis – Yet* (Cape Town: David Philip, 2006), p. 111.

[24] Walker, Reid and Cornell, *Waiting to Happen*, p. 126.

[25] Walker, Reid and Cornell, *Waiting to Happen*, pp. 126-127.

[26] Nattrass, *Mortal Combat*, p. 81.

[27] Iliffe, *The African Aids Epidemic*, p. 145.

opponents, social organisations, AIDS activists, scientists, pharmaceutical companies and the international public as they might pressurise the state into supplying antiretrovirals, "at the expense of its authority, its health priorities, and its wider development programme".[28] In his argumentation, Iliffe thus makes evident how questions of authority have shaped South Africa's AIDS policy. All in all, debates about the provision of antiretrovirals come down to the negotiation of costs as well as of political reputation and power.

To read AIDS medication in metaphorical terms as a 'treasure' would fall short of recognising the power relations that shape the realities of the South African HIV/AIDS epidemic. The conventional connotations imply that a treasure is extraordinary and accessible – possibly by means of violence – to a selected few only. In the context of HIV/AIDS, however, these implications need to be reconsidered: the call for a universal rollout of medication is inconsistent with the understanding of a treasure as unique. Paradoxically, however, the late and insufficient provision also adds to the value of antiretrovirals as they have not been accessible for everyone in need.

The controversies have frequently been described with war metaphors as a 'fight over medication', as a 'struggle', a 'battle' or, to cite the title of Nattrass's publication, as a 'mortal combat'.[29] Presenting the issue as a matter of life and death, these phrases highlight the seriousness of the epidemic for individuals, society and the state. The metaphors also mark AIDS medication as a 'treasure' for which it is worth fighting. In the late 1990s, the first major political and legal dispute between proponents of the medication and sceptical politicians was about particular antiretroviral drugs (Zidovudine and Nevirapine) that were shown to reduce the risk of mother-to-child transmission during pregnancy or delivery. Politicians were opposed to providing this medication, not least because of the high costs. They held on to this explanation even when the pharmaceutical manufacturers cut the price for poor countries by 75% and economists considered prevention programmes to be cheaper than treating HIV/AIDS in children.[30] In 2002, the controversy was finally settled when a Constitutional Court ruling ordered the Department of Health to provide a national prevention programme, finding that the government's policy had not met its constitutional obligation to advance adequate access to health care services.[31] Although antiretrovirals were then accessible for HIV-positive pregnant women to prevent an infection of their babies, the introduction of antiretrovirals for treating people living with HIV/AIDS caused another stir. Treatment programmes were not initiated until 2004 and made slow progress at first as they were not launched in all provinces until the end of 2005, albeit with varied

[28] Iliffe, *The African Aids Epidemic*, p. 145.

[29] Nattrass, *Mortal Combat*.

[30] Iliffe, *The African Aids Epidemic*, p. 143.

[31] Mark Heywood, "Current Developments: Preventing Mother-to-Child HIV Transmission in South Africa – Background, Strategies and Outcomes of the Treatment Action Campaign Case Against the Minister of Health", *South African Journal of Human Rights* 19 (2003), 278-315 (311-312). Nattrass, *Mortal Combat*, p. 98. Department of Health, "2008 National Antenatal Sentinel HIV & Syphilis Prevalence Survey" (Pretoria: National Department of Health, 2009), 24. <http://www.doh.gov.za/docs/reports/2009/nassps/index.html> (14 May 2010).

success.[32] In the Western Cape about every second person in need of antiretrovirals received the medicine, whereas in other provinces like KwaZulu-Natal, Mpumalanga, Free State and the Eastern Cape the coverage of therapy was much lower with about 20%, which means that only every fifth person in need of treatment received antiretrovirals.[33] By 2009, about 53% of the adults in need received therapy across the country.[34] Despite the positive trends, these figures also indicate that antiretroviral drugs can still be considered a 'treasure' because they are out of reach for a large group of people.

Unlike leading politicians of Mbeki's administration, South Africa's current President Jacob Zuma does not subscribe to dissident views on HIV/AIDS. Zuma's comments on the epidemic have met with public approval as they indicate political commitment and a break with the controversial standpoint long held and perpetuated especially by Mbeki and Tshabalala-Msimang.[35] In his presidential speech on the occasion of World AIDS Day 2009, Zuma spelled out his government's HIV/AIDS guidelines. He announced an earlier rollout of antiretrovirals: starting April 2010 every South African living with HIV/AIDS whose CD4+ count is 350 or less[36] qualifies for antiretroviral therapy.[37] Although it remains to be seen to what extent this programme will be implemented successfully and what effects it will have on the statistics of medical coverage with antiretrovirals, Zuma's AIDS policies have been received

[32] Nattrass, *Mortal Combat*, pp. 193-194.

[33] Nattrass, *Mortal Combat*, p. 131.

[34] Statistics South Africa, "Mid-Year Population Estimates 2009", 8.

[35] Despite his promising AIDS policy, Jacob Zuma became very much a talking point during his rape trial in 2006 when he admitted that he had had unprotected sexual intercourse with an HIV-positive woman and took a shower immediately afterwards to reduce the risk of infection. Backtracking on this statement after he was acquitted of rape, Zuma apologised for not being more responsible and using a condom (Nattrass, *Mortal Combat*, p. 170). Although respecting his regret, AIDS activists criticised that his apology cannot undo the effects of his behaviour and statements.

[36] Counting CD4+ cells, i.e. a particular kind of white blood cells that make up a central component of the body's defence system, is a means to measure immune system strength. People living with HIV/AIDS show a decreased number of these cells. The absolute figures describe the number of CD4+ cells per microlitre.

[37] Jacob Zuma, "Address by President Jacob Zuma on the Occasion of World AIDS Day" (1 December 2009) <http://www.anc.org.za/ancdocs/speeches/2009/sp1201.html> (2 February 2010).

In its HIV/AIDS treatment guidelines, the World Health Organisation (WHO) used to recommend that people living with HIV/AIDS commence treatment when their CD4+ count falls to 200 or lower, at which point symptoms of AIDS typically begin to show. Latest scientific findings, however, have proven that an earlier intervention with antiretrovirals reduces opportunistic diseases and death. In view of this evidence, WHO updated their treatment recommendations in 2009: HIV-positive people with a CD4+ count of below 350 are now advised to start therapy, regardless of their symptoms. World Health Organisation (WHO), "New HIV Recommendations to Improve Health, Reduce Infections and Save Lives" 30 November 2009. <http://www.who.int/mediacentre/news/releases/2009/world_aids_20091130/en/index.html>. (1 June 2010). The South African government under Zuma has already responded to these guidelines and updated its criteria of eligibility accordingly.

154 Ellen Grünkemeier

positively throughout South Africa because they are aimed at tackling and curbing the epidemic.

Social Responses to the Epidemic and to Governmental AIDS Policies

During Mbeki's presidency, discontent was growing in civil society, especially among AIDS activist groups, over what was thought to be an inadequate political response to the epidemic. In the controversies over the use of antiretrovirals for prevention and treatment, the Treatment Action Campaign (TAC), the "largest civil society body and the most effective national formation for organising people around HIV/AIDS in South Africa",[38] has taken on a particularly prominent role. In December 1998, Zackie Achmat and others founded this South African AIDS activist grassroots organisation which has strong human rights elements in that it campaigns for equal access to antiretroviral treatment and health care for people living with HIV/AIDS and for the prevention of HIV/AIDS. In its early years, TAC was mainly a "single-issue campaign",[39] promoting, as its name suggests, universal access to antiretroviral treatment. In its newsletter, TAC makes evident why the activists prefer antiretrovirals to alternative remedies although the infection is still not fully understood and although a healthy diet might also have a positive impact on people living with HIV/AIDS.

> TAC respects people's right to choose the course of treatment they follow according to their belief. But this is only part of the story. People with life-threatening illnesses are vulnerable and desperate. This despair allows for families, elders, leaders, opinion makers and health professionals to influence 'choices'. We urge individuals and families to take informed decisions based on scientific evidence. While certain herbal and other remedies may alleviate AIDS symptoms, no evidence yet exists to show they are equally safe and effective alternatives to antiretroviral medicines.[40]

The activists stress that the concept of 'choice' is misleading. Unlike other remedies, antiretroviral therapy has been clinically tested and found safe and efficient. TAC implores South Africans to make informed decisions; but, left with no research results on alternative treatment and with no clear guidance by the government, South Africans have to negotiate the variety of therapies by themselves.

From the perspective of the international pharmaceutical industry, AIDS medication is a 'treasure' as it turns a substantial profit. The manufacturers were TAC's primary targets in the fight for affordable treatment because "the government could not possibly subsidize antiretroviral treatment until drug companies agreed to drop their prices – or their patents – in South Africa".[41] In 2001, the TAC activists sided with the South

---

[38] Leclerc-Madlala, "Popular Responses", 849.

[39] de Waal, *AIDS and Power*, p. 38.

[40] Treatment Action Campaign, "Newsletter: Choice and Desperation" 24 May 2006. <http://www.tac.org.za/community/node/2210> (1 June 2010).

[41] Samantha Power, "The AIDS Rebel. An Activist Fights Drug Companies, the Government – and His Own Illness", *New Yorker* 19 May 2003. 54-67 (60).

African government in a legal case with pharmaceutical companies over intellectual property rights and the use of cheap generic antiretrovirals to treat people living with HIV/AIDS in poor countries. The negotiation was finally successful as the manufacturers reduced the drug prices and allowed developing countries to produce generic versions.[42] Despite this promising outcome, the government under Mbeki did not start to implement national prevention and treatment programmes, although antiretrovirals had become feasible. In response to this delay, TAC filed a constitutional claim against the government. According to section 27 of the South African Constitution (1996), the state is under an obligation to promote access to health care, food, water and social security. TAC's legal representatives argued in court that this constitutional right could be extended to include antiretroviral treatment.[43] The activists finally secured a ruling that forced the government to provide antiretrovirals to HIV-positive pregnant women.[44] Although this ruling was a major victory, TAC continued to demand a more comprehensive rollout of antiretrovirals not only as a prevention strategy but also as AIDS treatment. As a means to achieve its ultimate aim, the activists launched a civil disobedience campaign in 2003: they organised demonstrations, occupied government buildings and police stations and interrupted speeches of leading politicians, especially Manto Tshabalala-Msimang.[45]

As these cornerstones in the organisation's history show, TAC's political strategies have been marked by a critical and pragmatic engagement with government's AIDS policies.[46] The organisation was "able to mobilise social and political pressure, as well as utilise the power of the courts to force government to alter its direction".[47] All in all, South Africa's "state policy on AIDS owes much to tireless efforts by this group to prompt government into action"[48] and TAC continues to hold the government accountable for comprehensive health care services for people living with HIV/AIDS.

Zackie Achmat, living with HIV/AIDS himself, politicised his own health status and drew attention to Mbeki's AIDS policy by refusing to take antiretrovirals. Taking on the role of a representative of the South African AIDS epidemic, he refused treatment until it became accessible to all citizens through the public health care system. As a well-known AIDS activist, his stance generated international publicity for the lack of access to medication. In 2003, *The New Yorker* published a long article on him, tellingly entitled "The AIDS Rebel. An Activist Fights Drug Companies, the Government – and His Own Illness".[49] The documentary film *It's My Life* in the *Steps for the Future* film

---

<http://www.ansafrica.org/images/zackie/newyorker.pdf> (30 November 2009).

[42] Steven Robins, "'Long Live Zackie, Long Live': AIDS Activism, Science and Citizenship after Apartheid", *Journal of Southern African Studies* 30.3 (2004), 651-672 (663).

[43] Steven Robins, Bettina von Lieres, "Remaking Citizenship, Unmaking Marginalization: the Treatment Action Campaign in Post-Apartheid South Africa", *Canadian Journal of African Studies / Revue Canadienne des Études Africaines* 38.3 (2004), 575-586 (579).

[44] Nattrass, *Mortal Combat*, pp. 95-100.

[45] Nattrass, *Mortal Combat*, pp. 114-115.

[46] Robins, von Lieres, "Remaking Citizenship", 581.

[47] Nattrass, *Mortal Combat*, p. 12.

[48] Leclerc-Madlala, "Popular Responses", 849.

[49] Power, "The AIDS Rebel".

collection also explores Achmat's provocative decision.[50] Shot over five months, the film combines private and public images of Zackie Achmat by including sequences filmed at his home, at friends' houses or his doctor's office, at TAC rallies and in court rooms as well as original footage from news programmes. One scene shows a telephone conference with his friends, colleagues and the TAC executive members during which Achmat explains his refusal, although he suffers increasingly from opportunistic diseases and it was time he went on antiretrovirals:

> My position is based on an understanding that I want a right of life for myself but I want the right of life and I want to live in a political community in which that right is extended to every person. If such a political community does not exist and the only reason that you die [...] is because you are poor when you are sick, then I do not want to be part of such – on a conscience basis and on a moral basis – I could not be part of such community.

Achmat clearly states his priorities and puts the needs of the community first. He adopts this provocative stance in the name of the majority of South Africans living with HIV/AIDS, namely poor, black people who would otherwise remain faceless and voiceless since they lack political power. While many South Africans look up to Zackie Achmat as a hero, some disapprove of his drug strike, arguing that such martyrdom is not productive. Yet regardless of what people think of the sacrifice, the protest actions convey his human rights agenda. Achmat is well aware of the life-saving potential of antiretrovirals; still, stressing the universal 'right of life', he is unwilling to enjoy the benefits as long as only a small group of privileged people has access to the therapy. Achmat's stance and the human rights policy of the Treatment Action Campaign in general indicate how some established connotations of the notion of a 'treasure' do not hold true for this particular context and therefore need to be appropriated.

Zackie Achmat's position is so well-known in and beyond South Africa that he has frequently served as a point of reference in literature, as the following discussion of representations of antiretrovirals will show. Drawing on a range of texts and genres, I will explore the complex representations of the AIDS medication. As creative constructs, literary texts can function as sites for a negotiation of meanings and as aesthetically mediated references to the realities in contemporary South(ern) Africa.

Literary Representations of AIDS Medication

Edwin Cameron, a judge in the Supreme Court of Appeal in South Africa, wrote about living with HIV/AIDS in his book *Witness to AIDS* (2005).[51] His life narrative is

---

[50] *It's My Life* (Dir. Brian Tilley, South Africa, 2001), Steps for the Future Series. This series is a collection of films about HIV/AIDS in Southern Africa. The films emerged out of a collaboration of Southern African and international film makers, AIDS organisations and people living with HIV/AIDS. Further information can be found online: www.steps.co.za.

[51] Edwin Cameron, *Witness to AIDS* (London: I.B. Tauris, 2005). Further references to this edition will be included in the text (abbreviated as '*WtA*').

organised thematically rather than chronologically; in eight chapters, two of which are co-written with Nathan Geffen, a leading TAC member, Cameron discusses personal experiences of living with the infection as well as several topics linked with the epidemic in South Africa: the spread of the virus in Africa, governments' responses to HIV/AIDS, access to and costs of antiretroviral treatment, the role of the pharmaceutical industry and the impact of patent laws.

After being diagnosed with AIDS in 1997, Cameron starts an expensive antiretroviral therapy. At that time, the public health sector did not supply medication, but as a well-paid judge he has 'choices' and is given a "second chance" (*WtA* 41) at life and health.[52] In analogy to his work as a judge, Cameron tries to apply the court's rules of honesty and objectivity in his life narrative: he considers varied arguments and perspectives, he spells out both the benefits and downsides of the therapy. Powerful as they are in fighting the viral load, antiretrovirals "unavoidably affect other body functions – upsetting the digestive system, causing painful nerve abreactions (tingling, numbness) and redistribution of body fat" (*WtA* 17). Regardless of the long list of possible side effects, the positive results of taking the drugs are apparent when Cameron manages to climb to the top of Table Mountain after only four weeks of treatment. Improving his health and enabling him to work as a judge in the newly democratic South Africa, antiretrovirals are of value to Cameron. Contrary to less affluent people who cannot afford this expensive combination therapy, Edwin Cameron stresses that he belongs to the privileged South Africans who can pay for and benefit from this treatment (*WtA* 15). Nonetheless, he does not favour exclusive access to this 'treasure' but wants all South Africans in need of medication to benefit from HAART.

Not only does Cameron explore his own experiences but includes varied voices and positions different from his own. He sketches Zackie Achmat's stance on medication as well as the story of Simon Nkoli, an ANC-member and homosexual activist who died of AIDS-related diseases in 1998. Nkoli started an antiretroviral therapy but without success. As for the treatment failure, Edwin Cameron reasons that Nkoli's virus had become resistant to the medication. Unlike the "drug-naïve" (*WtA* 57) Cameron who benefits from a combination therapy, Nkoli had taken antiretroviral drugs successively as single medications. "By the time Simon died at the end of 1998, it was clear that the drugs had saved my life" (*WtA* 55-56).

Edwin Cameron also considers the availability of medical treatment in connection with the TAC member Christopher Moraka, a black, unemployed man from Nyanga, a township about 25 kilometres outside of Cape Town. He uses Moraka's example to explain and criticise the impact of pharmaceutical patent laws. Like Cameron a few months earlier, Moraka suffers from oesophageal thrush, a painful fungal infection of the throat which makes it impossible to eat or drink properly and can be fatal if not

---

[52] In the first chapter tellingly entitled "Second Chances" (*WtA* 9), Cameron relates court cases in which appeals against convictions and sentences are negotiated. Neither the accused nor the offences seem to be linked with the infection in the least. Still, Cameron establishes such a connection. Similar to the accused, whose appeals resulted in second chances, Edwin Cameron hopes for a positive prospect. "I, too, yearned for a second chance at life" (*WtA* 28). Because of his privileged situation, the infection is not fatal for him. In his narrative he stresses that he would like all South Africans in need of medication to be given such a second chance.

158   Ellen Grünkemeier

treated. Describing his own experiences and treatment, Cameron writes, "But I was fortunate. Judges in South Africa have medical insurance, and the insurance covered expensive medication such as fluconazole [a successful treatment against thrush]" (*WtA* 158). As the conjunction 'but' indicates, Cameron does not generalise his case but – well aware of his privileges – sets himself apart from others. Unlike Cameron, Moraka is unemployed, does not have medical insurance and cannot afford fluconazole. In 2000, a few months before his death, Christopher Moraka addressed the Parliament health committee, pointing out how poor people are denied access to life-saving drugs because of unjust patent laws working in favour of pharmaceutical companies (*WtA* 157-60). His general argument is similar to the position of the South African government and TAC activists in their joint legal case with international manufacturers over the production and use of cheap generic antiretrovirals to treat people living with HIV/AIDS in poor countries. Supporting Moraka's stance, Cameron points out how expensive treatment is.

> When Christopher testified before Parliament [...], Pfizer's branded product Diflucan had come down in price by about one-third. But it still cost over R80 per day. The two-week prescription for Diflucan that Christopher needed, supplied from a private pharmacy, would run to the unimaginable sum of R1120 – almost as much as the average monthly income of a South African household. (*WtA* 158-59)

The excessively high prices are, as Cameron explains, a result of patent laws which allow pharmaceutical companies to hold the exclusive right to produce the drugs, and thereby secure large profits. The market for fluconazole was very lucrative; and any concessions might have had far-reaching consequences for Pfizer, not only in South Africa but also in other parts of the world (*WtA* 162).

In 2000, in an attempt to put pressure on pharmaceutical companies, TAC organised its first civil disobedience campaign, the Christopher Moraka Defiance Campaign. The activists wanted Pfizer either to reduce its prices or to give another manufacturer the permission to produce generic drugs. Although Pfizer rejected their demands, the activists were successful in the end: the company agreed to provide the drug free of charge in many of South Africa's public health care facilities. Cameron calls the settlement "a significant step, and a wise, public-spirited corporate move" (*WtA* 165). TAC's protests brought into international focus the inequality in access to AIDS medication. Drawing attention to the deadly consequences of intellectual property rights and drug pricing, the activists generated negative and unwelcome publicity for Pfizer and, by extension, for the pharmaceutical industry in general. The chapter in which Cameron – jointly with Nathan Geffen – addresses these issues is entitled "'We are not the Red Cross' – Patents, profits and death from AIDS" (*WtA* 157). Cameron quotes an executive vice-president of Pfizer who stresses the difference between humanitarian organisations and the pharmaceutical industry when he tells a reporter: "We are not the Red Cross. We are a for-profit company" (quoted in *WtA* 184). While Cameron clearly acknowledges that manufacturers cannot simply be turned into charitable institutions, he still calls for a compromise, namely "a system of intellectual property protection that protects consumers as much as it benefits large corporations" (*WtA* 184).

As these exemplary cases indicate, Edwin Cameron looks outward throughout his life narrative in order to examine the complexity of the epidemic in South Africa. The analysis of the working practices of the pharmaceutical industry is but one example of how Cameron circles out of the private realm of his own body and life and into the public sphere. His text reads like a well-researched statement in which complex issues are addressed, explored and criticised: the epidemiology and virology of HIV/AIDS, intellectual property rights and the government's response – or lack thereof – to the epidemic. Cameron thus contextualises his own experiences and stresses that he can enjoy the benefits of antiretroviral treatment because of his privileged position. His attitude suggests that he appreciates the medication as a 'treasure', without, however, undermining the human rights argument that a broader public of people living with HIV/AIDS should be able to get access to this 'exclusive' treatment.

In *Khabzela. The Life and Times of a South African*,[53] the South African journalist Liz McGregor traces the life story of Fana Khaba, a young black man who has become known as 'Khabzela', a popular disc jockey of Johannesburg's youth radio station Yfm. In April 2003, Khaba announced on air that he was HIV-positive. With the financial support of his employers Khaba could have afforded antiretroviral treatment prior to the public rollout of HAART in South Africa, but after trying the drugs for a couple of days he refused antiretrovirals and trusted in alternative remedies instead. In January 2004, at the age of 35, he died of AIDS-related diseases. Compared to Edwin Cameron, Fana Khaba does not consider himself particularly privileged when he is offered antiretrovirals. Instead, he understands them as one treatment option among others.

Introducing the subject matter, McGregor opens the book with a detailed and unabashed account of Khaba's death.

> Fana Khaba died a horrible death. The HI virus had destroyed his brain, leaving him demented and hallucinatory. He could no longer move his arms or legs. He could neither defecate nor urinate. The colostomy bag attached to his bowel to drain his waste was leaking blood. Pus seeped from the wound left by the operation to remove his intestines. A vast bedsore had eaten away his right buttock. More bedsores festered on his back, hips, ankles and elbows. (*Khab* ix)

In these first few sentences of the preface, the author enumerates various aspects of Khaba's physical condition, so that the readers are directly confronted with his death in all its ugliness and agony. Yet, going on to call his death "premature" (*Khab* ix) and "all the more tragic because it was preventable" (*Khab* ix), McGregor qualifies this opening description by contextualising his death. Unlike many other people living with HIV/AIDS, she argues, Khaba has had the chance to avert his death because he could have had access to antiretroviral treatment which he declined (*Khab* ix). Being in the powerful position to make decisions about his health and medication is a clear sign of Khaba's privilege, setting him apart from most black South Africans who are historically at the receiving end of power relations. After having decided against antiretroviral treatment, however, he is left with little time or space to act, as McGregor visualises in the metaphor of a roller-coaster ride. "Fana was on a roller-coaster to self-destruction" (*Khab* 3). The trope can be decoded as an illustration of various ups and

---

[53] Liz McGregor, *Khabzela. The Life and Times of a South African* (Auckland Park: Jacana, 2007 [2005]). Further references to this edition will be included in the text (abbreviated as '*Khab*').

160   Ellen Grünkemeier

downs in his health status as well as a loss of control and agency. No longer able to change direction or to stop the ride, Fana Khaba heads straight and inevitably towards his own death, for which the journalist holds Khaba himself responsible, as the word "self-destruction" shows. To McGregor, his death is, however, of less concern than seeking an explanation for his decision to decline treatment. She focuses on "the central paradox of his death – why he refused the drugs that might have saved him" (*Khab* xi). Similar to her description of his death as 'premature', 'tragic' and 'preventable', the term "paradox" also highlights that McGregor does not regard Khaba's behaviour as rational or self-explanatory, but rather as influenced by a mindset that is different from her own. She therefore sets out to explore his motives.

Faced with Fana Khaba's AIDS diagnosis, his employers at Yfm studio management show a supportive attitude. Although the DJ works as an independent contractor and is not on a medical aid plan, the Yfm managers offer to continue to pay his salary and medical expenses until he is well enough to return to his post as a presenter (*Khab* 158). In return, they expect Fana Khaba to start antiretroviral treatment and to take time off to recover. Unsurprisingly, it is not a humanitarian offer; Yfm has a stake in this arrangement. To the radio station, HIV/AIDS has always been a significant issue. In an attempt to AIDS-educate its listeners, Yfm began to put on air the show "Youth Crossfire" in which youth can discuss sexual issues (*Khab* 100). With one of their presenters living with the virus, the managers could take the AIDS debate further. They want Yfm to become the first South African radio station to broadcast a regular show on people living with HIV/AIDS, hosted by Fana Khaba. Although both sides would benefit from this arrangement, the managers do not reach their aims. Fana Khaba starts antiretroviral treatment but gives it up after a couple of days.

Fana Khaba himself does not give reasons for his decision. "'Why?' I [Liz McGregor] asked Fana. He pretended not to hear the question" (*Khab* 3). Recognising Khaba's "antipathy" (*Khab* 72) to antiretrovirals, McGregor comes across the similar yet different case of Zackie Achmat. While the TAC leader declined antiretrovirals for political and moral reasons, no such motive becomes apparent in Khaba's case. When interviewed by McGregor, Fana's mother Lydia Khaba states that Fana has never been political. Even in the face of the tumultuous period of the 1976 uprisings in Soweto,[54] she describes her son as "just neutral. He would never take a stand" (*Khab* 36). Nonetheless, Achmat presents Khaba as a fellow AIDS activist in his speech at the DJ's funeral. Not only does Zackie Achmat use this strategy, but, as Liz McGregor remarks critically, almost all the speakers enlist Fana Khaba for their own purposes and, at times, competing messages (*Khab* 18).

---

[54] On 16 June 1976, black students in Soweto protested against the directive of the Afrikaner National government that wanted to impose Afrikaans as the medium of instruction in township schools. While this language issue and its ideological implications occasioned the march, further aspects aggravated the situation and played into the unrest, such as rising unemployment and the housing shortage among the black population; T.R.H. Davenport, *South Africa: A Modern History* (London: Macmillan, 1987), pp. 430-435. The Soweto uprising was a watershed event in the liberation struggle for years to come because the Afrikaner government was not able to regain control of society. Nowadays the events are commemorated on the day of the initial outbursts as Youth Day, previously known as Soweto Day.

Trying to find explanations for his rejection of the drugs, McGregor interviews his companions. Greg Maloka, one of Fana Khaba's colleagues and the general manager of Yfm, provides McGregor with two possible explanations, both of which seem "equally persuasive" (*Khab* 160) to the journalist. Firstly, the decision might result from Fana Khaba's character traits such as "his refusal to accept what was offered to him and his determination to achieve his dreams" (*Khab* 160). Had it not been for these qualities, Fana Khaba would not have been able to work himself up and become a DJ. Yet in the case of HIV/AIDS, Greg argues, this willpower has turned into a stubbornness that is counterproductive to his recovery (*Khab* 160). Secondly, Khaba's aim was to become well and therefore, in Greg's words, the DJ was willing to "take whatever steps would make him better" (*Khab* 161). However, when Fana Khaba began to suffer from dementia and was therefore unable to make rational decisions, he was overburdened by the variety of possibilities and recommendations, which is why, as Greg supposes, "at some point, he got overpowered by a particular belief and he thought all those western medicines were not going to help him" (*Khab* 161). Following this reasoning, Khaba's drug refusal was not the result of an active decision-taking process but rather a way of coping with what he believed to be the necessity to decide between antiretrovirals and alternative treatment. Sibongile Radebe, Khaba's fiancée, emphasises that Fana Khaba did take antiretrovirals but then stopped after about a week. Starting to feel worse, he believed that they were going to kill him (*Khab* 151 and 181). Bearing in mind the heavy side effects that accompany antiretrovirals, particularly at the beginning of the treatment, it might not be surprising that Fana Khaba had the impression that the drugs harmed rather than helped him. Sibongile argues that antiretrovirals "couldn't do much in his body because he didn't believe in them" (*Khab* 181). This comment conveys Sibongile's holistic understanding of treatment, according to which physical ailments cannot simply be treated with pharmaceutical or biochemical interventions because mental and spiritual elements as well as confidence in the medication are equally important. Sibongile therefore accepts Fana Khaba's decision and does not put pressure on him to take antiretrovirals without believing in their efficiency.

McGregor goes on to analyse why Fana Khaba could not live with the side effects and continue the therapy. She argues that "[a]cknowledging how ill he was and submitting to the treatment required to make him well would have required a temporary surrender of his independence, a reversion to an infantile state" (*Khab* 150). This "surrender" or "reversion to an infantile state" would have meant that Fana Khaba was no longer in control over his own life but, instead, dependent on chronic medication and on the support of others. His family in general and his mother in particular would have had to take care of him and look after him as if he were a small child again. In an attempt to comprehend Fana Khaba's situation, McGregor also draws on her own background. For a few days each month, McGregor takes an HIV-positive child out of an orphanage (*Khab* 150-51). Looking after the boy, she realises the great effort and responsibility of taking care of his medication even though the orphan is very obedient and accepts whatever medicine she gives him. To make antiretrovirals work for Fana Khaba, McGregor argues, he would have had to behave in a similarly compliant way and "revert to childish submissiveness" (*Khab* 151). Contextualising the situation, McGregor illustrates how Fana Khaba would have struggled with such a position that would have gone against his self-image. Taking his professional career and future into his own hands, Fana Khaba managed to make his dream of becoming a radio presenter come true against all odds. Known as "the DJ of the poor" (*Khab* 102), he never made an effort to disguise his humble background but encouraged poor black South African youth to follow his example (*Khab* 111-15). Furthermore, weakness and inferiority are incompatible with gender roles, in which men take up the dominant role and exercise power over women.

As for the reasons why Fana Khaba turned away from antiretrovirals and to alternative medicine instead, Sibongile argues along similar lines as Greg Maloka; she believes that "at some point he just got desperate and took whatever people said would cure him" (*Khab* 151). In his distress, Fana Khaba would try anything that might help him and put him back into the position of a man in charge of his own life. In the case of Khabzela, a person of public interest in South Africa, seeking treatment has what appears to be an empowering effect. To promote their individual remedies and alleged cures, many people visit and flatter him, trying to convince him to give their particular treatment a try. "Once again," McGregor argues, "there were people fawning over him. He had power. He could make a healer famous by trying out his or her cure" (*Khab* 151). Like the journalist, Angie Diale and Masi Makhalemele, two women who work as AIDS counsellors and who accompany the DJ for six months, are able to see through the attention that he receives. "All these doctors, traditional healers – all wanted a piece of him. They knew they could become famous through him" (*Khab* 156). Being once more the centre of attention, Fana Khaba feels appreciated and respected. Presented with a 'choice' of treatment options, he seems to be tempted by the prospect of a cure, as his "healing odyssey"[55] suggests. Following Manto Tshabalala-Msimang's recommendations on HIV/AIDS, he explores various alternative medications, including nutritional interventions, remedies with grand labels like 'Amazing Grace' and 'Africa's Solution' as well as herbal remedies prescribed by an African healer. It thus becomes apparent that the DJ does not so much value his privileged access to antiretroviral medication but rather aims at regaining his influential position in society as a man to whom people look up. However, the situation is deceiving because the attention is, similar to Yfm's offer of antiretrovirals, based on a strong (commercial) self-interest. The DJ does not so much return to being an active and powerful man, but is instead turned into an object or brand. Similar to those speaking at his funeral, the practitioners have their own agenda and use Khabzela to market their product.

Bringing together diverse voices and arguments, McGregor highlights the complexity of the DJ's behaviour. To explain his reactions, she contextualises and evaluates her research by taking into account various factors: the social context of Khaba's (family) life, his deteriorating health and dementia, the side effects of antiretroviral therapy, his despair in trying to get healthy again and to return to his life as a DJ.

The Zimbabwean author and medical doctor Patrice Matchaba goes a step further in his novel *Deadly Profit*.[56] Tackling the epidemic in Southern Africa, he not only thematises antiretrovirals but constructs a utopian plot in which scientists develop a

---

[55] Nattrass, *Mortal Combat*, p. 125.

[56] Patrice Matchaba, *Deadly Profit* (Cape Town: David Philip, 2000). Further references to this edition will be included in the text (abbreviated as '*DP*').

vaccine that prevents and cures the syndrome. Contextualising this discovery in medical history, it becomes evident how 'valuable' such a cure would be. While antiretrovirals have been shown to be life-saving as they delay the advent of the syndrome and alleviate its symptomatic diseases, the therapy still requires strict and life-long adherence to medication. A vaccine or cure, by comparison, promises to overcome the infection permanently. "Through most of history, the notion of a cure, a therapeutic intervention that achieves a permanent solution to a particular illness, was relatively rare."[57] The discovery and introduction of penicillin in the first half of the twentieth century provided a revolutionary therapeutic option for curing bacterial diseases, thus making medicine seem almost omnipotent in overcoming infections.[58] Despite their undeniable success, antibiotics are not to be mistaken for the ultimate cure because they are effective in treating bacterial infections only, not viral ones. The advent of HIV/AIDS in the 1980s highlights the lasting vulnerability of modern societies to infectious diseases. In this context, the development of a cure would mark a major scientific breakthrough. The rapid spread of the virus has made all the more apparent the need of a vaccine. Despite some promising steps of researchers and politicians, however,

> many pharmaceutical companies and smaller biotechnology firms that possess the expertise to conduct effective vaccine development have largely stayed out of the effort, owing to the probable cost and time required to create a successful vaccine relative to the size of a profitable market.[59]

As this contextualisation indicates, the development of HIV/AIDS treatments, cures and vaccines is not a mere medical issue but is also shaped by further social and economic interests.

In his medical thriller, Matchaba addresses the intersection of medical, economic and personal interests. GATO Pharmaceuticals, a US-American company run by Elizabeth Brown, focuses on research into a vaccine and cure for HIV/AIDS. Elizabeth has been personally affected by the virus because her brother John died of AIDS-related diseases after becoming drug resistant to antiretrovirals. As GATO's research undermines the powerful and established AIDS industry that promotes life-long adherence to AIDS medication, Elizabeth and her scientists are in danger. Attempting to put the scientists off course, opponents murder Stephen, GATO's chief research scientist, and beat up Reginald, a gynaecologist at a hospital in Cape Town who is in charge of the human vaccine trials. Elizabeth is deceived by her alleged lover, Thomas James, who uses her to get inside knowledge on confidential test results. However, the development of the vaccine is so advanced, the clinical trials are so promising and the research is so well-documented that the crimes cannot prevent GATO from achieving its

---

[57] Raymond A. Smith, "Cure", in: *Encyclopedia of AIDS*, pp. 185-186 (p. 185).

[58] In 1928, the English bacteriologist Sir Alexander Fleming developed what he called penicillin. The industrial production of penicillin encountered some initial difficulties which is why it was not used in patients until the 1940s. In 1945, Fleming received the Nobel Prize for Medicine for his discovery.

[59] Sam Avrett, "Vaccines", in: *Encyclopedia of AIDS*, pp. 729-732 (p. 731).

164 Ellen Grünkemeier

aims. In the end, Elizabeth and Reginald make public the vaccine test results and uncover their opponents' fraudulent practices. Nonetheless, the vaccine is not presented as the final solution because, six months later, some patients begin to show viral resistance. Despite its optimistic outlook, the novel is thus open-ended, implying the need for constant research and monitoring.

The discussion of AIDS medication is strongly shaped by the presentation and characterisation of Elizabeth Brown. Although she heads a pharmaceutical company and is GATO's majority shareholder, she is clearly set apart from other business people working in the HIV/AIDS industry. Introducing Elizabeth to the reader, the omniscient narrator focalises on Stephen who "liked her instantly" (*DP* 13). Stephen's favourable perception also shapes the reader's positive attitude towards her. Unlike her opponents in the pharmaceutical industry, Elizabeth is both professionally and personally involved in the epidemic. In a flashback (*DP* 18-25), the reader learns about her late brother John, his homosexuality, his infection, his treatment with antiretrovirals as a monotherapy, his drug resistance and finally his death. Elizabeth has been deeply impressed with John's empathetic doctor, realising that "the world was blessed to have people like John's doctor, men and women who genuinely dedicated themselves to the care of others [...]. In her line of business on Wall Street, the word compassion didn't exist. There was no monetary value to it" (*DP* 25). It is this experience and memory of John that makes Elizabeth stand out from the profit-oriented HIV/AIDS industry. Read in terms of the 'treasure' metaphor, it becomes evident that Elizabeth considers not only financial gains but is primarily interested in people's health. Stating that Lanco Pharmaceuticals, the leading manufacturer of antiretrovirals, "ridiculed our research into vaccine development" (*DP* 44), Elizabeth indicates that GATO's attempts at developing a vaccine are looked down upon by other manufacturers. Nonetheless, Elizabeth's business partners meet her with "respect for her corporate business intellect. At business school she had been the top student and she had done her research thesis on biotechnology in the pharmaceutical industry" (*DP* 13). Characterising Elizabeth by her education and intellect, the narrator makes clear that her unorthodox research plans do not result from naïve optimism but from well-informed decisions. Indirectly, the narrator thus exposes the derogatory remarks about GATO as a construct based on presuppositions rather than a critical evaluation of GATO's research. The negative image has been created and perpetuated by other pharmaceutical companies in an attempt to justify and secure their own supposedly superior position in the HIV/AIDS field.

Again and again, the powerful AIDS industry is featured in the novel so that readers can consider the virus in its complexity, not as a mere medical issue. Elizabeth is well aware of the economic dimension of the virus, not least because she has invested her own funds into GATO's research.

> [S]he had done this in the face of strong opposition and criticism from her rivals in the AIDS pharmaceutical industry. [...] None of them were interested in vaccine research and it was no secret that they were making more money treating AIDS with the various drug cocktails that now included the powerful protease inhibitors. This made business sense because HIV-infected patients had to take the drugs for the rest of their lives. (*DP* 17)

For GATO's opponents, an AIDS vaccine would not be a scientific breakthrough or 'treasure' but a disaster: "the era of vaccination, prevention and complete cure [...] would mean the collapse of an industry that based its income on the chronic, continued use of the HAART-drugs by HIV-positive patients" (*DP* 72). It is not until Stephen's murder that Elizabeth realises the extent of her adversaries' opposition; she comes to understand that "someone out there felt so threatened by their discovery of an AIDS vaccine that actually worked and that they were prepared to kill to make sure that it never got on to the market" (*DP* 71). Yet, remembering her late brother, Elizabeth becomes "more determined than ever to ensure that no one, no one was going to stop GATO Industry from releasing their results and launching their vaccine to the rest of the world" (*DP* 72). The repetition of the phrase 'no one' underscores her strong will to make the vaccine available.

In keeping with the generic characteristics of thrillers, it remains unclear for large parts of the novel who the rivals of Elizabeth and the scientists are. As in the quotes above, their opponents are referred to with vague phrases like 'someone out there', 'no one' or with the personal pronoun 'they', thereby setting 'them' apart from the characters associated with the GATO research. In fact, the text does not clarify who or what forces are behind the murder of Stephen and the attempted murder of Reginald. These questions are left unanswered, suggesting that the crimes and police investigations are not the novel's main concern. The attacks rather serve to emphasise how dangerous GATO's promising research is as it poses a threat to mainstream pharmaceutical companies. The forces opposing GATO's research remain faceless which implies that Elizabeth and her partners are up against a whole industry; they are not fighting individuals only. However, some intrigues and criminal networks are unmasked in the course of the novel, involving a corrupt US-American politician, Senator Brand. As a congressman and member of a Food and Drug Administration (FDA)[60] committee, he has misused his position and political influence. He has had access to confidential data on health research and – supported by his old school friend Thomas James, the Chief Executive Officer of a stock broking firm in New York – he invested money in certain fields. Even before the official approval and registration of antiretroviral drugs, he had Thomas shift money into companies manufacturing these drugs (*DP* 118-19). Brand's financial self-interest is the reason why GATO has faced obstacles. "[W]hen GATO made the first request for funding, he [Brand] did everything in his power to block this application on the grounds that the research was dangerous and unethical" (*DP* 119). Arguing that the virus might become resistant, multiply and spread uncontrollably through live vaccines, Brand uses supposedly scientific arguments to present GATO's research as threatening. As a result thereof the company does not receive financial support and the FDA does not give their approval for human vaccine trials (*DP* 120). In the end, however, Brand's illegal manoeuvrings become known; and confronted with his political downfall, Brand gets drunk and dies in a car accident (*DP* 123). As this sequence of events makes evident, the plot follows the

---

[60] In the United States, the Food and Drug Administration (FDA) oversees the testing and registration of medicines to ensure that the approved drugs are safe and therapeutically effective. Richard Jeffreys, "Clinical Trials", in: *Encyclopedia of AIDS*, pp. 144-147. Robert Marks Ridinger, "United States Government Agencies", in: *Encyclopedia of AIDS*, pp. 720-724.

principle of poetic justice: Senator Brand is 'punished' for his misdeeds. The same principle becomes visible in the case of the broker Thomas James who acts as Elizabeth's lover to get inside information which, in turn, helps him to manipulate shares. Thomas is affected by Brand's death because "he had lost a valuable Washington insider. Brand's information and insider trading tips had provided their company with almost eighty per cent of their profits in the last few years" (*DP* 141). Not only does he have to cope with this financial loss but in a television interview, Elizabeth uncovers Thomas's illegal involvement. "So, in front of the global audience, Thomas was restrained and handcuffed, read his rights and taken away, with his head down and his tail between his legs" (*DP* 146). This presentation of events underscores his defeat. The animal imagery and the passive verb forms suggest that Thomas is no longer in charge of the situation; instead, Elizabeth and the police are superior and in control. All in all, the cases of Senator Brand and the broker Thomas James serve to illustrate the scope and complexity of the epidemic. The AIDS industry not only involves people living with HIV/AIDS, doctors and researchers, but also politicians and business people who hope to benefit financially and/or politically from the virus. Influenced by different perspectives, these groups have different definitions of a 'treasure' in the face of the epidemic.

Elizabeth is well aware of the global imbalances of power and capital; and yet, it is her aim to make the vaccine available around the world. "It would be unethical to have an AIDS vaccine that was not affordable to the poor, who felt the burden of AIDS most" (*DP* 115). She has therefore come up with a special pricing system in which rich countries pay about three times the actual cost of the vaccine, thereby subsidising the launch of the vaccine in less privileged parts of the world (*DP* 115). This pricing scheme accentuates Elizabeth's understanding of what is 'valuable': from her perspective, the vaccine can metaphorically be read as a 'treasure', not so much because it results in considerable financial gains and high share prices of GATO Industry but because it can save people's lives. The plot and character construction of the novel – especially the explicitly positive representation of Elizabeth and her ethical response to the epidemic – contribute to the harmonious and optimistic ending, affirming the reading audience's hopes and wishes. Read in didactic terms, the novel thus aims to instil values of solidarity and moral integrity in its readers by presenting 'ideal' patterns of behaviour. The title *Deadly Profit* can be read along similar lines as a critique of established HIV/AIDS research which is primarily concerned with making money by selling antiretroviral drugs and testing kits rather than developing a cure. In the dedication, Matchaba spells out his political and educational agenda. "Although there is no AIDS vaccine at present, it is my naïve hope that this book will help change the AIDS research agenda, and the priorities of those that have the political, financial and intellectual resources to do so" (*DP* v). Matchaba thus sets the tone for the novel by addressing social power hierarchies and conflicting interests that have far-reaching consequences in times of the epidemic, of modern medicine and technology.

Yet, the ending of the novel is more complex than the utopian vision and euphemistic plot construction suggest. Although the vaccine is largely successful, about 30% of the people testing the vaccine begin to show an increased viral load after a couple of months. These findings imply that the virus has found a way around the vaccine and the scientists keep stressing that the vaccine is not "the final cure and answer to all [...] problems" (*DP* 170). Pointing out that antiretroviral drugs witnessed a similar backlash, the narrator stresses that this development is common in medical history and need not imply that vaccine research has come to a dead end.

> The same phenomenon had happened with the cocktail-therapy drugs. By the end of 1998, about 20 to 30 per cent of AIDS patients on the triple therapy had developed viral resistance. These patients then had to be put on new drug combinations. This worked for some of them, but it increased the incidence of side effects. Inevitably when the number of new drug combinations ran out, these patients eventually succumbed to this dreadful disease. (*DP* 170)

The vaccine can, in other words, still be considered a 'treasure', possibly even more so since people living with HIV/AIDS who become drug resistant to antiretrovirals might still benefit from the vaccine. Moreover, the generic classification of this novel as a medical thriller also indicates that Matchaba does not explore the positive qualities of the invention only. While some characters appreciate the cure, others perceive it as a threat to their commercial and political self-interests.

Conclusion

As the discussion has shown, the 'treasure' metaphor can serve as a useful analytical category. Until recently, AIDS medication was only available to the privileged few in South(ern) Africa who could afford the treatment. The trope signifies the importance of antiretrovirals as it marks AIDS medication as 'life-saving' and 'valuable'. These observations are not to obscure the fact, however, that metaphors create meanings and contribute to the cultural construction of the epidemic. Since they shape people's perception of HIV/AIDS, metaphors have to be scrutinised. In the close examination of texts and contexts, it has become evident that the 'treasure' metaphor does not account for the complexity of the epidemic. People living with HIV/AIDS, scientists, business people, politicians – they all attach importance to AIDS medication; still, the meaning of antiretroviral drugs, vaccines and cures is different to different groups of people in different parts of the world. Reading the texts and contexts through the lens of the 'treasure' metaphor does not call attention to the global imbalances of capital and power, to people's political agendas and commercial interests or to the aesthetic production of literary representations. Yet, these issues are of particular significance to a discussion of the HIV/AIDS epidemic in South(ern) Africa. All in all, the 'treasure' metaphor provides an apt category to approach the issue. Yet, for a detailed and critical discussion its connotations need to be re-examined and appropriated to meet the medical, political, social and ethical particularities of the epidemic.

Notes on Contributors

Dominique Claisse is *Maître de Conférences* in English at the Université de Valenciennes in France. Besides his specialisations in language teaching and its pedagogy, he has established research interests in American nineteenth-century literature, especially in the life and work of Nathaniel Hawthorne. His publications on Hawthorne include the essays "The Judge is Found Guilty, or the Sense of Justice in *The House of the Seven Gables* by Nathaniel Hawthorne" (2006), "The Missing Mother in *The House of The Seven Gables* by Nathaniel Hawthorne: A Study in Feminine Nature" (2005), and "Deep Roots and Travel Aspirations in Nathaniel Hawthorne's Early Romances" (2005).

Rainer Emig is Chair of English Literature and Culture at Leibniz University in Hanover, Germany. He is especially interested in the link between literature and the media and in Literary, Critical, and Cultural Theory, especially theories of identity, power, gender and sexuality. His publications include *Modernism in Poetry* (1995), *W.H. Auden* (1999) and *Krieg als Metapher im zwanzigsten Jahrhundert* (2001) as well as edited collections on *Stereotypes in Contemporary Anglo-German Relations* (2000), *Ulysses* (2004), *Gender ↔ Religion* (with Sabine Demel, 2008), *Hybrid Humour* (with Graeme Dunphy, 2010), *Performing Masculinity* (with Antony Rowland, 2010), and *Commodifying (Post-) Colonialism* (with Oliver Lindner, 2010). He is one of the three editors of the *Journal for the Study of British Cultures*.

Ellen Grünkemeier works as a research assistant in the English Department at Leibniz University in Hanover, Germany, where she teaches British Studies with a focus on literature and its cultural, historical and political contexts. Her main research interests include postcolonial issues and the New Literatures in English, especially African texts. She has co-edited (with Jana Gohrisch) a volume of essays on Anglophone African Literatures and Cultures entitled *Listening to Africa* (2012). Her monograph *Breaking the Silence: South African Representations of HIV/AIDS* is forthcoming with James Currey. Her current research focuses on political writing from nineteenth-century Britain.

Stefan Herbrechter is Reader in Cultural Theory at Coventry University in England. His research interests encompass English and Comparative Literature, Critical and Cultural Theory, Continental Philosophy as well as Cultural and Media Studies. Among his publications are *Lawrence Durrell: Postmodernism and the Ethics of Alterity* (1999), *Cultural Studies: Interdisciplinarity and Translation* (2002), *Discipline and Practice* (with Ivan Callus, 2004), *Post-Theory, Culture Criticism* (with Ivan Callus, 2004), *Metaphors of Economy* (with Nicole Bracker, 2005), *Returning (to) Communities* (with Michael Higgins, 2006), *The Matrix in Theory* (with Myriam Diocaretz, 2006), and *Cy-Borges: Memories of the Posthuman in the Work of Jorge Luis Borges* (with Ivan Callus, 2009). He has also translated important works of Cultural Theory and Philosophy from French into English (including works by Derrida, Cixous, and Stiegler).

Oliver Lindner is Professor of EFL Teaching (Literature and Culture) at Kiel University, Germany. His research interests include eighteenth-century literature, Daniel Defoe, British youth cultures and Science Fiction. He has published two monographs, *"Solitary on a Continent" – Raumentwürfe in der spätviktorianischen Science Fiction* (2005) and *"Matters of Blood" – Defoe and the Cultures of Violence* (2010), and three edited collections of essays, *"Teaching India"* (2008), *Commodifying (Post)Colonialism* (with Rainer Emig, 2010) and *Adaptation and Cultural Appropriation* (with Pascal Nicklas, 2012).

Jessica Malay is Reader in English Literature at the University of Huddersfield in England. Her main research interests are Early Modern Literature and Culture, especially the role of women and space. She has published the monographs *Prophecy and Sibylline Imagery in the Renaissance: Shakespeare's Sibyls* (2010) and *Textual Construction of Space in the Writing of Renaissance Women: "In" Habiting Place* (2006). She is currently pursuing a major research project on "Anne Clifford's Great Books: A Transformative Narrative of Identity and Place", which will among other things produce an edition of Anne Clifford's *Great Books of Records*.

Carl Plasa is Reader in English Literature and Critical and Cultural Theory at Cardiff University in Wales. His research interests include Victorian Literature, Postcolonial Literature and Theory; African American Writing as well as the literatures, cultures and histories of slavery. Among his publications are *Slaves to Sweetness: British and Caribbean Literatures of Sugar* (2009), *Charlotte Brontë* (2004), and *Textual Politics from Slavery to Postcolonialism: Race and Identification* (2000).

Karin Preuss holds a PhD in German and Comparative Literature from the University of Wales Swansea and has taught Comparative Literature at Johann Wolfgang Goethe University, Frankfurt am Main, Germany. Her research and teaching interests encompass aesthetics and poetry, monstrosity and representation, image making, Frankenstein's afterlife, and Nineteenth-Century to Twentieth-Century Studies. She has published articles on Comparative Literature and the intersection of music and writing. A book on unicorns in philosophy, literature and the arts is in preparation.

Marcin Stawiarski teaches at the University of Caen Basse-Normandie, France. He completed his Ph.D. thesis entitled "Temporal Aspects of Music in the 20th-Century Novel: Conrad Aiken, Anthony Burgess and Gabriel Josipovici" at the University of Poitiers in 2007. His research focuses on the intersections of music and literature as well as representation of time in fiction.

Russell West-Pavlov is Professor of English at the University of Pretoria, South Africa. He works predominantly on Postcolonial Literatures in English and French, across the southern hemisphere (Australia, Africa), with a particular interest in the politics and space and the semiotics of spatial representation. Among his recent major publications in this area are *Temporalities* (2013), *Imaginary Antipodes: Essays on Contemporary Australian Literature and Culture* (2011), and *Spaces of Fiction/Fictions of Space: Postcolonial Place and Literary DeiXis* (2010).